ALL COHERENCE GONE

And new Philosophy calls all in doubt,
The Element of fire is quite put out;
The Sun is lost, and th'earth, and no mans wit
Can well direct him where to looke for it.
And freely men confesse that this world's spent,
When in the Planets, and the Firmament
They seeke so many new; they see that this
Is crumbled out againe to his Atomies.

'Tis all in peeces, all cohaerence gone;
All just supply, and all Relation.

—JOHN DONNE, *An Anatomie of the World*

ALL
COHERENCE GONE

A STUDY OF
THE SEVENTEENTH CENTURY CONTROVERSY
OVER DISORDER AND DECAY
IN THE UNIVERSE

VICTOR HARRIS

FRANK CASS & CO. LTD.
1966

Published by Frank Cass & Co. Ltd.,
10 Woburn Walk, London W.C.1
by arrangement with the University of Chicago Press.

First edition   1949
New impression   1966

Printed in Holland by
N. V. Grafische Industrie Haarlem

For

S. M. H.

Foreword

THIS book owes much to the scholars who have preceded me in the study of topics close to my own. It is a pleasure to acknowledge such an obligation here as well as in the specific citations in my footnotes and Bibliography. Of the important pioneering work done in this field by Professor R. F. Jones, of Stanford, my readers will not need to be reminded. I particularly wish to thank also Professor Marjorie Nicolson, of Columbia, for sending me some very valuable unpublished material, and Professor F. Y. St. Clair, of the University of North Dakota, for making available his personal copy of his Harvard dissertation. For reading my manuscript in part or as a whole and for much excellent advice on its organization, arguments, and style, I am grateful to Professors G. E. Bentley, of Princeton; R. S. Crane and T. P. Cross, of Chicago; David Daiches, of Cornell; and Clarence Faust, of Stanford. My debt to Professor George Williamson, of Chicago, begins with his article, "Mutability, Decay, and Seventeenth-Century Melancholy," and includes his sympathetic criticism at all stages of this work. In addition, I am happy to acknowledge a generous grant in aid of research from the Graduate College of the University of Iowa, and many courtesies from the library staffs of the University of Chicago and the University of Iowa. Miss Rae Marsteller, Mr. James Brown, and Mr. Gwin Kolb have been very helpful with the proofs and the Index.

VICTOR HARRIS

IOWA CITY, IOWA
January 1949

Table of Contents

TABLE OF CONTENTS

[x]

Chapter I

THE DECAY OF NATURE

RECURRENT in man's intellectual history is a suspicion or a fear, and often a philosophical conviction, that his world is disintegrating. For this belief he finds many reasons. The race of men seems to grow feebler, society more confused, and all nature old and weary. This sensible decay of the universe, the corruption of plants or creatures or of the heavens themselves, is confirmed by the unresolved conflicts within man's mind. He has before him the tragic disparity between the ailing world he lives in and an ideal world which he envisages. Old men remember the happier days of their youth. Legend cherishes the dream of a golden or heroic age, of an era of giants or miracles, of a Garden of Eden untouched by sin or death.

The idea that the world decays—an idea inherited from the Middle Ages—was part of the Renaissance cosmic order. For two centuries it was particularly important to man's rational and spiritual life. What did this belief offer that so recommended it to the imagination, that brought to it such passionate allegiance? What was the change that finally outmoded the accepted world picture and substituted a different picture, another kind of order? These are the questions that I shall deal with in this study.

Throughout the sixteenth and seventeenth centuries there was still no serious challenge to the notion that the world was created for man's use and man, in turn, for God's glory. All the universe was included in a closely linked hierarchy of forms. Every unit held its appointed place in a magnificent harmony extending downward from God to the angels to man; from the heavens to the elements of fire, air, water, and earth; from macrocosm to microcosm; from

[1]

man to woman; from rational humanity to the brutish beasts; from the sentient to the vegetative; from the subtlest spirit at God's right hand to the grossest matter of ashes and dust.

But man, by denying his proper obedience to God, had violated the symmetry of the whole pattern. " 'Tis all in peeces," Donne lamented, "all cohaerence gone." The natural world was condemned with the moral; the sin of man took root in nature, and the whole was corrupted with the part.

The most optimistic hopes for man's achievements were always circumscribed by this consciousness of a fall. All studies were pursued only to recover some small part of what had been lost: "all Arts and Sciences in generall" were made necessary by man's Fall and the ignorance which resulted.[1] The aim of learning was thus only "to repair the ruins of our first parents."[2] "It cannot be without some great worke of God, thus in the old and decrepit Age of the World, to let it haue more perfect knowledge of it selfe," wrote Samuel Purchas about the extensive explorations of his age. "ALl Arts are but the supply of Natures defects, to patch up her ragged and worne rents, to cover rather then to cure or recover Mans fall."[3]

Based on this belief in a disrupted and violated natural order, the conviction that nature decays was reinforced by a variety of circumstances peculiar to the Renaissance. For one thing, the new astronomy of Copernicus, Kepler, and Galileo revealed yet another sign of the broken harmony of the universe: it extended the realm of mutability beyond the spheres within which it had customarily been confined, beyond the elements and into the celestial circles of the sun and the "fixed" stars.[4] The sun had declined nearer to the earth, and spots were discovered on its surface. New stars appeared and disappeared in the highest regions of the skies. There remained no natural constant which could restore the lost powers of the variable earth and its miserable creatures. The new science admitted the possibility of other habitable worlds and left the universe without a firm and stable center. The whole creation was seen to be involved in the fitful globe of mortality.

But these new ways of thought contributed less directly to the belief in nature's decay than to the general unrest and uncertainty of the times; and the scientists, by attacking the metaphysics in terms of which the doctrine of decay had been unified, eventually became the principal opponents of this doctrine. The increased concern over the world's natural corruption was more closely related to an intensified solicitude for man's spiritual good. In the soul's evil, man saw reflected the lost harmony of the whole creation. Immorality prospered in the worldly society of the Renaissance. An unsettled political economy further emphasized the insecurity of man's estate. The Reformation had attacked the authority of the universal church and had made doctrinal issues the province of every preacher in every pulpit. The disputes and the confusion made men more sharply aware of their individual burdens of sin, of the frailty of their mortal world.

Antichrist was in their midst, and men were unprepared for the day of judgment which was at hand. The six thousand years commonly allotted the creation were almost counted now. In the signs of corruption and decay could be seen God's warning that the end was near. Conversely, the imminence of this catastrophe, as established in Scripture and commonly accepted, was proof that men were actually watching and suffering the later stages of corruption. Any denial of the decay was an un-Christian denial that the world would end. Churchmen of all denominations were eager to defend the world's mortality against the Aristotelian doctrine of its eternity; and this desire, together with the popular expectation that the end would come soon, did much to bring converts to the belief in decay.

As men questioned more and more extensively the grounds of their natural and moral philosophy, the belief in the decay of nature, accelerated by, and at the same time contributing to, the general disquietude, became widely prevalent after the middle of the sixteenth century. At first it was not always distinguishable from the belief in the Fall of man and God's subsequent curse upon the earth. But in the 1570's and 1580's there grew up a more explicit concern over the progressive or cumulative corruption, over the

[3]

decay that did not stop with the original supernatural curse. In these years, also, the decay was generally believed to extend to the heavens, as well as to earth and man. By 1600 the idea had begun to exert upon the popular imagination an influence that lasted undiminished for several decades. In 1616, Godfrey Goodman, with the publication of his ambitious treatise, *The Fall of Man, or the Corruption of Nature,* gave the doctrine its most consecutive and extensive philosophical form and became recognized as principal spokesman in its defense. Throughout this period the concept of a decaying universe was reflected in the diverse work of encyclopedists, historians, astrologers, and popularizers of science; most particularly, it animated the exhortations of the preachers and provided the poets with a cosmic imagery of profound suggestiveness.

Opposition to the belief in decay was anticipated in the sixteenth century, but the common conception was not directly and comprehensively challenged until 1627, when George Hakewill, in *An Apologie of the Power and Providence of God,* attacked it for what he deemed its essentially irreligious leanings. John Wilkins, in the 1640's, and Henry Power and John Spencer, in the 1660's,[5] were prominent among those who offered arguments against it from the new science. In general, after 1635, when the conflicting statements of Goodman and Hakewill were openly and systematically juxtaposed in the third edition of the *Apologie,* any defense of the conventional position was likely to be incomplete and uncritical; and the belief in the natural corruption of the world ceased to be significant.

The two points of view were opposed in many different ways. Most obvious, though not most important, was the debate over the material evidence, over the actual signs which were recognized in nature. Often the entire controversy was ostensibly carried on in terms of these manifestations of decay. But to whatever extent the debate seemed to rest upon testimony of the senses or upon the corollary comparison of ancients with moderns, actually a decision could not be reached from what was seen and measured. The differences were not essentially descriptive or empirical but meta-

[4]

physical. The debate over the decay of the world was not simply a disagreement over the description of external nature; it was a major conflict between opposing philosophies.

More significantly, this conflict employed arguments from the purpose of creation, from its natural laws, its approaching end, and the relation of its separate parts to the whole design. Most parties to the controversy agreed, to begin with, that the world was made for man and man for God's honor; but there was disagreement on the kind of world which would best serve this end. Later came the introduction of a quantitative or material system, which rendered irrelevant the question of whether the world's decay or its constancy more enhanced God's honor; the scientists ultimately rejected the belief in decay not only because of the empirical evidence against it but also because it was based on a teleological view of the universe. In the realm of wholly natural principles the debate was over the original composition of the world and the subsequent effect of sin upon it. Since a continuous natural decay would presumably lead to a similarly natural end of the world, the discussion of the world's mortality also became an important part of the larger controversy.

These arguments were all encompassed in the most comprehensive argument from part to whole and, even more dramatically, in the analogical progression from the microcosm to the macrocosm. The world which was decaying was the harmonious philosophical whole in which the defection of a part proved the failure of all. It was the finite world whose beginning and end had been circumscribed, the world of natural and theological plenitude. The concept of man as microcosm seemed to be the most completely satisfactory and illuminating expression of the idea of decay, not so much because man thereby became a little world, as because the world became simply the greater man.

By this means a philosophical doctrine was given immediacy, emotional content, and imaginative complexity. Man was seen as the epitome of the world—its map, sum, symbol, index, and quintessence—as well as the end for which the world was created. If man sins, so went the reasoning, the world, too, is punished. If man is corrupt, the world's core must be rotten also. In the sixteenth and seventeenth centuries it was the loss of harmony, the loss of metaphysical unity, that was discerned and lamented. When the order and harmony of the parts are destroyed, then we may read in man's miserable condition the decay of the whole world.

The opponents of the belief in decay, separating revealed truth from natural knowledge, argued that, since only man is guilty, his sin could not be punished in nature. They rejected the analogy between microcosm and macrocosm because they found nothing in man to correspond to the immutable heavens or because they believed the world was not so completely known as to permit argument from part to whole, or even because they did not believe the world to be designed for man's use or tied to his destiny. In the end they willingly sacrificed the old philosophical unity for their new freedom of inquiry. In varying degrees men began to distinguish more sharply between reason and faith, man and nature, natural and supernatural, microcosm and macrocosm, and to insist on different laws for each and different ways of discovering truth in all.

Belief in the decay of nature has its obvious parallels in modern physical science, but such resemblances are more striking than important. For example, the theory of entropy, which measures the approach to an absolute zero of static uniformity (i.e., a breakdown of forms, complete "decay"), is applied only to parts of the universe and does not exclude the possibility of some compensating source of energy in the whole. The idea of a disintegrating and decaying nature has its similarities also with the Lucretian system of fortuitous atoms making and unmaking worlds without end, as well as with modern atomic theory; and there was in the seventeenth century a considerable revival of interest in Lucretius when the new science intensified man's efforts in natural philosophy. But the Lucretian world is almost the antithesis of the unified, ordered, teleological pattern of Goodman; and Lucretius was as often cited by opponents of the belief in decay as by its champions.

[6]

The analogy with our own times occurs more significantly in our attempts to find a basis for philosophical truth—on the one hand, in the metaphysical order and self-sufficiency of the whole and, on the other, in the independence and integrity of the parts. Once more we are asked to choose between empirical facts and self-evident principles, between the kind of knowledge which is fragmentary and that which is, certainly in its essentials, complete. Perhaps, because we no longer literally project our image into the physical world in the seventeenth-century sense, the analogy between microcosm and macrocosm has lost much of its power to serve the mind and stir the imagination. But we still must decide to what extent and in what ways man shall remain the center, and perhaps the end, of his universe.

Chapter II

THE FALL OF MAN AND NATURE

IN GODFREY GOODMAN'S *The Fall of Man* (1616) the belief in the world's continuous and palpable decay is explained more fully than in any other source. In 1616 Goodman was vicar of Stapleford Abbots, Essex. Five years later he became dean of Rochester, and bishop of Gloucester in 1625. The assertions of the vicar in 1616 had to be defended by the bishop in 1635, when the controversy between Goodman and Hakewill became public and explicit. A second edition of his treatise was published in 1618, and a third in 1629.[1] It was in 1627 that Archdeacon George Hakewill published *An Apologie of the Power and Providence of God*, attacking Goodman's position. Goodman's reply, together with Hakewill's answers, was, in turn, appended to the third edition of the *Apologie* in 1635.

It is worth noting that, although Goodman nowhere retreats from the position which he took in 1616, he objected to the printing of the 1629 edition, a reluctance which may have been due to the dignity of his rank or possibly to the forcefulness of Hakewill's attack in 1627. Perhaps the latter explanation is more plausible, for Goodman afterward asked Hakewill to print his (Goodman's) objections to the *Apologie*, thus publicizing and heightening a controversy which had been up to that time oblique and certainly impersonal.[2]

In the exchange of arguments and rebuttals in the third edition of the *Apologie*, we find the issues of the controversy most fully and most clearly stated. Goodman, in his original work, takes as his thesis the Fall of man from grace. The daily growth of man's corruption and the sensible decay of the physical universe, though

[8]

precisely enunciated and defended, are offered only as proof of the Fall. Hakewill's attack, furthermore, is professedly not directed against Goodman in particular but against the "common streame." "THE opinion of the Worlds Decay is so generally received, not onely among the Vulgar, but of the Learned, both Divines and others," Hakewill complains, "that the very commonnesse of it makes it currant with many, without any further examination" or proof.[3] Even in 1635, when the two are at last publicly and pointedly opposed, Goodman defends not so much the decay as the mortality of the world, a procedure which, though pertinent, results in a certain amount of arguing at cross-purposes. Goodman is, nevertheless, the most persistent and voluminous writer for his side of the quarrel, and we may best see the problem as it was recognized in the seventeenth century if we begin by defining the doctrine of the world's decay in Goodman's terms.

I. GOODMAN'S DISTURBED AND PROMISCUOUS METHOD

The *Fall of Man* is divided into three parts, the first dealing with "the peculiar punishments of mans sinne," peculiar, that is, to man; the second with "mans condition in generall"; and the third with those punishments "which are related in Scripture to bee the punishments of the first sinne."[4] Since it is Goodman's purpose to prove man's fall from grace and the resultant corruption of man and world, he argues that the Fall both caused the corruption and is demonstrated by the corruption. Proof of the Fall is thus the recital of man's ills and of the world's inadequacies.

Part I (pp. 1–63), devoted chiefly to the miseries proper to man "in regard of his constitution," divides these unique punishments roughly into two groups: those seen in the corrupt "natural actions" of the body and those derived from the presence in one being of a corruptible body and an incorruptible soul. Natural corruptibility is shown in the preponderance of evil over good and in the existence of contrary qualities. Goodman indicates, though not yet at length, that man's place is at the center of the universe; that the punishment for his sin may be extended to the sublunar world and even to the heavens; and that, since God intended a perfect universe, any departure from perfection is corruption and decline.

Part II (pp. 64–205) is a description of man's miseries other than those deriving from the peculiar nature of his body and soul. The first portion (pp. 64–108) elaborates upon man's troubles as compared with the lesser ills of other creatures, which were originally intended to be completely subservient to him but which are so no longer. A description of man's vices, called "miseries of the minde," and his vanities, "wherein our pleasure may seeme to consist," makes up the remainder of Part II.[5]

Part III (pp. 206–403) is allotted principally (pp. 214–347) to those punishments of original sin "which are generally related in Scripture": punishment of the creatures, enmity between man and beast, barrenness of the earth, man's nakedness, his tilling of the earth, the conflict between man and wife, the curse of God, the confusion of tongues, the pain and degradation of birth, and death itself.[6] Part III then continues with the "transition from the death of man, to the death of the whole world," where the world's corruption is established by application of the analogy between microcosm and macrocosm.[7] The world will not be annihilated but purified in the final conflagration. The need for faith and the limitations of reason are stressed. There is a sanctifying grace, which will be restored to man when he returns to religion. Man's sin and his need for this grace are proved by philosophy, reason, poetry, and—in the comparison of ancients and moderns—empirical and historical "observation."

In these three parts, which constitute the body of the text, Goodman attempts to prove that, because man and the world are corrupt, man must have fallen from a higher and better estate. The appended Corollary (pp. 404–45) is concerned with the manner of this fall. In the text proper the design is "to proceed in such manner & forme, as that my proofes might serue to inforce the naturall man by the light of his owne reason, to confesse his owne corruption." But now, Goodman admits, "I must ingeniously and truly confesse; though mans knowledge discerneth his fall, yet by the same knowledge he cannot possibly conceiue the manner of his fall."[8]

In attempting not merely to establish the Fall but to account for it, Goodman thus does not presume to appeal to reason unaided. He discusses at length the limitations and the scope of proper Christian investigation, until actually the Corollary resolves itself into a contention that the explanation of man's Fall, though not demonstrable by reason, is as fully in accord with reason as is the fact that man fell. In Parts I–III the "reasonable" proof of the Fall is to recognize it in its consequences: man's corruption and the decay of the world. But in the Corollary, where we are not dependent on reason, we are concerned not with the results of man's sin but only with the occasion and the cause.

The argument of the entire book rests heavily on a teleological interpretation of the universe. Man, according to Goodman, was created perfect, for God's glory; and the world, with all its other creatures, was designed for man's use and pleasure. The miseries of man are then explained as the signs of his fall from this first state of grace: "fall of man appeares in the miseries of man.... The greatnesse of our woe shewes the large extent of our sinne."[9]

The ordering of the work is thus in terms of the kinds of miseries (or punishments) which man endures. Part I deals with the sufferings arising out of man's own nature; Part II, with those inherent in man's relation to society—both the moral society of mankind and the larger, natural society of all the creatures. Since Goodman directs his treatise to "natural" man, he places in his first two sections the punishments, and thus the proofs, most readily apparent to reason.

In Part III, though still undertaking to prove all by reason, he appeals also to the authority of the Scriptures. All human woe is, of course, due ultimately to Adam's Fall, but in Part III Goodman discusses those punishments which are specifically promised and explained in Scriptures as the result of original sin. In the Corollary are discussed certain tenets which, though beyond reason, are not contrary to reason.

This procedure invites a certain amount of overlapping. For

example, in Part III, the mean travail of man's birth is a punishment "related in Scripture," whereas in Part II it is portrayed as a suffering natural to man by contrast with the easier birth of the creatures.

Again in Part III man's nakedness is God's promised punishment; in Part I this nakedness is a natural state of man's body and one which brings him shame and suffering. Goodman recognizes that his three divisions

"seeme rather as seuerall degrees of one and the same foundation, which is laid vp and buried in the tombe of our miseries: and therefore I pray pardon me, if I be not ouer strict and curious in my method, though I speake promiscuously, and confound them together: for miserie betokens confusion. A confused stile, and a disturbed method, is fittest to discourse of our miserie."[10]

This confusion, which certainly exists, is nevertheless one of details; the larger pattern is consistent enough. The whole work is a lament, frequently eloquent and even lyrical, over the unhappiness of man. The reasoning is resolved into one argument: man's sufferings can only be punishments of his sin, and we need but see his misery to know that he is fallen; the miseries of man are thus the "signs" of his corruption. Man's corruption, in turn, causes (and proves) the world's corruption; the great world, too, is mortal in the death of the little world.

The progression throughout is from points which are wholly demonstrable by reason to those which are merely not contrary to reason. The constant tone of lamentation further binds the parts together; the cumulative weight of Goodman's grief and humility adds to the persuasiveness of the work. This unrelenting exhortation, which is both additive and repetitive, is directed to the aim of making man recognize his own corruption and the decay of all material things, so that he may return to the contemplation and service of God.

II. GOODMAN'S STAR: THE LIGHT OF REASON

A careful analysis of the text, in order to realize the full import of Goodman's argument, must inquire beyond the stated pattern.

That the principles derived from such an examination are pertinent to the contemporary controversy over the decay of nature will be apparent as we later bring into the range of this study the writings of other men who, on one side or the other, are deeply concerned over the vision of corrupt mankind languishing in a decrepit world.

In the first place, it is the rational appeal to "natural" man which professedly determines the scope and design of Goodman's treatise. "I will lay aside Scripture, Fathers, Councels, the vniforme and Catholicke consent of the whole world," he promises; "Reason and common sense shall stand in the forefront, and beare the whole brunt of the combat."[11]

He even apologizes that he must "sometimes vse the phrase of Scripture," for he will be guided only by "a starre, the light of reason, the contemplation of nature." It is important to note that there is no conflict between the light of reason and the contemplation of nature; reason is the right reading of nature. Where reason fails to understand nature, it is because man's reason, like the rest of nature, has been corrupted. The "natural" man is simply man without or before the "fulnesse of knowledge" found in the Gospels.[12]

Because Goodman is interested in showing reason misled by the senses, he sets up a conflict between reason and the senses, whereas no such conflict exists between reason and the natural world itself. It is possible for Goodman to say, therefore, that natural alterations are "insensible"—i.e., that decay may not be apparent to the senses— "yet in reason, you shall easilie discerne the vndoubted tokens of the worlds ruine."[13] The charge made by Hakewill, that man's observations (via the senses) and his studies of nature do not reveal a corrupted world, is thus, if not forestalled, at least anticipated.

Furthermore, the God who revealed the mysteries of faith is the same God who laid the foundations of nature, and "the mysteries of faith must necessarily presuppose the groundworke and foundation of reason."[14] Therefore, there should be no disparity between man's view of nature through his use of reason, on the one hand, and through faith, on the other. By either means the truth of the

Fall and corruption may be discovered. Goodman would prefer merely to accept God's word, but, in appealing to the natural man, he has renounced the use of Scripture, confident that by reason alone we can know our sin and the world's corruption.

In the course of his treatise Goodman finds it desirable to justify this procedure by defining, somewhat broadly, the whole scope of reason. Its principal function is to reveal to man his sin, so that it would "seeme a naturall knowledge" that we are decayed and corrupted. Reason thus lessens man's pride and draws him to religion and, eventually, to God. The three uses of philosophy are to acknowledge God, to show the harmony of nature and grace, and to prove God's miracles "transcendent above our naturall reason."[15] Whatever is natural, as opposed to the miraculous, can be proved immediately by reason. The decay of nature—and this becomes a most significant part of Goodman's argument—derives from the basic principles of nature and can thus be established by reason unaided.

In order to validate further the use of reason to prove the corruption of the universe, Goodman shows in the appended Corollary how other matters of faith are also verifiable in reason. If by reason alone we may ascertain, for example, the existence of God, as well as the creation of the universe, the time and order of the creation, the freedom of man's will, and the inevitability of the world's end, it follows that the Fall and the corruption need not be beyond reason. Goodman in general upholds the efficacy of reason in confirming the articles of faith, whereas Hakewill contends that such questions as the beginning or ending of the world or the time and manner thereof are not conclusions but principles and have no antecedents.[16]

Goodman admits that the ancient philosophers, following reason without revelation, say little about the decay of nature, but he argues that even among these writers there are many who "seeme to intimate as much in effect." He finds in the Platonic doctrine of an ideal good an implication of a better state from which all is now fallen. Similarly, he holds that ideas about the transmigration of souls have "vndoubtedly some reference to the first infusion of mans soule," proving the Fall and corruption by showing that the soul needs "to change the place of her dwelling."[17]

The Platonists' dictum that *cognitio nostra est reminiscentia* is another indication that they recognized a prior and better state, which man, through his studies, tries to recover. The Aristotelian concept of privation, which plays an important part in Goodman's demonstration, serves to establish the basic corruptibility of nature.[18] The very need for natural philosophy shows that man's learning is defective, as the need for moral philosophy shows his conduct, his laws, and his government to be decayed.[19] By such reasoning Goodman makes the mere existence of arts and sciences among the heathen presume their implicit acknowledgment of the Fall.

Though a defense of reason is called for by his method, Goodman does not, however, overlook the limitations of reason. We may prove, for example, that man fell, but the manner of that fall is merely in accord with reason, not provable by reason. All truths in the secret realm of God's providence are altogether "above" reason, and into these Christian mysteries we must not pry. The weakness of man's reason is, in fact, part of God's curse after man sinned, and all we have left are "those few sparkes of reason, which now lie raked vp in the dead embers of our nature."[20]

Goodman points out the discrepancy between the things which man understands and those he wishes to understand, between his intellectual powers and his aspirations, and he cites the differences of judgment in individuals and the conflicts among the various schools of philosophy. The "obscure, darke, hidden, secret notions, which are the principles of al our knowledge ... seeme rather to belong to the cognizance of common sense, then of the reasonable soule," common sense here being identified with the intuitive perception of axiomatic truths or first principles. Man's arts and sciences were needed to cover the nakedness of his ignorant, sinful soul, and "those night-watchings and great labours in the Vniversities, are only vndertaken to supply natures defects."[21]

[15]

Goodman thus defends reason, but only as it is sufficient to show man his corruption, for the limitations of reason are those of man fallen; and, when the Fall is accepted, the powers of man (including the rational powers) are seen to be weak and corrupted. By the light of nature we cannot aspire to a full or spiritual understanding; the light of nature reveals the corruption of nature, and that alone. Beyond this, man can satisfy his curiosity only by faith and submission.[22]

III. ENGINE OF JUSTICE

Man's responsibility for the decay and his general relationship to God can be understood in the light of this subordination of reason to faith. Whereas God's justice is reasonable, according to Goodman, the extent of God's mercy is miraculous. The sin and Fall of man and the corruption of the world can be discovered by reason. But the original grace with which man was created and the ultimate grace which must erase his sin are both to be known only by faith. Goodman's proof of the corruption, a proof aimed at natural man, finally depends on his assumption that there had been some prior perfect state from which both man and world had declined. The argument from reason depends on the article of faith.

There is, to begin with, a Creator. Proof of the Creator, judged desirable in a treatise appealing to reason and offered as a truth within the range of reason, is given at length in the Corollary. This proof is established principally by discovering the workman in his workmanship: the harmony and simplicity of the design are evidence of a single Creator, not the result of chance.

The created world had a beginning and, being finite, will have an end. The precise manner of beginning and end cannot be demonstrated, but the record of the one and the promise of the other, as related in the Scriptures, are the most reasonable possible. Goodman elaborates these points, not to answer any challenge to the actual existence of a Creator, but to establish the finitude and mortality of the world.[23]

The purpose of the creation was to enhance God's honor; "the end of mans creation consists not in man himselfe, who vndoubtedly shall tast and see corruption." Corruptible man could never have been the ultimate aim of all creation. Because man was destined to fall, the glory of God must therefore be the end of being. A belief in the decay of the world does more honor to God than does a belief in its inviolability, Goodman argues, for it shows man his misery and returns him to religion. Religion seeks to make man know his own miseries and by such means to bring him to the worship of God: "before wee can raise man, he must first acknowledge his fall."[24]

When God first created man, "the nature of man was innocent and incorrupt, as being Gods owne immediate workemanship." The perfection existed "inwardly in the faculties of his soule, outwardly in the right rule of his senses, and the gouernment of his flesh," so that man was thus "sanctified in the wombe, sealed vp with original grace." This original grace is the postulate upon which Goodman's entire demonstration depends, "the principall intent and scope of my whole speech"; for, if man were or could have been corrupt in the beginning, his present corruption need not be a punishment of sin and a proof of the Fall. The Fall depends upon a state of grace to fall from; the state of grace itself rests upon no prior premise in reason. "Gods intent in the creation," asserts Goodman to natural man and religious man alike,

"was onely according to the nature of goodnesse . . . to impart his owne being and attributes to the creatures: but when I finde sorrowes and griefes in man, I begin to enquire, where is the originall? for in God there is no sorrow, no griefe, no maladies, no afflictions, no diseases, no death: God did only desire to impart himself; whence proceedes the malignitie? were it not, that some after-corruption hath stained mans nature."[25]

Man, then, was created innocent and without corruption. He had free will, but this was not evil or the seed of evil, for his sin could not spring from his own flesh or from nature, neither of which could initiate sin. The evil came from without, "from some spirit, that is maleuolent and opposite to nature, and intends noth-

ing more then the corruption of nature." This malevolent spirit
acted upon the understanding, and thence upon the will, both of
which, though "good in themselues," were "capable of euill."[26]

Goodman is careful to point out that the essential qualities in
man's nature were subject to no defection, and that only in those
which were accessory and accidental did man enjoy a free election.
Furthermore, man could have overcome his temptation either by
his natural strength or by reliance on original grace, for God warned
him against the occasion of his fall. Thus, though God's prescience
specifically comprehends the voluntary actions of man, *"the freedom of mans will subsisting with the ouer-ruling hand of Gods
prouidēce,"* God had no actual part in man's sin.[27]

Indeed, God offers a sanctifying grace to compensate for the loss
of original grace. To regain salvation, man need only recognize his
Fall and take "a dislike and a distaste in nature." His miseries
become a preparation for the return to grace, so that his punishments are the means to greater bliss, his corruption the highway
to redemption. Goodman wants to awaken us to our miseries; our
punishments must deter us from further evil. Knowing our nature,
we should turn from it to God. Goodman thinks of himself as cur-
ing mankind by lancing the wound and applying the salve.[28]

The argument proceeds from original grace to corruption and
then, in turn, to the grace that is in redemption. Though Goodman
does not actually reach the *resurgam* in the course of his treatise, his
professed text is *Ne laeteris quia cedidi, resurgam.* As we have seen,
he explains the corruption by contrasting it with the prior state
from which man fell. The corruption is also seen as the promise
of the final salvation. Why would God have shown us our illness,
he asks, if there were no cure? From the present decay Goodman
derives both the original and the ultimate perfection. This is as
close as he comes to establishing grace by reason alone.[29]

In spite of man's sin, however, God does not renounce him or
abandon the corrupted world. To preserve is as difficult as to create,
and the universe could not continue without God's constant care.
Left to themselves, all things would return to nothing or to the

original chaotic mass in which matter had first been created. Moreover, any actual corruption of nature, once it sets in, is irreparable
without God's direct intervention: "the wound and corruption of
nature, by ye strength of nature, is incurable."[30]

To some extent God allows the corruption, brought on by sin, to
destroy the order of the universe and the happiness of mankind. He
leaves man to himself, more now toward the end of the world than
formerly, withholding his continued good influence, so that man's
corruption is expedited and his miseries aggravated.[31]

But God's justice is outweighed by his mercy, and he will not
permit the total destruction of his creation; an excellent order will
still be preserved, and there will be no complete return to the "un-
digested chaos." The decay of the world and the miseries of man
are not merely punishments; they are reminders, intended in the
end to save men. All is corruption; this we must know and lament,
but we are not to despair, for God's providence will sustain the ailing universe:

"... God created all things of nothing, therefore shall all things
returne againe vnto nothing? This is a false consequence; for
being once produced, the same power shall vphold and continue
them, which laid their first foundation; euery thing containes in it
selfe a power, or rather an impotencie to returne vnto nothing
['impotencie' here is not 'inability,' but 'compulsion,' or inability
to do anything different]; and no creature in it selfe is independent, but seeing it hath stood with Gods mercie first to produce
them, it cannot but stand with the goodnesse and constancie of his
will, still to continue them, and to preserue his owne most excellent
workmanship. So that now all things relie not on the weaknesse
of their own foundation and pillars, but on the inuincible strength
of Gods power, the most certaine assurance of his promises, the
most infallible effects of his prouidence: so that howsoeuer the
production was, whether by creation, generation, alteration, &c. yet
we shall not neede to doubt or feare the corruption."[32]

Goodman's demonstration of the Fall always requires this
emphasis on God's mercy, for only a merciful God would create
man perfect in the first place. On the other hand, the argument is

reciprocal, and the best proof of God's mercy is, in turn, man's original and ultimate grace. Since the Fall, God has been merciful by restraining the violent contraries which otherwise would destroy man and world alike. Any enjoyment of happiness on earth is, in fact, a specific, merciful act of God. England's peace and prosperity under present and recent rulers, when the world everywhere else has become more corrupt, is a sign of God's pointed and benign grace. An "especiall warrant and protection vnder Gods owne signet" permits certain lands to remain unpoisoned by the corruption of nature, as proof of God's mercy and nature's original integrity. God increases or decreases his mercies according to our sins and our deserts, though even our miseries show his goodness, for the punishment is always less than the crime warrants, and the ultimate mercy—redemption—is, of course, greater than we deserve.[33]

Goodman contends, indeed, that the very decay and destruction of the world are merciful. To preserve infinitely a corrupt and sinful world would not be in accord with God's goodness: "therefore hee suffers the world of it selfe to decline by degrees." The last and irrevocable destruction is an act of mercy, for

"before it [the world] *comes to that extreame old age, weakenesse and miserie, God takes pittie on the world, thus languishing in a lingring disease; and seeing death is the wages of sinne, God doth suddenly interpose, hee burnes and consumes the world with fire, that so hee may purge and purifie it."*[34]

Hakewill's denial of this is direct and unequivocal: the punishment of man and the final conflagration of the world are acts of justice, not of mercy.[35]

On the whole, however, Goodman believes that our corruption is our punishment, and our miseries the fruits not of God's mercy but of his justice. If we accept the creation and the manner of creation as merciful, then original grace will have been established, and the present condition of man must be essentially a sign of justice rather than of mercy, and therefore evidence of man's Fall. The effects of justice are, of necessity, subsequent to the creation and are coexistent with sin rather than with mercy.

[20]

The punishment is not too great for the crime. The unborn children of the race participated in Adam's offense, and "mans sinne, like an hereditarie disease," is "together propagated with his seede." It may seem strange that the individual sins of men, which are forgiven after simple repentance, are greater than the original sin of mankind, which can be forgiven only by Christ's intercession. But the burden of original sin, common to all mankind, is aggravated by each personal sin, and the particular punishment of each man is thus added to his share of the common punishment. All in all, God's justice is less severe than his mercy is gentle. At the beginning God was merciful in not permitting man to sin more desperately and irretrievably; in the end he is merciful because his justice leads us to repentance and eternal grace.[36]

Justice may be administered both by supernatural means (conjunctions of stars, opening of the earth, etc.) and by natural means (noisome climates, etc.), so that the punishment as well as the sin becomes inbred, renewing itself out of nature. The plague, for example, is one of "Gods immediate and extraordinary actions... but sure I am that God is the God of nature, and hee can vse naturall meanes, for the punishment of mans sinne: thus plagues are sometimes foreseene and foretold."[37]

Manifestations of justice include not only the miseries of man and the conflict between man and creatures (because God first intended man's complete supremacy) but also the corruption of the earth and of the heavens. To these assertions of Goodman's, Hakewill later replies by holding God's judgments to be specific and supernatural (the Flood, the burning of Sodom and Gomorrah, the curse at the time of the first sin); the punishment may be visited upon nature but cannot take root in nature.

Goodman sees the corruption as so inherent in nature, once nature has become corrupt, that only God's restraining hand delays a precipitous and chaotic end. God "created not the elements thus rebellious, but leauing them to themselues, then began the insurrection." He keeps control over the various parts of nature

[21]

"like a cunning States-man," so that the opposing parts are equally matched and the outcome doubtful, until

"in a time best knowne to himselfe, hee shall no longer interpose himselfe as an vmpire; but vnbridle them; and giue them free power to reuenge their owne wrongs, and worke their owne wrath, and then shall follow the dissolution of nature. Thus one and the same cause serues as a present token of mercy, and as a future engine of iustice."[38]

IV. HOUSES OF CORRUPTION

Upon this view of man's relation to God, Goodman constructs a complex but consistent universe, defining man's place in the integrated whole, his function in the hierarchy of created things. The ordering of God's work is absolute and consummate, its unity comprehending not only the spheres of heaven and earth but all the creatures as well. The elements are "adiacent and contiguous," and the world is round, so that "all things might be better prest and compacted together." The linked harmony of the creation proves the unity of God.

Man, the union of spirit and body, has his place at the very heart of this pattern. He is "the center in the middest of the circumference; a little Microcosme, in whom all the creatures are vnited." Thus it is that God, taking the nature of man, "sits in the very middest of his creatures, imparting himselfe infinitly to all."

Just as man is created for the glory and service of God, so the universe is designed for man. It is man "for whom the whole fabricke was created, to whose vse and seruice all creatures were directed"; "Certaine it is that the heauens were ordained for man, and for man alone the whole earth was created."[39]

This premise—that all the world is contained in man and intended for his use—is fundamental to Goodman's argument, for it explains what would be otherwise incomprehensible: the corruption of heaven and earth as a consequence of man's sin. Only if man is the end and sum of all creation, only if the whole world is thus circumscribed within its principal part, can man's transgression bring suffering to the other creatures and decay and disorder to the framework of the universe.

The progression from the corruption of man to the corruption of the world, as supported by this unity and symmetry of creation, is immediately effected by one simple analogy: man is "the mirrour of nature . . . a little world epitomized, an abridgement of nature," and that which is applicable to man is applicable to the world. Man's violation destroyed the perfect symmetry of the whole; the little world set the great world on fire. Throughout most of his treatise Goodman devotes himself to proving the corruption of man, turning to the decay of the world only when he is three-fourths of the way through Part III and making the transition explicitly in terms of microcosm and macrocosm:

"me thinks I haue subdued the little world, and brought man as a captiue or slaue, through much misery and sorrow, at length to the place of his execution; and hauing now possest my selfe of the fairest fortresse, or tower in nature (man that is a little world), I cannot here content my selfe, but I begin to enquire, whether there are as yet more worlds to be conquered? and behold in the second place, I will fall vpon the great world, and I will attempt with Archimedes, to shake her foundations, to threaten her ruine, in this generall corruption and dissolution of man: for this punishment (*morte morieris*) though it principally concernes man, yet the whole world cannot be exempted from it, being directed and ordained onely for mans vse, containing in it selfe the very same seedes, and causes of death and destruction; and as it is most fit and agreeable to our present condition, that being corruptible in our selues, we should likewise dwell in houses of corruption."[40]

Refutation of the belief in decay is very often accompanied by a denial that there is any true resemblance between microcosm and macrocosm. Hakewill, for example, asserting that the analogy distorts our understanding of the universe, constantly **distinguishes** between man, who for his sin was cursed by God, and the world, which knows no sin and cannot be corrupt.[41] Goodman agrees that only man, having reason and free will, is capable of sin, but he believes that man's sin could and did poison the whole world.

This concept of microcosm and macrocosm, of part and whole, is a principal point on which the controversy over the decay of nature turns. When man is no longer the center and focus of the pattern, no longer the epitome of spiritual and material, it becomes impossible to find in his miseries the decay of the whole universe.

According to Goodman, then, it is by means of man that corruption is introduced into the world, and it is fitting that man suffer more than do the creatures or the inanimate bodies. Most of the punishments which man endures, frequently indicated as specific punishments of the first sin, are unique and peculiar to man. Since only man is capable of the transgression, the punishment "chiefly and principally" is his. God's justice "must onely bee exercised vpon man: for all the rest of the creatures are carried with the violence and streame of their nature; only man hath a discoursiue reason."[42]

Even the earth, which feeds the creatures freely, begrudges man its grain. The Flood and the final conflagration are "principally directed for man as the fruites of his offence." The conflicts arising from a corruptible body and an incorruptible soul are man's alone. Many of the other troubles of man which Goodman takes up are punishments which only man must bear.[43] The weight of God's wrath which man must carry is so preponderant, in fact, that Goodman proposes to rest his whole case on his recital of man's miseries, "and by man alone the fall & corruption shall manifestly appeare."[44]

But, because the whole creation is so closely woven, some of the guilt and punishment is visited upon the creatures also. Man's sin affords them an "example and president." If man, being *"nexus & naturae vinculum,"* breaks his proper pattern, "it must necessarily follow, that all the rest of the creatures, which were bound and knit together in man, should likewise be inordinate, & ouerflow their owne banks." The creatures shared in God's original curse of nature and groan under the burden of man's sin. After all, they are wholly designed for man's use, and their suffering cannot be too great if it serve for man's admonition and as a "remembrancer of his sinne."[45]

Because their suffering is caused by man's sin, it is only justice that they should, in turn, become instruments for man's punishment. One creature mocks man, another annoys him, many can hurt him, and the lowliest of all—the serpent—can deal him a mortal wound. There exists now a constant antipathy between man and beast, and man no longer enjoys his ordained superiority. The creatures conspire against man, because man, forsaking his rank and casting off his majesty, has put on the "qualities and beastly conditions" of the creatures.[46]

The earth and the heavens also feel the effects of man's sin. Goodman's universe is still a geocentric one, "the earth as the center, the heauens for the circumference; the earth as an immoueable stocke." He dismisses as absurd the Copernican hypothesis,[47] but he recognizes that "the whole world is but a point, & carries no sensible quantitie in respect of the heauens."[48]

In other words, although he has not accepted a heliocentric astronomy, even without Copernicus he can be aware of the relative smallness of the earth. In his philosophy, God can "square and proportion the heauens for the earth," even if it be an infinitesimal point of an earth.[49] Thus the teleological picture of a decaying universe does not require the earth to have the relative dignity of vast size, and the impact of the new astronomy is not so great as it would be if it introduced the earth's insignificance as a new element in the whole design.

What Goodman does depend on is the dignity of the earth's position at the center, and his closely knit universe has none of the incomprehensible distances which Copernicus realized must exist between solar system and stars. According to Goodman's conventional pattern, the universe is continuous, with hell at the center of the earth, then concentric spheres of the elements and the planets, all ultimately inclosed within the sphere of the fixed stars.[50] Man, master of the earth, secure upon the solid center of the universe, is thus given a place in the physical creation corresponding to his metaphysical importance as the aim and epitome of all God's works.

Decay and corruption begin with man, then, but soon extend beyond man; because of sin "the earth is cursed," and "by the earth the whole world is implyed, for it is the center which points out the circle." If man, for whom all else was created, declines, then assuredly the world cannot be excused from corruption, and the heavens as well as the earth are brought into the realm of mortality and decay. "Now I haue brought man to his graue," Goodman cries, "and together with man the whole fabricke of nature . . . I haue cast the heauens and the earth vpon him, and together with man intombed the whole world."[51]

To some extent it is the corruption of man and earth which vitiates the cordial, life-giving influence of the heavens, but the heavens themselves are decayed also. From this extreme position Goodman does not retreat. Hakewill agrees that the heavens were made for man and that decay in the heavens would be a sufficient cause (and sign) of decay on the earth; but he denies that the argument can extend from the sphere of mortality to the sphere of immortality, challenging Goodman again and again to prove corruption of the heavens from actual observation.[52]

The corruption of heaven and earth, as with the corruption of the creatures, is, in turn, a further instrument of man's punishment. The infection, contracted from man, is hatched in the earth and there perpetuated, just as man's sin and corruption are bred into the very seed of man. One of the punishments "related in scriptures," as explained in Part III of the *Fall,* is that the earth shall bring forth thorns and briars, the soil shall be barren and venomous, and man shall suffer from the corruption he has brought upon nature. Nature further punishes man by tormenting and deluding him; she gives him appetites and desires which cannot be satisfied and promises him a contentment that he can never attain.[53]

Though usually Goodman's argument proceeds from man to nature, in the fashion outlined, it may operate conversely as well, from nature to man, for the homogeneity of the creation means that any defection found in one part must be a sign of a defection in the rest. The design of his entire work is, of course, to prove man's Fall by showing the present corruption of both man and world,[54] and Goodman actually begins his study with a statement of the world's corruption, only then advancing to man. The weeds of the earth argue the weeds of man's mind. Nature abounds in evil, inclines unto evil, is violent with contraries, and requires art to repair her ruins. For these reasons "it cannot be denied, but nature in generall is much corrupted; which doth more argue the corruption of mā in particular, being that whole nature is directed to man."[55]

Thus, although the man-to-world, microcosm-to-macrocosm progression certainly determines the usual pattern of Goodman's reasoning, he is able also to derive the first step from the second and to submit the world's corruption as proof of man's corruption. It is only the demonstration, however, which sometimes proceeds from nature to man; the corruption itself is always rooted in man and spreads thence to nature.

V. INBRED SEEDS OF CORRUPTION

The appeal to natural man requires that Goodman not only prove the decay of nature analogically and teleologically but that he establish, as well, the inherent natural corruptibility of all created things. This he does in a series of conventional arguments, which show, in addition to the contrast between the original perfection and the world as it is now (a contrast which may be inferred simply from the Fall of man), a current and progressive deterioration in all things.

The natural tendency toward decay is established in various ways. For example, decay in the whole is derived from decay of the part, and death of the species from death of the individual. Signs of the world's approaching end, itself proved by the natural weakness leading it to destruction, are, in turn, used to demonstrate this natural and inbred corruptibility. The most important arguments from nature are based on the principle of privation and on the conflict of contrary motions.[56]

The inherent tendency to corruption is expounded early in Goodman's text. Even before he proceeds to his main discourse on the miseries of man, he gives a preliminary list of reasons for the corruption of nature. True, he here uses these reasons to prove the Fall (nature is not now perfect and thus must be declined from its original excellence), but they indicate also the grounds for his belief in corruption as a process rooted in nature:

"... first, that nature so much aboundeth in euill; secondly, and is so much enclined vnto euill; thirdly, considering how the heauens stand affected to the earth; fourthly, how elements amongst themselues; fifthly, how mixt creatures one to another; sixthly, and in themselues what defects and imperfections there are; seuenthly, how Art serues like a cobler, or tinker, to peece vp the walles, and to repaire the ruines of nature."[57]

The first two and the seventh deal with the shortcomings of nature relative to an ideal perfection which must have existed before the Fall; the third through the sixth elaborate upon the conflicts which abound at all levels of creation.

More specifically, the first proof of nature's corruption stresses the variety and range of evils as contrasted with the rigorous simplicity of the good: "there is but one state of a sound and whole constitution; but diseases, and distempers are numberlesse: to euery vertue, there are many vices opposed; to euery meane, there are many extreames." This is closely related to his second argument, that such a preponderance of evil continues to increase. It is easier to destroy than to build, Goodman points out. There is one tedious way to be born, but "infinite by-waies" which lead to sudden death.[58]

This assertion of the tendency to decay occurs, as we have seen, just before the long treatise on man's miseries gets under way (pp. 14–27), and it appears once again (pp. 349–50) immediately at the end of this treatise, when Goodman effects his transition from microcosm to macrocosm. In an argument that decay extends to the creatures as well as to man, he gives these three reasons:

1. The farther from the fountainhead, the greater is corruption.

2. Corruption in the "singulars" argues corruption in the kinds.

3. All nature has a tendency to decay.

The progression from individual to species is a variant of the part-to-whole line of reasoning. The other two points, the first a consequence of the third, repeat the earlier assertions that nature is inclined unto evil. When the corruptibility is established, the corruption itself must follow, and Goodman proceeds at once to compare ancients and moderns, and to give detailed empirical signs that the world's corruption is evident. "See then," he says as he takes the step, "the generall intent and scope of nature tending to corruption, must likewise argue that nature her selfe in generall, shall at length be tainted with the same corruption."[59]

But even when the principle of corruptibility is recognized and the results of corruption are apparent, Goodman writes, the actual process may not be evident to the senses: *"the Sunne moves swifter then an arrow, yet seemes to stand still; much lesse is the dissolution so easily discerned."* Natural alterations are often insensible, and the corruption, discernible by reason, is difficult to prove from observation. By "reason" Goodman means, of course, the demonstration proceeding from prior knowledge; and he derives the palpable, perceptual "signs" of decay from the true pattern of the universe as he understands it. Forced to it by Hakewill's attack, he advances a period of three centuries as long enough to reveal the growing corruption, and *"in every 300 yeares,"* he says, *"I do undertake to shew an apparent change and decay in nature."* This span serves also as the dividing line between ancient and modern.[60]

The doctrine of physical corruptibility implies that corruption has a basis in natural law, that the corruptible part corrupts the whole, that the original curse of God has taken root in nature. In other words, the evil is bred by natural means. Explanation of this inbred corruption is principally in terms of privation and the conflict of contraries. Goodman sees privation wherever *"a thing is capable to be, and ought to be, but is not."* Coetaneous with matter and form, privation is common to all creation. It is defect, the lack of that which should be present, "a kinde of nothing," and thus to be distinguished from negation or the absence of something which was never intended.[61]

When this potential force is set in motion, it disrupts the balances of nature and releases discords which eventually lead to dissolution. It is the means by which corruption takes root, the principle of nature *"whereby out of her weakenesse shee is apt to bee worne out with use."*[62] Providing a perilous balance between matter and form, it is the potential of change and hence of decay. Because of privation, anything which is mutable is also corruptible, and the process of decay is cumulative and irreversible.

Privation indicates denial or deficiency and, therefore, also a potential good greater than that which actually exists. The corruption is recognized and understood by contrast with this ideal good. Absolute perfection is impossible in corrupted nature, and the greater the apparent perfection, the more menacing is the potential evil of privation. Because "euery thing containeth in it selfe the inbred seedes of corruption," we find that the more perfect the creature is, the more apt for corruption. The finest wool soonest breeds the moth; the fairest beauty is first to wither. The tendency is always away from perfection and toward greater corruption.[63]

In addressing natural man, Goodman insists that privation (and hence the corruptibility of nature) existed prior to the Fall. But if nature were subject to decay before man sinned, how, then, can Goodman offer the decay of the world as proof of the Fall of man? We should repeat that the principle of privation is enough to account for the wholly natural inclination toward decay. Yet to explain the difference between the mere absence of a greater potential good and the definite lack of that good, Goodman invokes once more the argument from the intended purpose of the creation: a better state of being were possible "were it not that some curse had altered the course of nature, whereby that, which formerly was onely a bare negation, should now be conceiued to be a naturall priuation."[64]

But again, why only a bare negation before the Fall? Goodman answers that God had then restrained the natural privative action and that, even prior to man's sin, only God's grace had held off the corruption of the world. Innocent man and the perfect world around him were therefore always subject to decay; but, before the harmony of the universe had been violated, all were and would have continued to be preserved by the special favor and mercy of God. In proving the corruption to be natural, Goodman must show the preservation of the world—before as well as after the Fall—to be miraculous.

Now that the corruption is under way, God's intercession prevents, or at least postpones, the complete natural destruction of the world. Nature, being once fallen, "could not raise her selfe by her own naturall power." She has only the necessity or the "power" of returning to nothing. God mercifully retards the process of corruption. When he relaxes his benevolent vigilance, the dissolution will be accelerated: "as nature was made of nothing, so it should [then] haue a power to returne againe to the same nothing, as being the first matrix or proper place, whereunto of it selfe, being left to it selfe, it is naturally inclined."[65]

The principle of privation, borrowed from Aristotelian natural philosophy, is thus made to support the Christian tenets of original grace and the Fall of man. Not only was corruption possible in the original state of nature; without the explicit saving grace of the Creator, it was inevitable. But, since evil is simply the lack of good, there was no evil before man sinned. Known only in relation to good and having no independent being, evil must have been introduced into nature since the creation. It cannot be positive, for it is "in it selfe a meere defect and priuation," just as darkness is caused by lack of light. Sin is the falling-away from good, and the punishment of sin is the removal of the grace which the world had enjoyed.[66]

The tendency to decay, the privative necessity for returning to nothing, once it has been put into effect by the Fall, is, according to Goodman, implemented by the contrary motions in perpetual conflict throughout nature. Man's soul, for example, is immortal because (and only because) it is "exempted & freed from the opposition and contrarietie of elementarie qualities," which opposition is "the only motiue and inducement to corruption," whereas the physical world will decay because of its *naturall principles and composition subsisting of contrary qualities, and these ever active and opposing each other."*[67]

The conflict rages on all levels, beginning with the basic incompatibility of the elements and extending to the mixed bodies, which are the "pitch't field, the place appointed for the combate and encounter of the elements." Mixed bodies are those combining the elements or humors, and they include man (though not his soul) and all other creatures. The conflict in man is heightened by the particular and unique opposition of body and soul. The mixture of elements accounts for the conflict within each creature (for example, the melancholy and discontent of every man), within any one species (the factions and quarrels among men), and among different species (the hostility between man and the other creatures). Finally, even "the heauens, and the earth, seeme to conspire the one against the other."[68]

The decay is gradual despite the general conflict, but only because God partially restrains the contrary motions. He keeps control over the various parts of nature so that some balance is achieved, until such time as he releases all the disruptive forces and thus permits the world to work its own dissolution. Hakewill's answer here is the same as it is in refuting privation and the general tendency to decay: prove decay in the immutable heavens, and he will grant the rest.[69]

The corruptibility of the world is further argued from a number of inferences, serving to characterize the whole by some part, the end by the beginning, the unknown by the known. All these patterns are ultimately subsumed under the more sweeping analogy between microcosm and macrocosm, the corruption of man extended to include the corruption of the world.

At times Goodman contends that the part actually corrupts the whole. The diseased member will destroy the whole body; one man with the plague will infect a city. At other times Goodman's argument is simply that the corrupt part is a sign of the whole. A monster is a flaw in the particular, but it implies a flaw in the general as well. The surface blemish shows the inward illness; for, "if any one branch or leafe doe miscarrie, the roote is vnsound; so is it in the outward workes of nature, these being corrupted, doe vndoubtedly argue the corruption of nature." If the part is corrupt, Goodman contends, the whole must be corruptible, *"and by the decay of all individualls, wee judge of the decay of the world, which subsisting of the same principles cannot bee exempted from the same lot and condition."* The world grew from nothing and must return to nothing; it was perfected by degrees and must decline and die by degrees.[70] Hakewill answers in kind, that a supernatural beginning promises a supernatural end; and, in general, he replies to such arguments by denying the analogy, maintaining that an imperfect part may fit into a perfect whole.

One of these points assumes particular importance in the controversy—decay of the individual as extended to decay of the species. The only eternity possible, Goodman believes, would be that of the individual, and "eternity by succession" introduces death and decline. Just as the world "dies daily in the singulars, so at length it shall faile in the vniuersals, and in the kindes of the creatures."[71] To some extent death may be compensated for by birth and corruption balanced by generation, so that the process of dissolution is delayed; but not even this comfort is granted to man, for at man's death his soul is irretrievably lost to nature.

All the species on earth have declined, and some, indeed, have actually disappeared. Only the angels and spirits are freed from corruption, because only these have immortality of the individual rather than of the species. "It would implie a contradiction in nature," says Goodman, "if the parts and the whole were not of like condition," i.e., equally corrupt, and it would be equally illogical to "suppose a corruption of the singulars, and an eternitie of the kinde." The succession of individuals may postpone, but it cannot prevent, the corruption of the species.[72]

The natural corruption of the world is proved also by the approach of the final fire. The signs of the end, as given in the Scriptures, are "natural"; that is, the destruction may be effected by means of the principles inherent in the physical universe. Only if this were true, could the end of the world be foreseen as it now is, Goodman argues. He cannot conceive that the world will be destroyed with *"no token, nor signe thereof, to appeare in nature."* The final destruction will come about, if God does not prevent it, as a continuation and acceleration of processes already in operation. When the world grows desperately sick and near death, her light shall be put out. All nature "shall stand in an vprore, the heauens with the elements, the elements with the heauens, and all together confounded."[73]

Conversely, it is the corruption which proves that the end is near. The signs of decay are also signs that the world is wearing down toward its finish. This circularity of argument, whereby the world's corruptibility establishes its mortality and its mortality, in turn, establishes its corruptibility, is not unique in Goodman's dialectic. It is the result of an incomplete adaptation to rational or empirical evidence of principles which Goodman himself held by faith and revelation.

Though we know that the end approaches, we cannot know the date. Fifteen generations seem to mark off each epoch of the world's history: from the creation to the Deluge, from the Deluge to Christ, and from Christ to us; "that which remaines, it is the sound of the trumpet." Man's wickedness is a sign of the coming end, and "now in these latter daies, when the world is almost come to an vpshot, when the period of time is now approching," it is no wonder that God withdraws his favor, permitting man to neglect the common good for "his owne priuate and present commoditie." Our sins will be judged, and the necessity of the justice hastens the judgment. The end is near: "when the hangings and furniture are taken downe, it is a token that the King and the Court are remoouing; nature now beginning to decay, seemes to hasten Christs comming."[74]

The end will be in a sense the completion of decay, for all the present forms of things will be dissolved. But it will also be a reversal of the decay, for there will be new and purified forms. Goodman believes that the end of the world will in a sense be its beginning. There will be *"a death and corruption, but no Annihilation."* After the destruction of the world which we know, there will follow some perfect purged existence neither wholly spiritual nor wholly material, a world which will last for eternity.

Such a "purifying" destruction is best effected by fire, whose property it is to gather the homogeneous and separate the heterogeneous. Fire draws out the elixirs and quintessences, is the nearest element to the heavens, and provides the best means for passage of bodies from terrestrial to celestial and spiritual. The fiery end may well be close at hand, for the fiery constellations are predominant and the general combustion may be kindled at any time.[75]

In the arguments appended to the *Apologie,* considerable space is devoted to debating this problem of the world's mortality, which receives relatively little attention in Goodman's original argument. His thesis at first is, of course, simply that the general decay proves the Fall of man; but, when pressed by Hakewill, he finds it necessary to defend at length the natural mortality of the world, and he is eager to press the implication that Hakewill's heathen position would assume the present world to be eternal.

He even declares, possibly (as Hakewill accuses) in an attempt to evade the defense of his argument on decay, that the principal purpose of the *Fall* is to refute any belief in the world's eternity, maintaining that only a belief in decay completely precludes the eternity of the world as we know it. Hakewill answers that he supports merely the *possibility* of eternity, and he insists that whatever end there is must be supernatural rather than the result of nature's wearing-down. Thus Hakewill's point is merely that the world would not come to an end of itself, by any natural means, whereas Goodman contends that its innate corruption makes its end and the return to chaos inevitable, even without the final conflagration.[76]

[35]

VI. SIGNS OF CORRUPTION—MAN

Goodman's interest in the decay of the world is in the corruption as evidence of the Fall. But a corrupt world, punished for man's sin, still need not be a decaying world. The difference between the perfect original creation and the present evils of man and nature need not imply a constantly degenerating world, as we discover from the writings of many of Goodman's contemporaries. The appeal to natural man, however, and the forcefulness of the exhortation are both served by seeing the corruption as a continuous process, culminating in the now imminent end of the world. The decay so conceived is established first in the theoretical concept of natural corruptibility and then in the sensible evidence of decline from one age to the next.

Yet Goodman does not separate these two procedures. The signs of decay, the elaboration of which makes up the bulk of the treatise, are predominantly flaws which were introduced at the precise moment of the Fall; but indiscriminately listed among these are also the signs of continuous deterioration since the Fall. The distinctions which dictate Goodman's organization are rather those among the kinds of human miseries. The major pattern of the treatise is the catalogue of man's ills, in which "the fall & corruption shall manifestly appeare."[77] I now turn to an examination of these outward evidences of corruption, ignoring at this point, as does Goodman, the differences between the corruption that accompanied the Fall, on the one hand, and the subsequent decay of a corruptible universe, on the other.

Goodman is constantly reminding us that his whole treatise is a sermon on the miseries of man, a lament and a prayer which will bring man back to God. It is an intense and highly emotional appeal to man's self-pity and his fear of the unknown. The ills and weaknesses of the flesh are proof of man's corruption and the decay of all the world. The purpose of every argument is to reveal the corruption before it is too late; the whole work is not so much dialectic as homiletic.

[36]

Goodman sees his own corruption and humbly offers it as a sign and admission of all corruption: "if I haue spoken any thing, or shall hereafter speake in this Pamphlet," he says,

"vnaduisedly, illiterately, without good order or methode; acknowl-edge (I beseech thee) the generall punishment of whole mankinde, which more especially discouers it selfe in my weakenesse, the con-fusion of tongues. I am confounded, I am confounded, poore silly wretch that I am, I am confounded, my minde is distracted, my tongue is confounded, and my whole nature corrupted; in me, in mee alone, see the punishment of whole mankinde, learne now to be compassionate, and pitifull, for I cannot altogether excuse thee; *Nihil humani à te alienum putes,* here is thy benefite indeed, my weakenesse appeares, the presse hath proclaimed it, this Pamphlet can witnesse it; and thine is yet vndiscouered."[78]

The evidences of man's decay, whether peculiar to man or rela-tive to the rest of creation, whether named in the Scriptures or simply recognized in nature, are found in the miseries of man's body, in the miseries of his mind and spirit, and in the indications of the decline of society.

The miseries of the body first appear in man's instinctive or nat-ural actions, all of which are "tainted and defiled." These actions shame man, bring him bodily hurt, and enslave him. If he must eat in privacy, what are we to say of the grosser exercises of his body? His blushes, included by Goodman under the natural actions of the body, are a confession of the corruption that cannot be concealed. He punishes himself with his fears and his self-accusations. He is better equipped to destroy than to preserve himself. His old age is a disease and a punishment.[79]

The corruption is apparent also in the natural restrictions upon the body. The soul cannot leave and return. Man cannot converse with angels. He is ruled by his habits and his occupations, nor can he ever free himself, for "mans nature is corrupted, mans nature is corrupted: and therefore with patience we must endure the yoke, no longer sonnes of a louing mother, but seruants and slaues to a step-dame."[80]

[37]

Man's birth is mean and dangerous, his life short, and his death inevitable. He is weak and helpless when he is born, sometimes dying and sometimes causing death at birth. He comes into the world head first, without weapons or defense, and knows only confusion from his first day. His brief stay on earth becomes even briefer. His body can be embalmed and thus preserved, but the days of his life are few; since the Flood these days are fewer still.

Death is specifically "the last punishment of the first sinne," and without sin there would have been no dying, "but some happie translation." Because the soul is lost to nature, man's death is irreparable and against the whole scope and intent of nature, and "in the death of man, and of man alone, the corruption and nothing but the corruption of nature sufficiently appeares."[81]

Man's body is weak and susceptible to pain and disease, more so now than ever before. The cunning and activity of his wit are little and always decreasing. He suffers the miseries of decrepit old age. His body is smaller and weaker than it once was, and he no longer has his wonted ability to engender. The world's population declines, and the females now outnumber the males. Man is physically weaker than the animals, has poorer natural instincts, is more unclean. All is confusion and suffering, and the suffering is proof that man, for whom the world was created, is being punished for his sin.[82]

Miseries of the mind and spirit are even more oppressive, for here Goodman includes all vices and sins. He points out that lust invites disease and that other failings of the mind bring on sufferings of the body. Man's reason is weak and variable among men. Unlike angels, which understand by "infusion" what is proper to them, or beasts, which encompass their proper province naturally by their senses, man cannot comprehend the truths that should be his by reason and God's grace but must busy himself to make his "owne obiects" intelligible.[83]

Because his understanding does not enable him to judge, man thus confuses the virtues and the vices and indulges in the vices, too stubborn ever to recognize and admit his error. His learning, a repetitious jumble, is a remembering of those truths he should have known naturally or instinctively; because he has forgotten them, we know he is corrupt. Because the first sin was "curiositie of knowledge," this limitation of man's reason is a particularly appropriate punishment, and the extremes of madness and idiocy are properly peculiar to man.[84]

The vanity and delusion of all man's hopes are further signs of the corruption. His desires are transitory, bringing him only unrest. There is no enduring happiness on earth: beauty causes lust and then fades; honor but increases pride; wealth brings cares and dejection; learning ends in confusion; and pleasures belong to the ephemeral realm of the fancy.

Goodman preaches this contempt of the world so that "hauing no true ground of happinesse in our selues, wee might cast vp our anchor of hope vnto heauen." Joys are illusory, always in the past or in the future. Man's desire for knowledge is never realized, and, worst of all, he is ignorant of his own soul. His will is "deluded with showes, vaine hopes, false promises, receiuing no manner of contentment."[85]

There is no satisfaction in man's dwelling, apparel, diet, goods, or the comeliness of his own person. Clergy, gentry, lawyers, judges, citizens, and nobles alike endure sorrows and servitude. Because of his sin man must labor; man alone is so punished, and, though destined to be the lord of all creation, he must serve both the earth and the creatures, tilling the soil and tending the flocks.[86]

His degenerate passions and his fears also indicate his corruption. Even his good actions come from evil intentions. He enjoys the misfortunes of others and seduces his fellows into sharing his own evil. His smallest sorrow outweighs all his joys; and sleep, his greatest joy, is the very image of death. He is afraid of death, anticipates his misfortunes, fears hell and damnation, and worries always about the future. Even his most generous passion—his sympathy for others—causes him grief and sorrow. He suffers shame, and poverty of spirit; notice how servile are his common salutations, and how he must clothe the nakedness of both body and soul. The root of his corruption is within himself. He is constantly tormenting himself with self-accusations, self-mortifications, and reproaches, and sometimes he gives clearest proof of his inner corruption by becoming a "self-homicide."[87]

Many of these ills are directly attributable to the conflict in man between the body and the spirit—the combination in one entity of the corruptible and the incorruptible, the sensible and the intelligent, the material and the spiritual. This unhappy union is not "the speciall difference" or the defining and distinguishing characteristic of man, though it is, of course, peculiar to man. It is rather one of the explicit punishments of man's sin, and it accounts for the first nine of the twelve punishments which Goodman lists as the direct result of the Fall, and to which he devotes most of Part I of his treatise.[88]

The spiritual soul, "exempted from any elementarie composition," must nevertheless be coupled with the base body. It is no wonder that neither part of man understands the other. The two belong to different worlds, "and therefore in reason should not admit any fellowship or societie betweene themselues, much lesse be the members of one and the same corporation." The understanding is betrayed by the body, so that sense rather than intelligence dominates man, whose concern is thus with particulars instead of generals and whose actions are guided by his passions instead of by his rational soul.[89]

The conflict between body and soul is paralleled by further conflict on all levels of human activity. Contrary qualities may cause opposition between individuals or between nations. Or the disparity may be between the inner and the outer man, between inner wisdom and outward ugliness, or inner baseness and outward beauty, whereas "in all other creatures, the comelines, beautie, and fit proportion of the outward limbes, signifies the good inward conditions." Contradictions appear in men's humors, their ages, their sexes, and even among the various faculties of the soul. Wit and memory, for example, are not frequently found together; and the wit of one man will seldom comprehend both mathematics and metaphysics. Such disproportion and contention cause men to be melancholy when alone and carry them into quarrels and factions in society.[90]

The corruption of body and spirit thus brings about the decline of society, the third great indication of man's Fall. His moral and social conduct is indefensible. He thinks of himself alone. His dealings with his fellows are corrupt and full of impostures, more now than in the past, and a "Machiauelian policy" prevails in his affairs.[91] Having lost his sovereignty over beasts and nature, he now has it only over woman, and even woman has become rebellious. There are many abuses of marriage, the worst being the practice of marriage after divorce.

The diversity of fashions, the use of tobacco, the drunkenness, and, finally, the theaters, with their "changes and variety of fortunes, feares and iealousies in loue, and somtimes tragicall conclusions," are evidences of the same decay. The confusion and disputes in religion are among the clearest signs of God's curse, and, though we have the gospel and thereby a fulness of knowledge impossible in nature alone, religion has declined by degrees, at least since Noah. Indeed, Goodman laments,

"I am fallen into a cold sweate, and am suddenly stroken with great feare and confusion...for when I obserue the course of things, the seuerall actions and inclinations of men; when I consider the diseases of these times, together with all the signes, tokens, and symptoms; alas, alas, I feare a relapse, I feare a relapse, lest the world in her old doting age, should now againe turne infidell, and that the end of vs be worse then the beginning."[92]

Many of the disturbances which Goodman records are reflections of an unsettled economy. Housekeeping is conducted on a humbler scale than in the past. Food and clothing are less attractive than formerly and harder to obtain. Prices are higher, and more things are scarce. Coin has decreased both in value and in quantity. All wealth, in fact, has greatly diminished. As a result, the economic and military strength of nations is constantly decreasing, as we may see in the reduced armies and the meager shipping today. The "inclosing of common fields" is a current practice "vnknowne, or els vtterly detested and abhorred, by the former and better times of our forefathers." By this device public lands were fenced off and used for pasture only, with consequent shortage of crops, unemployment, and "vitious and dissolute courses."[93]

Goodman objects, however, to any effort at altering these circumstances and, without exception, mourns the passing of the older society. As the feudal paternalism breaks down, he notes only his regret at the decrease of alms. Just as to discredit antiquity in religion is to *"open a gap to all innovation and projecting, which may passe under the faire pretence and colour of reformation,"* so in social matters if we admit changes, *"how apt shall we bee for innovation, what daunger of a mutinee; the country boares may rise in sedition."*[94]

Only England is exempt from these troubles; the government is good and the people are happy. There is now "such a generall Peace," so much justice and security, that plots and uprisings seem impossible. We have peace, in these declining days of the world, by special dispensation from God, who has given us rulers so good (referring especially to Queen Anne) that even "the corruption of mans minde could neuer frame vnto it selfe, the lest seeming or supposed occasion of complaint or grieuance."[95]

VII. SIGNS OF CORRUPTION—NATURE

Throughout his treatise, then, Goodman is concerned primarily with man—man's sin, man's Fall, man's punishments, man's miseries. Not until late in Part III is there a formal transition to the corruption of the world. By this time Goodman considers his thesis established; when man's corruption is recognized, his Fall is beyond question, and there remains only to draw the inevitable inferences about the decay of the world. Goodman has persisted, thus, with his professed plan of proving all corruption "by man alone."

This procedure does not exclude earlier references to a corrupt world, since the barrenness of the earth, for example, is a specific punishment of man as contained in God's curse and related in Scripture. But such references are incidental to his proof of man's corruption, and only in the thirty-odd pages near the end of Part III does he promise to concern himself with decay of the macrocosm. After making his transition, quoted at length earlier in this study (p. 23), in terms of the little-world : great-world analogy, Goodman need only point out instances of the great world's decay. It is here also that he adopts the method of comparing present conditions with past.

Two important observations may now be made. First, this brief section of Goodman's work comprises his only considered treatment of the ancients and moderns and, similarly, the only consecutive or extensive presentation of decay as a continuous process.[96] But he uses the same premises and the same method he has been using up to this point: all sufferings or imperfections are the results of man's sin; the decay of any part is the decay of the whole. Second, in even this disproportionately small section of his text, expressly allocated to signs of corruption in the macrocosm, Goodman still is more concerned with man than with nature.

Because man's original sin is the cause of *all* corruption, two sets of distinctions disappear: first, that between the Fall and the continued decay and, second, that between decay of the microcosm and decay of the macrocosm. Thus we confirm once again Goodman's dependence upon man as symbol and epitome of the world which was made for his pleasure and which suffers for his sin.

Decay in the macrocosm is thus, for Goodman, simply a reflection and extension of decay in the microcosm. Flaws either in man or in nature are offered as proof of corruption in both. The decay of nature, considered as a corollary or even a mere restatement of the decay of man, is discovered both in the earth and in the heavens. The earth, since the Fall, has become barren and even poisoned, although the poisons need not be immediately or universally operative. Briars, weeds, and thorns, which were not in Eden, are the fruits of sin. The losses sustained at the Flood were never recovered, and the "pits," "layers," and poor soil of today may be attributed to the confusion of the elements which then existed.

The base, mean creatures show the earth's corruption, for if she were sound she would not be busied with begetting these contemptible objects. Being defective, however, "and not able to produce couragious Lions, braue Vnicornes, fierce Tigers, stout Elephants, shee makes it her taske and imployment to be the mother, and midwife of wormes, of gnats, and of butterflies." The earth seems to be "frozen, and congealed with coldnesse in the Sunnes absence; or else to be scorched and consumed with heate, by his ill neighbourhood, and nearer accesse." We have "excessiue drought in the spring, excessiue moysture in haruest; the spring alwaies annoyed with an East winde, which nippes the tender bud; and the Autumne alwaies molested with a boysterous Westerne winde, which scattereth the fruites before they are ripened."[97]

Most of the world cannot be lived in because of inhospitable rivers, climate, soil, mountains, deserts, wildernesses, and seas, although the hot zones of the earth, once unfit for man, are now habitable as the earth loses its strength. The mountains are being washed away, the rivers clogged, the land encroached upon by the sea. In all climates alike, nature has lost her original virtue and can no longer fulfil her functions alone but must submit to the "high contempt and indignity" of depending upon man. The earth must be tilled, plants tended; beasts and men alike must be trained; "nature is to bee taught and instructed by her hand-maid, to receiue her last and finall perfection from her vassall and slaue, that ill-fauoured ape, mistrisse Arte," the "learned gossip" who "serues like a cobler, or tinker, to peece vp the walles, and to repaire the ruines" of the world.[98]

The decay of nature extends to the heavens as well as to the earth, to the circumference as well as to the center. This is Goodman's boldest assertion, and in terms of this point alone Hakewill is willing to decide the entire controversy. For Goodman, all the disturbances upon the earth, "the diuersitie, the stormes, and the tempests, the famine, the pestilence," are signs of the corrupt heavens. The "reciprocal opposition" between heaven and earth, he argues further, was certainly never intended. It is most strange "that the heauens being Gods blessed instruments to continue life, quicken sense, stir vp motion, yet with their malignant and disastrous aspects, should cause the ouerthrow of man." Designed to increase the earth's fruitfulness, the heavens now accelerate its decay. Nevertheless, it remains clear that "the root of this dissention" was first bred and still remains not in the heavens but in the earth, "from whence proceeds the first occasion of these tumults."[99]

At times Goodman seems to state the more easily defended view that the heavens themselves remain unharmed and beneficent, while only the corruption here below prevents their good influence from penetrating to the earth. In discussing the extent of damage at the time of the Deluge, for example, Goodman says that, although "these sublunary contagions could not infect the stars, yet were they able much to hinder the goodnes of their actions and operations, as likewise to eclipse and obscure their beauty." But the corrupt earth would eventually renew itself if the heavens were not also corrupt, and the fault does not lie with the earth alone: "since the fruitfulnesse, or barrennesse of the earth, proceedes from the influence and disposition of the heauens; in the last place I dare accuse the materiall heauens, as being guiltie, conspiring, and together ioyntly tending to corruption."[100]

Some of the signs of this celestial mutability—meteors, the three-day darkening of the sun—are supernatural, Goodman concedes, and are not to be taken as evidences of decay. Such supernatural actions, however, serve (as did the Flood) simply to hasten and affirm the natural inclination. Corruption of the heavens is also slower and less perceptible than corruption on earth and, consequently, more difficult to prove from natural observation. The indications are, nevertheless, sufficient and, to Goodman, incontrovertible.

The sun's power is diminishing, as we see by the reduced heat that reaches the earth. There are spots or blemishes on its surface; and its position in the heavens is steadily declining, according to the measurements of ancient and modern astronomers. Our calendars clearly record the running-down of the universe, for the *"decay of the world is not so much as the losse of ten summer dayes, yet these were lost in the* Julian *yeare."* Oddly enough, Hakewill does not consider this a significant loss and will not bother to deny it; ten days, he answers, are "very little indeed ... if the decay bee no more then so, wee need not feare any hasty dissolution of the world by the decay thereof."[101]

The comet of 1572 and others have come and gone, says Goodman, in the sphere of the supposedly fixed stars. The moon, scarred and spotted, resembling man in its mutable and changing countenance, is the very symbol of decay. There is no phenomenon of the heavens, in fact, which does not contribute to this impression of universal alteration and impermanence; and here once more (as with the earth and creatures and all the sublunar world) corruption in the macrocosm is accepted as fitting because of the whole world's inclusion in and dependence upon the microcosm:

"And thus being mortall of our selues, wee dwell in houses of clay, the roofe of this world, as well as the foundations shall together be mooued; for wherefore serues the diuersitie of seasons, the day and the night succeeding each other, Summer and Winter, the rising and setting of Starres, the different and contrarie motions, the various aspects and oppositions? but that in some sort they partake of our nature, and shall haue their part and portion with ours."[102]

Chapter III

HAKEWILL'S DEFENSE OF NATURE

GOODMAN'S position is untenable; his philosophy is a philosophy of despair. This is the argument of George Hakewill, who is moved to protest against the prevalence of the belief in the world's decay, and more especially against Goodman's defense of that belief. In 1627, encouraged by the praises of his friends, he completed and published the work which he had begun some years earlier, *An Apologie of the Power and Providence of God in the Government of the World*. A second edition, *"revised, and in sundry passages augmented by the Authour,"* appeared in 1630; and in 1635 there was a third edition, further augmented with *"the addition of two entire bookes not formerly published."*[1]

Changes incorporated into the second edition were relatively insignificant.[2] The third edition, expanded and changed in many minor ways also, adds fifteen new sections,[3] plus the whole of Book V, devoted entirely to the controversy between Goodman and Hakewill, and the whole of Book VI, engaged in a more general refutation of opposing views. Book V is especially valuable to this study because, although it gives no over-all picture of the conflict between the two philosophies, it isolates most of the specific points about which Goodman and Hakewill quarrel. For this reason, but also because of the generally richer body of reasons and illustrations, the third edition is used as the text for this discussion.[4]

I. THE QUARREL WITH GOODMAN

Although there are many evidences of Hakewill's debt to Bacon, Bodin, and other contemporaries who regard with distrust the doctrine of a decaying universe, Hakewill is among the first to attack this doctrine explicitly and at length; and he properly considers himself the apologist for an unpopular point of view. "I have walked," he believes, "in an untroden path, neither can I trace the prints of any footsteppes that have gone before mee."[5]

This, at any rate, is his customary position, though in "The Epistle Dedicatory," and later when he has recited his impressive catalogue of authorities in Book VI, he contends that the opinion of the world's decay is a common mistake "rather as being commonly entertained among the vulgar then among the learned," though even the learned, who "with their milke sucked in this popular errour," at times reflect the general ignorance.[6]

It is to be noticed also that Hakewill addresses himself to the "common error" rather than to Goodman's exposition in its defense, until in Book V of the third edition the conflicting opinions are juxtaposed and Goodman's objections are answered, paragraph by paragraph. A sentence of praise from Goodman is even included among the "testimonies" which follow the Preface in the second and third editions of the *Apologie: "FOr your booke as you treat on a subject wherein much learning may bee shewed, so truly you have shewed it abundantly, and I thinke there is no ingenuous scholler but doth worthily esteeme and commend it. &c.* Your loving friend and brother to be commanded, *Godfr. Gloucester.*"[7]

Goodman prefaces Hakewill's fifth book (which has a separate pagination and a new series of signatures) with a statement giving some of the circumstances of the debate. "GOod Reader," he begins, "it may seeme strange unto thee, that a man of my yeares and place should interpose in a controversie of this nature." Since Hakewill had challenged his position, however, he now feels obliged to reply, though he has not neglected his "better studies, but allotted for this exercise onely the houres of my recreation."[8]

Hakewill seems to be annoyed at Goodman's somewhat condescending cordiality and at his repetitious and circuitous objections. The bishop, he says, "hath highly honoured me by stooping so low, as to enter the lists with a man of my ranke," but as to the argument itself, "I am yet where I was." To Goodman's protestations

that the debate is a concern only of his leisure hours, Hakewill replies later in Book V that he can well believe it, "but in very truth
my Lord, (if you will give mee leave to deliver my minde freely)
if you indeed desire (as you pretend) to finde the truth, and to give
satisfaction to others as well by answering, as opposing, you will be
enforced to make it somewhat a more serious studie then hitherto
you have done, or to yeeld mee the bucklers." The same point is
made again still farther on when Hakewill asks three things of his
adversary:

"First that you will seriously intend it and make it somewhat
more then a recreation, as hitherto you pretend to have done; Secondly, that you will unfold your selfe in a clearer and more per-
spicuous manner, that I may not bee forced onely to guesse at your
meaning, and sometimes perhaps to mistake it: And lastly, that
you will take more particular notice what your selfe and I have formerly written both in mine *Apologie* and other papers sent you
since."[9]

Throughout all these exchanges it is Goodman who is more
sanguine in the hope of finding common ground and Hakewill
who, unwilling to accept expressions of good will as pertinent to
the argument, persists in the systematic and uncompromising refutation of Goodman's every point. According to Goodman, *"after
some little agitation of questions betweene us, it is not impossible
but we may agree in the conclusion, as no doubt we doe at this time
agree in the intention."* But Hakewill sees little hope of reconcilia-
tion until Goodman first resolves the contradictions within his own
writings; and he demands of Goodman that "you should either
professe your selfe satisfied with my replies, or shew me why you
are not; one of the two till you be pleased to doe, it is altogether
impossible (as I conceive) that any agitation of the question, should
ever bring us to agree in the conclusion."[10]

The actual points of disagreement are discussed in some detail
later in this paper, and it is perhaps sufficient to say here that
neither is in the least convinced by the other or is even willing to
make any significant concession to the other, and that Hakewill,

opposing one authority with another and offering empirical evidence which Goodman is unprepared to refute, opposes Goodman's theoretical position with a consistent and fully developed philosophy of his own.

II. TO HONOR GOD AND FORTIFY MAN

Hakewill sees this conflict, "touching the shippe wherein we all sayle, whether it bee staunch or no," as a good deal more, of course, than a quarrel with Goodman. A man who believes in the decay of the world does not know or understand God's universe, Hakewill contends, and, what is more important, he will be discouraged from the repentance and the virtuous effort which can effect his soul's salvation. Hakewill explicitly justifies the writing of his *Apologie* on three main grounds: for the honor of God, the redemption of man, and the restoration of philosophical truth.

It is the third of these which governs the organization of his argument and the selection of his evidence, but it is the more pragmatic desire to fortify man's spirit and lead him to grace which moves him to undertake the work originally and which sustains him in his eloquence once it is begun. "If then we come short of our *Ancestours* in *knowledge*," he says in "The Epistle Dedicatory,"

"let us not cast it upon the deficiencie of our wits in regard of the *VVorlds decay,* but upon our owne *sloth;* if wee come short of them in *vertue,* let us not impute it to the *declination* of the *VVorld,* but to the malice and faintnes of our *owne wills;* if we feele the scourges of God upon our Land by mortality, famine, unseasonable weather, or the like, let us not teach the people that they are occasioned by the *VVorlds old age,* and thereby call into question the *providence,* or *power,* or *wisedome,* or *justice,* or *goodnesse* of the Maker thereof; but by their and our *sinnes,* which is doubtlesse both the truer and more profitable doctrine."[11]

As Hakewill elaborates upon his position, he names five "Reasons inducing the Authour to the writing and publishing of this discourse":

"*Whereof the first is the redeeming of a captivated truth....*
The second is the vindicating of the Creators *honour....*
The third is, for that the contrary opinion quailes the hopes and
blunts the edge of vertuous endeavours....
The fourth is, for that it makes men more carelesse, both in re-
gard of their present fortunes, and in providing for posteritie....
The fifth and last is, the weake grounds which the contrary opin-
ion is founded upon, as the fictions of Poets, *the morosity of old*
men, the overvaluing of Antiquity, *and disesteeming of the present*
times."[12]

The search for truth is so worthy and so satisfying that he would
hold it sufficient reward in itself. If his opponents argue that belief
in the world's decay induces greater modesty and humility by reminding men constantly of the approaching end, Hakewill answers that no virtue can be achieved at the expense of truth, "what
faire pretence soever of piety, or charity, or humility it may put on."
It is, however, the practical, hortatory end that animates Hakewill's
argument even at this point, so that truth is sought not abstractly
and simply for its beauty and sovereignty but also because it yields
infinite content to the soul and helps to repair the image of God
in man.[13]

His second reason is incorporated into the title of the work: *An*
Apologie or Declaration of the Power and Providence of God in
the Government of the World. He hopes that by bringing men to
his point of view he will vindicate *"the Creators honour,* the reputation of his *wisedome,* his *justice,* his *goodnesse,* and his *power;*
being all of them in my judgement by the opinion of *Natures decay,*
not a little impeached and blemished."[14] To admit the possibility of
the world's decay, he argues, is to question the excellence of God's
work and thus the power of God himself. Here Hakewill is constantly and categorically at variance with Goodman, who accepts
the world's decay as the result not of God's weakness but of man's.

When critics object to his begging of the question in the book's
title, Hakewill answers at length in Book VI by quoting authorities who prove God's providence "from the constant government of

the world," and by elaborating upon his proposition *"That the preservation of the course of nature, and consequently of the world from decay, suites best with the* Divine Providence; *inasmuch as it serves most to advance his glory, by the evidencing and illustration of his Attributes"*: i.e., his eternity, immutability, ubiquity, love, wisdom, power, truth, justice, and beauty.[15]

Hakewill's most pressing and most practical reason for writing the *Apologie* is that he might improve the hopes and thus the virtuous endeavors of men. We must not permit ourselves to yield on the assumption that all our efforts are futile. By recognizing the unimpaired excellence of the creation, we are stirred to be more constant and diligent in the performance of our own duties, nor do we waste our energies in lamenting the better times which are gone. By discovering the unbroken harmonies of nature, we are united more closely in amity among men, understanding order, and giving obedience to our superiors.[16]

"The doctrine of *Natures* necessary *decay*," Hakewill reasons, "rather tends to make men worse then better, rather cowardly then couragious, rather to draw them downe to that they must bee, then to lift them up to that they should and may bee, rather to breed sloath then to quicken industrie." When Goodman objects that the hope of better things on this earth may excite new and violent passions in the lowly and may thus put us in *"daunger of a mutinee"* or an *"innovation,"* Hakewill assures him that "there is not so much feare of Innovation from the country *Boares* ... by meanes of my opinion, as of lazines and murmuring in them by meanes of yours, if they be once persuaded that nothing can bee improved by industry, but all things by a fatall necessity grow worse and worse." Against Goodman's thesis that men will be moved to virtue by the contemplation of a corrupt, decaying world around them, a world obviously nearing its end, Hakewill always affirms God's goodness, the perfection of God's creation, and the weakness only of the resolution, the hope, and the efforts of men: when men fail, "the fault is not in the age but in themselves."[17]

Closely related to this point, and in a sense prior to it, is Hakewill's assertion that men who believe in the world's decay do not "care much for repentance, or call upon God for grace," for they think themselves living in a depleted time in which no hope can prosper. If their resolution for the present is weakened, so much more so is their hope for the future, and they are not moved to be provident of posterity.

"For when they consider how many thousand yeares *nature* hath now beene, as it were in a fever *Hectique,* daily consuming and wasting away by degrees; they inferre that in reason she cannot hold out long, and therefore it was to as little purpose to plant trees, or to erect lasting buildings, either for *Civill, Charitable,* or *Pious* uses, as to provide new apparell for a sicke man, that lies at deaths doore, and hath already one foote in the grave."[18]

Hakewill's fifth and last reason for undertaking the *Apologie* is the *"weake grounds which the contrary opinion of the Worlds decay is founded upon,"* or, more properly, his conviction that because these grounds are manifestly weak he need only reveal them in order to discredit his opponents and their philosophy. As he sees it, belief in the world's decay originated in the *"fictions of Poets,"* specifically in the myth of the golden age, for that *"pretty invention"* has made such an impression on men's minds that it can hardly be rooted out.[19] Hakewill shows in some detail how wicked and brutish men's lives often were in earlier times and how all ages and all places in the world's history have had their good and their evil alike. Indeed, if the world had grown steadily worse, we would need, in order to describe the present age, metals far baser than any we know.

And, just as the poets are responsible for introducing the concept of a declining universe, so we must look to "the *morosity* and crooked disposition of old men, alwaies complaining of the hardnesse of the present times," and to the "excessive admiration of *Antiquitie,*" to understand how this concept came to flourish in the popular mind. As to the former, "old men for the most part being much changed from that they were in their youth in complexion and temperature, they are fill'd with sad melancholy thoughts, which makes men thinke the world is changed, whereas in truth the change is in themselves." Hakewill condemns, also, too great a love for antiquity, though he is careful not to condemn antiquity itself. He would have men recognize the good of former ages, without despairing of good in their own age and without veneration for what is past merely because it is past: "Antiquitie I unfainedly honour, and reverence, but why I should bee bound to reverence the rust and refuse, the drosse and dregs, the warts and wenns thereof[,] I am yet to seeke."[20]

These, then, are Hakewill's reasons for writing and publishing his treatise. Redemption of a captivated truth is first named and honorably pursued but, as a motivating force, is perhaps least urgent among the reasons offered. The work is more significantly what in its title he indicates it to be, an apologia for God's power and providence. That God is more honored by the world's preservation than by its decay is vindication of Hakewill's thesis, justification of his labors, and sufficient basis for conversion of the doubtful. Finally, if in an age of excesses, wickedness, and indifference to the teachings of the church, he can move men to greater piety and more virtuous efforts by giving them more hope in the present and in the future, then this aim becomes, for a man who is himself pious and virtuous and hopeful, his strongest incentive.

Hakewill thus alleviates the gloom and the melancholy which brought forth Goodman's laments; but it may be anticipated at this point that even Hakewill does not speak with radiant optimism as the apostle of progress. If the world is no worse, neither is it essentially better, and in any case it is the sinful, mortal world, the world which must be eschewed for heaven and salvation, the world which, though it does not decline of its own weakness, will some day be utterly destroyed by God in his righteous anger.[21]

III. THE ORDER OF THE PARTS

The ends that Hakewill proposes are, on the whole, well served by the organization of his treatise. In Book I he presents general arguments, drawn from theology, common sense, natural philosophy, reason, authority—arguments stated in Goodman's own terms. Then for almost five hundred pages, through Books II, III, and most of IV, he addresses himself to empirical evidence, or "proof by instances," showing that the heavens are as perfect and as efficacious now as they ever were and that the sublunar creation, although subject to the vicissitudes of mutability, compensates for each loss with a corresponding gain, so that there is no constant, natural, or inevitable decline and no decay either in quantity or in quality. Finally, he devotes the last part of Book IV to proving that the world will be completely consumed by fire and that its end will not be natural but supernatural.[22]

It is in the first part of his work, "Of this pretended decay in generall," and the last part, on the world's mortality, that Hakewill shows his skill as preacher and dialectician; the central core of the *Apologie* is, by contrast, a product of his enormous scholarship, made effective for his audience by the accumulated weight of his illustrations but even more by the prestige of the authorities cited for these illustrations. The importance of the appeal to authority, in Hakewill's argument, can hardly be emphasized enough. The evidence against the "signs" of decay will eventually make untenable the belief in a decaying world; but, before such evidence could be acceptable, Hakewill had to satisfy his readers that only a universe whose constancy and integrity are unimpaired is in accord with God's providence and power. In this demonstration he tries to make the orthodoxy of his views justify the admission of his evidence.

In Book I, he summarizes his procedure for the entire work. He will begin with a general argument and then move, in turn, to the heavens, the elements, mixed bodies, and, finally, man. He will go on to reason that the world will end miraculously by fire rather than naturally by decay, and he will conclude with an exhortation "for the stirring of men up" to prepare themselves for the day of fire and judgment.[23]

The most important thesis developed in Book I is the warning that mutability must not be confused with decay. Hakewill grants temporary and recurrent vicissitudes of all kinds to be the burden of sublunar creation but denies that these vicissitudes portend the decay of nature. Any lack in the parts, he contends in direct opposition to Goodman, is supplied by the perfection of the whole, and any apparent evil in the parts is designed for some good in the fabric of the whole. Furthermore, there can be no defection on the earth so long as the influence of the heavens remains unimpaired, and in the heavens there is not even mutability, far less decay.

But if, indeed, the world were declining steadily, Hakewill goes on, it would have been completely destroyed by this time, and, if not completely destroyed, then at least men could prophesy the date of the imminent end; since the first of these conditions obviously does not prevail and the second is contrary to God's design, there can be no constant and progressive decay of nature. Furthermore, a beneficent God will not suffer his handiwork to be wasted away; the power which created the world will still support and maintain it. In the course of Book I, Hakewill also explains the prevalence of the opposing opinion, justifies the publishing of his work, and refutes not only the principal arguments directed against him but also the authorities in whose names these arguments are supported.

Books II–IV are simpler and more unified in design. The first five chapters of Book II deny the decay of the heavens, specifically in terms of the celestial substance, motion, light, warmth, and influence. The last four chapters descend to the elements and the mixed bodies. In Book III, Hakewill argues against the decay of man, the first five chapters being devoted to man's age, size, and strength and the last five chapters to his arts and sciences. In Book IV, chapters i–xii deal, in the same fashion, with man's morals and manners. Book III is a great deal longer than Book II, and the first twelve chapters of Book IV, in turn, a great deal longer than Book III.[24] Since the accounts of the past are rich in records of the institutions and accomplishments of men and because Hakewill's purpose is to inspire men to virtuous endeavor in the present, the apparent disproportion, wherein half the entire work is devoted to the description of arts and conduct, is both explained and justified.

Books II, III, and the early chapters of IV are not devoid of arguments from first principles, or arguments which must ultimately be resolved as questions of faith, or even arguments no stronger than the authorities that they depend upon; but in this section of his work Hakewill relies predominantly on his own observations and on the records and measurements that had been accumulated for two thousand years. The progression here from the heavens to the elements to mixed bodies, then to man's body, his wits, and his manners, is, on the whole, a progression from the pure or elemental to the compound, from patterns of investigation established in Christian metaphysics to the levels of simple description in secular and natural history. It is also a progression from a position shared with most of his readers—that the heavens do not decay—to one which opposes the common view of degenerating morality. Hakewill's interest in the material witness of the senses accounts for his much more detailed and specific contrast of ancients and moderns than is found in Goodman's *Fall*.

In the last two chapters of Book IV, after insisting that the world does not waste away, Hakewill asserts that it is, nevertheless, a mortal world. He begins chapter xiii by vigorously dissociating himself from unorthodox ideas about an eternal universe and then undertakes his demonstration that the end of the world by fire is a Christian truth and (though the event itself will be wholly supernatural) a gentile and a rational truth as well. Finally, in chapter xiv, he shows the destruction of the world to be a terror to the wicked, a comfort to the godly, and an admonition to all. Partially because his belief in the world's end has much of the same meaning for him that a belief in its decay has for Goodman, the *Apologie* falls short of a complete and final repudiation of Goodman's position.

Book V, added in 1635, presents a long series of Goodman's objections, with Hakewill's answers interposed. These are divided into arguments from natural philosophy, from metaphysics, from theology, proofs by instances, and "other arguments," this last, miscellaneous category making up over half of Book V. Goodman's objections usually turn upon the interpretation of some universal

law or of a principle of faith and rarely attempt to refute the
empirical evidence that Hakewill has amassed. Consequently, only
a few pages are required for the "Proofes by instances." In fact,
Goodman specifically charges Hakewill with neglecting the general truths in favor of the particular examples:

> "YOu will be pleased to consider that generall truths are ever
> best proved and confirmed by generall grounds, principles, rea-
> sons[,] axiomes, and not by instances; yet truly Mr Archdeacon
> though your booke bee full of good learning you are a little defec-
> tive in these generall reasons and grounds, and your proofes doe
> most consist of instances."

It is Hakewill's reply (and this is perhaps his best description of his
method) that his "instances" are "drawne out for the better illustration and strengthening of the rule, all rules being first grounded
and built upon the observation and induction of many instances,
and then the instances serve to add both light and life unto them."[25]

In Book VI, also added in 1635, Hakewill cites at some length
further authorities for some of the points on which he had been
challenged. Once more he defends his opinion as most consonant
with God's providence, because, he writes, the divine attributes are
best recognized in a world free from decay. He finds it easy to see
also why great churchmen and thinkers have proved God's providence by the preservation of the world, not by its decay. Again he
elaborates upon the practical usefulness of believing that God's universe is above corruption and natural disintegration. And, finally,
he returns to the quarrel over the disposition of the world after its
destruction, holding for utter abolition, against the opinion of
Goodman, Suarez, and others that a restoration of some sort is
possible.[26]

Books V and VI, although amplifying many points and clarify-
ing a few, introduce almost no new arguments, and their principal
contribution to this study is in the coupling of Goodman's objections with Hakewill's replies. These two books show that, despite
Hakewill's original emphasis on historical and empirical particulars, the real dispute, as represented by the challenges and defenses

in Books V–VI, is metaphysical and theological.

IV. FLYING TO THE MIRACLE

In the body of his discourse (Books I–IV) Hakewill deals principally with either the elementary assertions of faith or the empirical
testimony of witnesses that he considers reliable. Unlike Goodman,
he distrusts the processes and products of reason. In contrast to
Goodman, who directs his argument to the natural or reasonable
man, he insists that the most important tenets of human knowledge
are questions of faith, questions which cannot, therefore, be proved
by reason alone.

The existence of God, for example, is accepted as a principle
rather than as a conclusion demonstrable by reason. To Goodman's
contention that the Creator may be proved from the complexity, the
limitations, or the "mutual relations" of that which is created (there
must be a compositor where there is a composition), Hakewill
answers that such reasons may bring probable, but never positive,
demonstration. A beginning in causality may perhaps be proved,
but not a beginning in duration.[27]

That the world had a beginning and will have an end are also
matters of faith, according to Hakewill, though reason may grope
at such truths. In Book V, Goodman explicitly attacks this position,
once more offering the world's beginning as a self-evident rational
truth and deriving its end from its beginning. It is Hakewill's
invariable reply that, since beginning and end are supernatural,
they are beyond the compass of "naturall reason," which "by the
light of nature can rise no higher then ordinarie naturall causes."[28]

Since Goodman foresees a continued decline of the world toward
a possible natural ending and Hakewill admits only the supernatural ending, both are consistent in their arguments: the natural end
is predictable in reason; the supernatural end is wholly a doctrine
of faith. If reason is not properly limited, if it attempts to comprehend the things of the spirit, says Hakewill, it infringes upon the
sovereignty of faith and thus inclines toward atheism. The choice
between the two philosophies, as Hakewill makes the choice, de-

pends neither on the vindication of man's powers nor on the glorification of his future; it depends rather on his humility before God.

When Goodman protests that his own position is more reasonable, Hakewill answers that his is more religious. When Goodman accuses Hakewill of "flying to the miracle," Hakewill asks if it is possible to be a Christian and not fly to miracles. Unless we are willing to admit that some things are wholly beyond natural explanations, he continues, "truly my Lord wee may burne our bibles, and shut up our Churches, and renounce our profession, so as while you plead so much for the reasonableness of your opinion, I much doubt it will at last relapse upon irreligion."[29]

What procedures, then, are most important for Hakewill? To some extent the very deductive processes which he seems to eschew, and especially is this true in Books I and V and throughout his treatise wherever he encounters "an argument drawn from reason," which he undertakes to answer in his own terms. Such answers often are grounded upon the first principles of faith, prior to which no argument can be admitted. But often Hakewill is dependent also upon the "instances" which make up a large part of Book II and almost all of Books III and IV—the records, measurements, and testimonies, the natural and social histories, all of which reflect ultimately the witness of the senses. He regards such evidence, however, less as the testimony of the senses than as conclusions and judgments of reliable authorities; for, though he uses the primary and particular data of past and present to strengthen his hypothesis, he considers the senses the least reliable witness of all, as far beneath reason as reason is beneath faith. In this manner, therefore, while defending an opinion upheld by faith and reason and supporting his findings with pertinent material evidence, Hakewill depends heavily upon the appeal to authority.

The best authority, of course, is the Scriptures, acceptance of which is not to be distinguished from an act of faith itself. The only controversy here arises in the selection and interpretation of the passages used in argument, and he and Goodman often oppose each other with biblical quotations.[30] The Church Fathers are sec-

ond only to the Scriptures in their reliability, although Hakewill, as
does Goodman, makes a point of marshaling also the heathen writers on his side. The *Apologie* is especially rich, too, in its citation of
contemporaries—Vives, Leroy, Bacon, Briggs, Hooker, Du Bartas,
Camden, Bodin, Ralegh, to mention but a few. Not all authorities
are infallible, of course, but they are overthrown only with the help
of other and better authorities.

Hakewill finds no fault, for example, with the assumption underlying Goodman's taunt that the authors whose support he en-
lists are few, poor, and contemptible *"in respect of those whom you
acknowledge to be your Adversaries."* He does not question the
principle but merely defends and expands his own list of "authors."
"I have done with my testimonies," he says at one point. "Now if
in the mouth of two or three witnesses every truth shall stande,
much more in the mouthes of two or threescore, against whom lies
no exception, neither can be suspected of partiality; Which number I have the rather thus mustered up together."[31]

V. A CONSTANT AND INVIOLABLE NATURE

In spite of many essential disagreements, both Goodman and
Hakewill seek a belief that will bring salvation, and both combine
arguments (though not in the same proportion) from faith, reason, the senses, and authority; hence it is not surprising that there
should be similarities as well as differences in their ideas about the
natural universe. Like Goodman, Hakewill holds that the world
was created out of nothing, for man's use, according to an *"Archetype"* which "still is in the Creatour himselfe." But Hakewill goes
on to insist that God will not permit "this goodly and beautifull
frame" to "runne to ruine." The providence that sustains the world
is not a special or miraculous one, he believes; it is rather the "first
law and command still operative in the creatures of God," the
simple and inevitable extension of the creation itself.[32]

The question of the world's decay must not be decided from the
weakness of the creatures, he repeats, but from the goodness, wisdom, and power of the Creator. Decay in the universe must imply

a flaw in the Creator, and the providence as well as the power of God must be found in the preservation, rather than in the decline, of the world. A constant, inviolate world is in accord also with God's eternity and all his glorious beauty, "the stabilitie of the Creature either implying these, or shadowing them forth unto us, which the decay cannot doe."[33]

The world, created perfect in the image of its divine archetype, was designed for man's use; even *the starres were made for men, and not men for the starres.*"[34] If men were removed from the world, God could receive no glory or satisfaction from the rest of creation and would have no reason for sustaining it. But man sinned, and for his sin he is cursed. To this extent Hakewill and Goodman are in agreement.

Hakewill denies, however, that man is the microcosm, the epitome of the world, and that man's sin can affect the other creatures, the earth itself, or the heavens. Only men and angels could be the agents of their own Fall, and only they can suffer from their sins. It is not the world which needs to be saved, but man: "the sinne of man could not alter the worke of God, or marre that sweet harmony which hee had set in it." In so far as God placed a specific curse upon the earth also, as a further punishment to man, the curse is operative upon nature. But it is not extended to the heavens, and it does not bring "an irrecoverable consumption, or a languishing sicknesse" even to the earth. Hakewill concedes that there may be excesses or defects in nature, put there to remind us of our Fall, but he emphatically denies that "the whole frame of nature should thereby be disjoynted and become subject to corruption, and a universall declination."[35]

Hakewill thus believes that any changes discernible in the frame of nature are supernatural and not results of a natural, inbred principle of corruption. The state of nature may change, but its powers remain inviolate. The creation itself was such a supernatural work as the end of the world will be. The new star of 1572 was not "the effect of *Nature,* but the *supernaturall* and *miraculous* worke of *Almighty God* ... & the like may be said of all such *Comets.*"

The destruction of paradise and the Flood were also the direct operation of God's will and came suddenly, without long preparation. When God stopped the sun from moving, he did so against the ordinary processes of nature. If the Holy Land once was more fruitful than it now is, we may credit God's special favor and not nature's decay. The long lives of the patriarchs may be explained as God's provident way of populating the world and preserving a continuity in man's learning. Any particular signs of nature's failure may be due to God's special and immediate judgment, although the more usual circumstances of compensation and mutability in nature must be first explored as possible causes.[36]

There is no dispute between Goodman and Hakewill about the existence of "extraordinary judgments" of God. The issue is whether or not the universe decays even according to the ordinary working of natural laws. Hakewill believes that such a natural or inbred decay could have been introduced neither before nor after man's Fall. Before the Fall, God pronounced his creation good, and there was no evil to punish. Any decay introduced after the Fall would be "forraine or accidentall," and clearly not a basic principle of nature. Thus "nature not onely before the fall, but since is kept inviolable, save only in men and Angels, who wilfully cast themselves away."[37]

VI. THE CONSTANT WITHIN THE CHANGING

Nature is inviolable, then. For Hakewill this means all of nature—heavens, elements, creatures, including man. In his argument Hakewill begins with the heavens and moves methodically down to man, exactly the reverse of Goodman's procedure, which was to begin with man and then find decay in the universe. Goodman finds signs of decay most easily in man; Hakewill finds the constancy of nature secured in the heavens. The incorruptible heavens, Hakewill reasons, "cannot but by their *quickning virtue* and vitall efficacie impart likewise an incorruptibility to these inferior bodies"; if the heavens are unchanged, the rest of nature will be renewed.[38] Each man argues most shrewdly from his most widely accepted premise, Goodman starting with the corruption of man, Hakewill with the immutability of the heavens.

Because the heavens and lesser bodies were all formed from the same first matter, the whole creation is incorruptible, according to Hakewill. Natural dissolution is impossible anywhere in the universe because the first matter cannot be destroyed except by the miraculous hand of God. The elements and mixed bodies, made up of contraries, are always changing, even though they are not subject to corruption. But the heavens are more than incorruptible; they are immutable, having a form "so excellent and perfect in it selfe, as it wholly satiateth the appetite of the *matter* it informeth."[39]

This form which perfectly satisfies the matter invites no change in the heavenly motion, light, heat, or influence. When matter is perfect, it tends neither upward nor downward and moves in a perfect, circular pattern. The light is incorruptible because it derives from incorruptible matter, as also because it stems directly from God himself, the first thing created by him and the nearest to him. Heat is caused in turn by light, and therefore it too is not subject to decay.* Finally, there is no decrease in the efficacy of the heavens as they work upon the earth. It is difficult to read the signs or anticipate the influence of the heavens, but we know that "as *heat* pierces where *light* cannot, so the *influence* pierces where the heat cannot." If there is no change in the substance, motion, heat, or light of the heavens, neither can there be a change in the effect upon the earth.[40]

All apparent signs of decay in the heavens are necessarily deceptive. If more spots seem to appear on the moon, perhaps "by the helpe of the new devised *perspective glasses,* they have beene of late more clearly and distinctly discerned then in former ages," but no actual change has occurred. Or a supernatural explanation can be

---

* The celestial bodies are not hot of themselves but generate heat in the earth and its creatures, which, composed of the elements, are capable of receiving heat. Hakewill argues also that the sun, because it is incorruptible, is not hot; for, if it were hot and fiery, it would be subject to alteration and corruption by an opposite quality. This argument, of course, begs the question, for his opponents hold it to be corruptible because it *is* fire.

resorted to, as in the case of the 1572 star in Cassiopeia; these *"extraordinary unusuall apparitions"* are intended either as warnings or as prophecies. If the sun seems to move nearer to the earth, either there is definite range of variation, with maximum and minimum figures of declination, or else the measurements of the astronomers have been in error. The North Star approaches the Pole more closely now than in the past, but it will return, just as other stars have their "times of *accesse* and *recesse,* to and from the *Pole*."[41]

Eclipses do not damage the sun or moon and probably do not damage even the earth; if some harm actually is done the earth, time will make it whole again. Comets do not belong to the immutable realm of the heavens but develop from "a passing hot and dry exhalation" upon the earth and are "inflamed" in "the highest region of the ayre." The one admission Hakewill makes is on an issue which he considers too trivial to argue over—that we have lost ten days by the Julian calendar.[42]

There is no decay or corruption, then, in the heavens. There may be a seeming failure, or errors in measurement, or regular cycles that we have not discerned, or changes brought about directly by the Creator, but there is no natural decay. Not even the scriptural prophecy that the heavens shall wax old like a garment can be understood to promise decay, for to wax old "doth not necessarily imply a *decay* ... but sometimes doth only signifie a *farther step* and accesse to a finall period in regard of duration."[43]

Hakewill has now strengthened his argument materially; for, if there is no decay in the heavens, the losses sustained on the earth can always be restored. The heavens *"guide* and governe, nay cherish and maintaine, nay *breed* and beget these inferiour bodies." Many times in Book V, Hakewill challenges Goodman to prove a dissolution in the heavens. Any other evidence, he argues, is worthless for proving the decay of the world.[44]

But Hakewill shows that this dissolution in the heavens cannot be proved, even by analogy with any possible decay in the earth. The sin of man could n . : of itself infect the heavens. God's curse upon the earth did not change the actual principles of nature on the earth; certainly, it did not reach into the heavens. Nature was no accessory to man's crime, the heavens least of all. Furthermore, the influence moves always from heaven to earth, and there is no reciprocal power centered upon the earth. The perfect form of the heavens, completely realized, will not permit of their being acted upon from without.[45]

The analogy between the microcosm and the macrocosm will not establish even the mutability of the heavens, far less their decay; for the two worlds "subsist not of the same principles, nor are in all things alike." Decay of the parts or of the individuals is compensated for in the great world but not in the little. By regarding the heavens as free "from all kind of corruption" and the elements as repaired "with equivalent compensation," Hakewill rejects the similarity of the great and little worlds and explains the preservation of the whole. The debate over the relation of part to whole and over the operation of contrary qualities is discussed more fully later in this paper; we may simply observe here that such questions of natural law are introduced in the attack on the analogy of microcosm and macrocosm. The easy figure of speech, says Hakewill, distorts the true picture of the universe:

"...this little world carrying in it foure humours, answering in proportion to the foure elements, whereof one alwayes is so predominant, as it finally conquers all the rest, findes the same seedes to be the instruments of its dissolution, which were the principles of its constitution. But in the great world it is not so, if we looke up to the heavenly bodies, we shall never there behold hanging out any flagge of defiance; no bloudie colours displayed, no armies ranged; wee shall heare no drumme, no trumpet sound an alarme to the battle; the matter and forme like man and wife, are there married by such a sacred and inviolable knot, as they never jarre, and are wearie of each other, but everlastingly imbrace each other in a most lovely & amiable manner; nor can possibly bee divorced but by the hand of that eternall Priest who joyned them."[46]

The elements, then, are mutable, but they do not decay. Plants and animals must decay and die, but the elements persist, holding the same proportions among themselves, keeping *"by mutuall exchange the same dimensions in themselves."*[47] The earth may sometimes encroach upon the sea, or the sea upon the earth; but the elements are unchanged in the whole pattern, as a river is unchanged while continually gaining and losing its flood of waters. Hakewill devotes four chapter in Book II to his evidence that air, water, and earth are ruled by laws of compensation, not of deterioration. When Goodman cites God's curse upon the earth, Hakewill answers that the curse is a specific supernatural punishment and therefore does not change the principles of nature. The Flood, similarly, was not a sign or a cause of decay or "a losse without a reparation," but simply a "confusion of the elements."[48]

The elements change in form, but not in quantity or in quality. The earth, for example, has lost none of its size or its natural powers. Though some mountains wear away, the diameter, the circumference, and the proportions of the whole earth do not vary. Or, if any difference is found, it must be attributed to the units of measurement or to the lack of skill in the measurer. The earth is as rich as it ever was in minerals and metals; even if a decrease could be proved, it would not be a natural loss but the result of man's greed.[49]

Nor is there any loss of fertility. The earth is able to bring forth trees as great and herbs as powerful as in the past. Wherever the land may seem to fail, the failure may be due "to the curse of God upon that accursed nation which possesseth it, or to their ill manuring of the earth," but not to any decrease in the efficacy of the soil itself. Our vineyards are less fruitful now because the peace with France has made French wines cheaper, and we no longer cultivate our own vineyards so industriously. There is no increase in the growth of "thornes and thistles & poyson-some herbs," which, had we remained without sin, would have been more helpful than harmful to us.[50] In any case, there is compensation for all losses, and the land which is barren in one time will be fruitful in another.

Similarly, where in one place the water invades the land, in another the land encroaches upon the water. Old rivers are filled in, and new ones are cut. Some lands are engulfed, but towns which once were seaports are now a hundred miles inland. Consequently, the balance between earth and water remains constant. The balance between mountains and valleys is kept in the same way. The reductions in mountains are repaired by earthquakes and other means, though there is little enough lost, says Hakewill, when "instead of barren mountaines wee shall at length have fat and fruitfull valleyes."[51]

The weather is no worse now than it was earlier, in spite of the common opinion that winters are colder, summers not so kindly as they have been, storms fiercer. Part of Hakewill's demonstration, in fact, is intended to show from the records that "the World in former ages hath been plagued with more *droughts, excessive raines, windes, frosts, snowes, hailes, famines, earth-quakes, pestilences,* and other contagious diseases, then in later times." Even if he should admit that we have our troubles today also, because of our sins, he asks what this has to do with the universal decay of nature. Or else we merely imagine things to be so bad now:

"men for the most part, being most affected with the present, more sensible of punishments then of blessings, and growing in worldly cares, and consequently in discontent, as they grow in yeares & experience; they are thereby more apt to apprehend crosses then comforts, to repine and murmure for the one, then to returne thanks for the other. Whence it comes to passe that unseasonable weather, and the like crosse accidents are printed in our memories, as it were with red letters in an Almanacke; but for seasonable and faire, there stands nothing but a blanke: the one is graven in brasse, the other written in water."[52]

The earth is not impaired, nor are the species that grow upon it. The waters change and flow but are always the same in quantity and quality. The air mixes good and bad in its great variety of climates and weathers but remains temperate on the whole. The fire has lost nothing of its "active and masculine efficacie." If the elements are all inviolate, then inviolate also must be the creatures made up of elements and living upon them. They have not grown smaller; they live just as long as they ever did. There are no more monsters now to be found among them than were found former-ly.[53] And all this must be said equally of the fish in the seas, the animals upon the earth, and the birds in the sky.

But to say that the creatures in general remain unchanged is not to say that each individual creature is incorruptible, for all bodies under the circle of the moon are subject to change and decay. Their eternity is in succession, in the species; and, because "the same *species* of hawkes; of horses, of whales, of oakes, of men exists at this very present which was created in the beginning," the mixed, sublunary bodies may be seen to retain their integrity according to the true course of nature.[54]

VII. ANCIENTS AND MODERNS

Chief among the creatures, subject to the common mutability but, like the others, free from natural corruption or decay, is man. He is distinguished from other creatures by his reason, his freedom to choose between good and bad, and thus his moral responsibility for his conduct. We may therefore attribute his miseries not only to the general vicissitudes shared by bodies under the moon but also to God's direct punishment for his sins. But this punishment is enough to explain his hardships, and there is no need to assume that the principles of natural law have been altered.

Even before the Fall, man was mortal because he was composed of contrary elements and humors. But God's providence, working through the care of the angels and "harmony" of man's soul, made him immortal by special privilege. Though man is no longer in this sense invulnerable, neither is his nature, or the nature of the whole world, so changed as to imperil God's creation. Hakewill argues that, since there is no decay in the heavens, the elements, or the mixed bodies in general, neither is there any reason to suppose that man decays. But because this discourse is intended, after all, for man's study and profit, he goes on, he will compare in some detail the men of today with those of earlier times:

"first, in regard of *age;* secondly, in regard of *strength* and *stature;*

[69]

thirdly, in regard of *wits* and *inventions;* fourthly, in regard of *manners* and *conditions.* And if upon due consideration and comparison it shall appeare that there is no such decay in any of these as is supposed, the *Question,* I trust, touching the *worlds decay* in generall, will soone be at an end."[55]

Man lives as long now as he did in the past. Certainly, his lifespan has not been shortened within the last two thousand years. Admitting that the records show the patriarchs and others in the first ages of the world to have lived longer, Hakewill chooses to explain this as "some *extraordinary priviledge*" rather than as the ordinary course of nature. The world had to be populated, and the sciences had to be established. Since the time of Moses, when the span was three-score years and ten, the age of man has not abated. A constant decrease is surely not part of nature's pattern, for Adam was not so old as some who followed him, and in modern times there are instances of men (among the Florida Indians, for example) who have attained the age of two hundred and fifty years. If there is actually any decrease, it is not the failure of nature but our own fault: mothers no longer nurse their children; we allow "*hasty marriages* in tender yeares," when nature is "yet greene and growing"; but most important of all, "the pressing of *Nature* with *over-weighty burdens,* & when we finde her strength defective, the helpe of strong waters, hot spices, and provoking sauces, is it which impaires our health, and shortens our life."[56]

Men do not decline in age, therefore not in stature either. If such a decline were inherent in nature, men today would be far smaller than they are. Besides, before a decrease in man's size can be proved, we must show a decrease in the heavens and the elements, and this we cannot do. If ancient records show the frequent occurrence of giants, we have also much recent evidence of the same sort. And ancient truths must not be confused with ancient fables, spread by Homer and others among the poets. Many of the giant-like bones which we find are probably bones of animals anyway. In all the records, much "no doubt was *fained,* much *mistaken,* much *added* to truth thorow errour, or an itching desire of *Hyper-*

bolicall amplifications"; yet even if it is true that there were more giants in the past, when miracles were more in fashion as direct manifestations of God's power, "a diminution of the stature of mankinde in *generall* cannot from thence be sufficiently inforced." Further evidence that there has been no decrease in size lies in the fact that ancient units of measure and weight were no greater than ours; ancient armor, beds, doors, altars, and seats were no larger; and the ancient diet prescribed no more food than we eat today. For all individual instances the law of compensation prevails.[57]

Man's strength remains as constant as does his stature. The same medicines serve their purpose in the same proportions; modern physicians draw as much blood as Galen did.* Men today have as many teeth and as long a gut. The fertility of parents has not decreased. Nor are men more susceptible to diseases now than formerly, nor have the number of diseases increased; the sweating sickness, leprosy, and the French disease are even less prevalent now than in past ages. Though if in any way we are indeed weaker because of our excesses, there is, nevertheless, no fear that the race will decline. The face of mankind, Hakewill writes, "is daily decayed and daily renewed but the face of individuall man decayes daily without any compensative renewing."[58]

In his wits, his arts, and his learning in general there is a similar fluctuation, without decay. The soul is not decayed, either as a whole or in its principal faculties—imagination, judgment, and memory. All learning is, in fact, relatively modern, there being little "that can plead the antiquity of 2000 yeares, & none of 3000," and studies of the last hundred years are much advanced over those of earlier ages.[59]

In metaphysics, for example, the Christian divines of today understand much that the ancient philosophers were ignorant of. Civil history, which flourished in Greece and Rome and then declined, has achieved new glories of late; ecclesiastical history prospers now

---

* Diana "a noble Lady of *Est*," "bled onely at the nostrils 18 pounds, besides what was spilt on the ground; upon her apparell, in napkins and other linnens about her" (*Apologie*, p. 244).

[71]

that it has been freed of its excess of saints and martyrs. As to poetry, there are many who prefer Virgil to Homer; and Sidney, Tasso, Bartas, and Spenser are in many ways equal to the very best of the ancients. Painters in this age are surely greater than ever before. Modern grammarians, translators, and annotators far excel those of former ages. Rhetoric is recovering after a period of eclipse. Logic became obscured and too complex in the hands of the school philosophers, but modern methods have improved the study.[60]

Modern inventions and sciences are far advanced over those of the ancients, and this century may be favorably compared with any preceding one. To the necessary groundwork laid by the ancients we have added paper, perspective glasses, watches, porcelain, and many other useful and important items. Now that we have the printing press, books are "redeemed from bondage," and another total decay of learning is made unlikely. The compass is probably a modern invention; certainly, navigation is much advanced today, as witness the work of Drake, Hakluyt, Purchas, and others. The new Gregorian calendar mends the defects of the old. By comparison with modern stratagems and engines of war, the ancients were childish in military matters.[61]

Moderns are superior also in mathematics, natural philosophy, topography, and astronomy, correcting many errors of the ancients. The science of anatomy belongs to modern times, neither the Greeks, the Romans, nor the Hebrews having practiced it. The knowledge of herbs and simples has been revived in recent times. To Paracelsus, a modern by comparison with Galen, must go the credit for introducing to these parts of the world "the use of *Hermeticall, Spagyricall,* or *Chymicall* Physicke"; and his followers have now "changed *Aristotles* three principles of naturall bodies, *matter, forme,* and *privation;* into *Salt, Sulphur,* and *Mercury;* and from the severall temper of these three, they affirme all sicknesses and health to arise."[62]

Hakewill turns, finally, in the longest of his four books, to the virtues and vices, and finds that "as in the *Arts* & *Sciences,* so likewise in matter of *manners,* there is a *vicissitude,* an *alternation* & *revolution,*" which seems to govern the pattern of human affairs.

[72]

In the total of good and evil, however, the moderns must have the advantage, for the ancients lacked the guidance of Christianity, and only Christianity can draw men to the greatest virtue and the best society. With the conversion of Constantine and then again with the Reformation, the church has had much of its primitive purity and integrity restored.

Errors and heresies have been gradually eliminated, our sermons have been "exquisite and effectuall" of late, the Scriptures have been more soundly interpreted in the last century, and even our controversies have "sharpned the spirits of *Divines*," and "made the grounds of *Christian* Religion to bee better understood." Certainly, Christianity, even in its most corrupt state, is to be preferred to the pagan religions, with their worship of images, idols, and devils, and, worse still, men. Among the ancient gods are to be found strumpets, adulterers, sodomites, murderers, and thieves, "*old Gods* and *new Gods, hee Gods* and *shee Gods, citty Gods* and *countrey Gods, common Gods,* and *proper Gods, land Gods* and *sea Gods,*" and, finally, in the complete depravity of those times, passions, diseases, vices, weasels, mice, and onions![63]

True wisdom and virtue, Hakewill argues, rest upon true religion. Largely because of Christianity, moderns are more virtuous than the ancients, in works of piety and charity, in sacrifice, gratitude, and love. The golden age is a poetic myth, and the present is as good a time to live in as any. The ancients were defective in planting virtue, the Stoics holding "that all sins were equall," the Epicureans "that soveraigne happinesse consisted in pleasure," both doubting the immortality of the soul, "whereby they opened a wide gappe to all licentiousnesse." The Romans were cruel to Jews and Christians alike, loved war and slaughter, encouraged suicide, strangled their children, exploited their workers and slaves, robbed temples, and engaged in numerous other immoral practices. The Gauls, Saxons, and Greeks were also unjust and barbarous.[64]

Finally, in spite of our excesses, we are moderate and even abstemious by comparison with some of the ancients. Roman luxury, for example, included

"*monstrous excesse in all kinde of uncleannes & incontinencie, in*

[73]

*diet, in apparrell, in retinew of servants, in buildings & furniture of
their houses, in bathings & annointings of their bodies, in prodigall
gifts,* and lastly, *in setting forth their playes and Theatricall
shewes."*

Hakewill then proceeds to develop each of these categories at some
length, enlarging especially upon items of dress and toilet. They
wore frizzled hair, spoke with small voice, pressed their clothes
artificially, used "slibber-sauce" on their faces, wore clothes of
"light and whorish colours," and Suetonius reports that Otto even
shaved every day. The women were, of course, worse still, and

"did not blush to have it knowne, that usually they painted not
their faces onely, but their very eye-browes.... They frisled and
curled their haire with hot irons.... They likewise dyed their
haire.... They also wore haire which they bought, instead of their
owne.... Besides, they used artificiall teeth in defect of naturall.
... Lastly, they had infinite little boxes filled with loathsome trash
of sundry kindes of colours and compositions for the hiding of their
deformities, the very sight and smell whereof was able to turne a
mans stomacke."[65]

   In his discussion of the arts and sciences, and even more so in his
discussion of manners, Hakewill's method is thus seen to be a detailed comparison of the ancients and moderns, wherein the moderns prove to be at least as virtuous and able as the ancients, taken
century by century or age by age. Since, in Hakewill's philosophy,
there is no decline in any of the powers of nature, all changes in its
present condition must necessarily be temporary. Moderns have, in
addition, the advantage of continuing their studies where the ancients left off, though, as Hakewill quotes from Vives, we are not
dwarfs upon the shoulders of giants: *"non est ita, nec nos sumus
nani, nec illi, homines gigantes, sed omnes ejusdem staturae."*
In a sense it may even be said that we ourselves are the true ancients, "the times wherein wee now live being in propriety of speech
the most ancient since the worlds creation" and thus meriting any
respect due simply because of venerability.[66]

[74]

VIII. A KIND OF CIRCULAR PROGRESS

Notwithstanding the better part of four hundred pages which Hakewill devotes to the comparison of past and present, however, this comparison plays a relatively minor part in his total controversy with Goodman. In the first place, Goodman is not extensively concerned with the problem, since his argument rests upon the difference between actual conditions and a hypothetical state of perfection before the Fall; the miseries of man are related primarily to the original and exemplary perfection of the universe, not to the circumstances of any other age with which itemized comparisons are possible. Nor is Hakewill much concerned with the ancients and moderns in Books I and II, where he lays the whole foundation for his position, establishing the general principles whereby the mutability of the parts is distinguished from the decay of the whole. In Books III and IV, in which he gives detailed comparisons of the present with particular points in the past, he is merely fortifying an argument which he considers already won.[67]

Hakewill thus depends less on the comparison of ancients and moderns than one might assume. In order to answer Goodman, who, attempting to discover a natural basis for corruption, sets up a series of principles or proofs "drawn from reason," Hakewill also takes up each of these principles in some detail. He does so primarily in Book V, however, as Goodman once more makes an issue of them, and their consideration does not determine the organization of his treatise. His position may be summarized in the statements that "to the Authour of Nature it is every way as easie to make as unmake," and that nothing is destroyed "but some other thing is instantly made of it; so as in the totall summe nothing is lost."[68] Hence the whole cannot be characterized by its parts, nor the species by any individual therein.

To Goodman's contention that privation makes all nature corruptible, Hakewill answers that, even if privation be admitted, it is a merely negative principle. It "implies an endlesse circle of corruptions and generations by turnes," just as the phenomenon of night presupposes both a precedent and a subsequent day. It governs the fluctuations in nature while at the same time, far from operating for nature's destruction, it assures her continuity and integrity. It does not show nature inclining toward corruption, "because privation hath reference to the bringing in of a new forme, and not to the casting out of the old."[69]

Hakewill admits the conflict among contrary elements and hence the mutability of the sublunar world, but he denies the presence of contraries in the heavens. What destroys the creatures, the rocks, the trees—all subcelestial bodies, in fact—is not time itself but this conflict of the elements; and he cannot suppose there is a body below the moon "so equally tempered, or evenly ballanced by the Elements, that there shall bee no *predominancie,* no struggling or wrastling in it." There, however, we have an end to Hakewill's concessions. No struggle occurs in the heavens, which do not share in the elementary qualities or conflicts.[70] Prove decay, prove conflicts, in the heavens, and it will then be granted that corruption is a natural law and that the whole world inclines toward decay.

Another point stressed by Goodman is that corruption increases as we move farther from the *"first mould."* Hakewill considers this his adversaries' main argument, "the *Pole-deede* of their evidence," and undertakes to refute it in some detail. Such an argument would imply a decay simply "in *processe of time,* whether *man* had *sinned* or no." Violent motions (the arrow sent from a bow) may decrease as they leave the source, but, with natural motions (the falling of a stone) the contrary is true, according to Hakewill. And when it comes to preserving the world, God's hand may be said to go along with the arrow, sustaining all things in their original force. Nature would not "so farre degenerate, as to runne her selfe out of breath," if she were left completely to herself. Primogeniture, which Goodman advances as a natural law, is no more than a convention of society: actually, the younger brother is often wiser than the older, the son greater than the father.[71]

Goodman's argument that the decay of the world is apparent in the decay of its parts is opposed by Hakewill at every level. The elements, for example, "sometime losing what they had gotten, and then againe getting what they had formerly lost," retain a perfect balance by means of a *"reciprocall compensation."* The mixed bodies decay in their particulars but are preserved in their generals. Because "the parts that are whole have a greater inclination to keepe themselves sound, then to be corrupted," the sound part may often cure the corrupted part. The decay or death of an individual man cannot indicate the decay of the race of man, far less the decay of the whole universe, the decay of the parts being "supplyed and repaired by an equivalent compensation" in the great world but not in the little world.[72]

Thus from still another point of view Hakewill attacks the analogy of the microcosm: believing that the macrocosm contains the immutable heavens and is therefore not subject to the laws that govern the microcosm; that the sin of man was not visited upon the heavens; that the heavens influence the earth and not the earth the heavens; that the heavens are composed of a matter without contraries and a form so perfectly realized that it does not permit of alterations; and that there is "nothing in man correspondent to the heavenly bodies, by which the great world is preserved from decay," he now attacks the comparison once more in a corollary to his proposition that the whole cannot be inferred from its parts.[73]

Goodman's part-to-whole argument includes the progression from decay of the individual to decay of the species, a progression which Hakewill denies repeatedly during the course of Book V. According to Hakewill, the death of the individual is actually required for the preservation of the species, "the perpetuitie of both being in a naturall course incompatible, impossible to consist together." Life is thus maintained not by each individual but by a succession of individuals. For Goodman, such succession is simply *"an earnest of the dissolution,"* but Hakewill sees it as God's way of reconciling the eternity of his creation with the obvious mutability of his creatures. Man, for example, "because a *species,* by succession becomes eternall," and the lost part is recovered in the whole: the river is still the same, though every drop of water in it be changed and renewed.[74]

All species continue as they were created, without deterioration, nor have new harmful ones arisen. Hakewill implies once that even the death of a species would be no sign of a decaying universe; but usually he insists upon the permanence of species—as though he were willing to decide the issue on this point alone. The burden of proof rests with Goodman, who must "have either broken or un-linked that inviolable chaine of generations and corruptions, suc-ceeding each other by turnes in these sublunarie bodies, or showne a perpetuall and universall decay in all the celestiall bodies, specially in the Sunne since the first Creation," before he can properly de-clare the world to be decaying.[75]

Another argument "drawn from reason" is Hakewill's thesis that if nature inclined toward corruption, the world would have ended long ago.[76] This proposition, recurring frequently through-out the *Apologie,* is perhaps the purely logical counterpart of his appeal to the senses: the so-called "signs of decay" actually point in no one direction, whereas, if the world were declining, they would be unmistakable beacons of corruption—if there were any world left at all. That this argument was effective is attested by Samuel Fell's testimony, prefaced to the second and third editions of the *Apologie,* that he was converted to Hakewill's opinion by just such reasoning.[77]

Hakewill uses this approach at various levels. If the world were steadily decaying, *"Adam* should have beene the *tallest* and *longest-liv'd"* of all men, and today we would be no bigger than rats—if, indeed, we still survived. If the various species constantly decreased in strength and fertility, man and beast alike would have been ex-tinguished. If corruption overbalanced generation, "the world had long since beene utterly dispeopled." If the weather were constant-ly growing worse, "wee should by this time have had no weather to ripen our corne or fruites," and we would not be here to com-plain. If the heavens shared the conflicting qualities of the elements, they would long ago have been destroyed by their own flame. If na-ture in general had been decaying through all the past ages,

"the vigour and strength of it must needes have beene *utterly ex-hausted and worne out.* If in every *Centenary* of yeares from the

Creation, or since the *floud,* some small abatement onely should have beene made ... nothing else could now be left unto us but the very *refuse* and *bran,* the *drosse* and *dregges* of *nature:* and as heavy things sinke in rivers, but strawes and stickes are carried downe the streame; so in this long current of time, the *kernell* and *pith* of *Nature* must needes have beene spent and wasted, onely the *rinde* and *shells* should have beene left to us. The *Heavens* could not by their warmth and influence have beene able sufficiently to cherish the *earth,* nor the *earth* to keepe the plants from starving at her breasts, nor the *plants* to nourish the *beasts,* nor could the beasts have beene serviceable for the use of *man,* nor *man* himselfe of abilitie to exercise the right of his dominion over the *beasts* and other *Creatures.* The *Sunne* by this time would have beene no brighter then the *Moone* or *Starres, Cedars* would have beene no taller then *shrubs, Horses* no bigger then *Dogges, Elephants* then *Oxen, Oxen* then *Sheepe, Eagles* then *Pigeons, Pigeons* then *Sparrowes,* and the whole race of mankind must have become *Pigmies,* and mustered themselves to encounter with *Cranes.*"[78]

But the world does continue to exist, and without any clear evidence of deterioration. There are changes in every age, temporary losses; but, however great the lamenting, these changes constitute a mutability, not a corruption or decay. The sum of the argument is that the world does not grow worse with time; though, when all things are considered, it is probably no better either, for the principles which govern the whole are unchanged. There is, instead, "a kinde of *circular progresse*" in all things: "they have their *birth,* their *growth,* their *flourishing,* their *failing,* their *fading,* and within a while after[,] their *resurrection,* and *reflourishing* againe." Such a *"wheeling* about of all things in their seasons and courses" is incompatible with any perpetual, cumulative decrease.[79]

In so far as Book I of the *Apologie,* dealing with the "decay in generall," has any unity, this unity lies in developing the distinction between mutability and decay. The principle of compensation may be recognized in nature (the fluctuations of land and sea, mountain and valley, etc.), established in reason (losses in the parts are recovered in the whole), or simply accepted in faith, for *"all things worke together for the best to them that love God.*" It serves to drive a wedge between the microcosm, which dies, and the macrocosm, which permits of mutability but not of decay. It characterizes especially the history of men, in terms of which Books III and IV are so fully elaborated. There never was any age "but hath exceeded all others in some respects, and againe in other respects hath beene exceeded by others." If men "degenerate in courage, or age, or strength, or stature, or wits in one place, they grow more masculine and vigorous in another, and in the same place at another time."[80]

IX. DESTRUCTION BUT NO DECAY

The doctrine of compensation precludes despair, but Hakewill's hopefulness is offset by his intense concern over the mortality of the world. The world's end is inevitable and reminds men of death. No date may be anticipated for the end, however, and the very fact that there will be a last day must be accepted in faith alone. That the world was created step by step does not mean that it will end piecemeal, and we cannot reason from "a graduall perfection supernaturall to a graduall declination naturall."[81]

A decaying world would permit us to anticipate the date of the end and thus pry into the working of God's providence, whereas, actually, God's judgment at that time, as it was at the time of the Flood, will be wholly miraculous and beyond our calculations. The coming of the Antichrist could not help us fix the date, for he was expected very soon by Cyprian, Gregory, Lactantius, and others, and he has probably been on hand for some time already. Surely, if in Paul's day, "the egge were then layed, shall we imagine that the Cockatrice is not yet hatched?" Even the signs which we have been promised before the end—"the *Subversion of Rome,* and the *Conversion of the Iewes*"—will not reveal the intended date, although because these signs have not yet appeared we know the end cannot be immediately at hand.[82]

Hakewill objects, in other words, to any attempt at making the end of the world natural or reasonable. It cannot be deduced from natural law, is not evident in nature, and cannot be assumed on any grounds except God's promise.[83] No Christian can doubt that the world will end, but there will be no "natural means" used, such as are insisted upon by Goodman, and therefore no signs or preparations for the end. The destined end of the world cannot therefore be used to prove its decay, for "Annihilation is the immediate worke of the Creatour, and equivalent to Creation, so is not decay." Actually, God intends to destroy the world with fire, so it cannot "be well conceived why he should ordaine or admit such a dayly, universall and irrecoverable consumption," which would bring an end without fire.[84]

If the world were steadily and irredeemably decaying, its complete destruction could be construed as an act of God's mercy, designed to spare man further suffering; and it is just so that Goodman construes it. Hakewill is equally consistent in attributing the destruction to God's justice. It is God's mercy that sustains the universe in its original integrity, but the end of the world is the occasion of his judgment, when the good will be rewarded and the sinful will be punished. The last chapter of the *Apologie* is devoted in its entirety to a consideration of "the uses wee are to make of the consummation of the world, and of the day of Judgement." It will serve as a *"terrour to the wicked,"* as *"a speciall comfort to the godly,"* and as admonition and instruction to all.[85]

When the judgment is effected, the material world "shall bee totally and finally dissolved and annihilated." Divines have variously believed that at this time all creatures will be restored to their original perfection or that only the heavens and some two or more of the elements will be restored or that possibly an entirely new world will be created. The last of these potentialities is maintained by Goodman and is extensively refuted by Hakewill, who argues that the Scriptures promise a complete destruction of the world, and "to renovate it, is not to destroy it." Once man is redeemed unto everlasting life, he no longer needs the world that told him of God's power, for he sees God face to face.[86]

Any existence that we enjoy after the judgment will thus be a spiritual one directly in the company of God and the angels and not here on this earth, in whatever fashion this world may have been renewed. Hakewill objects to Goodman's use of the links of generation as applied to the world, whereby a new world may be said (even in a *"metaphysicall sence"*) to grow out of the old. And, finally, he argues that the conflagration will not be simply a purge, wherein the world will be restored in some purified state but that (the quality of fire being what it is and the Scriptures calling for total destruction) the end of the world will in all ways be the end of everything we have known in this material universe—the heavenly bodies, the elements, the creatures, and the mutable bodies of men.[87]

X. GOODMAN VERSUS HAKEWILL—THE ISSUES

This completes the summary of Hakewill's philosophy, with particular emphasis upon the points at which he conflicts with Goodman. The controversy between the two men is resolved into a series of differences, combining to form consistent arguments for and against the decay of the world. In terms of these differences, as elaborated by the principal protagonists, contemporary concern over the future of the universe may perhaps be better understood. The remainder of this study undertakes to show not so much the extent to which thoughts of a decaying universe pervade the writings of the period as the prevalence of these thoughts in the form that they take: frequently in the dialectic of Goodman and Hakewill, less frequently in other terms and with other arguments. The fundamental areas of divergence may be briefly synthesized as follows:

Goodman and Hakewill agree that the world is designed for man's use but disagree over whether God's glory is better served by a corrupt or a constant universe. Both argue in terms of a provident God: Hakewill finds providence in the constancy of the world, Goodman in the decay that makes men repent. Hakewill believes that the relationship between God and man must be accepted entirely on faith, but Goodman is more sanguine about the ability of human reason to verify or arrive independently at the tenets of faith. Each man feels it necessary to justify his point of view within a completely teleological framework, and the debate over the decay of the world, when conducted over the issues raised by Goodman and Hakewill, is thus directed to doctrinal ends held in common by all parties to the debate.

There is disagreement also over the original constitution of nature and the effect of sin upon it. Goodman believes in an inbred, natural corruption. Privation in all the universe makes possible a return to nothing, he holds, and the dissolution is effected by means of the contrary elements and qualities which make up all material bodies. Because of man's sin, God released these contraries and permitted the process of disintegration to set in. This process, wholly in accord with all principles of nature, cannot be halted or reversed except by the direct intervention of God. Where Goodman traces a decline in the *conditions* of nature, Hakewill insists that the *powers* of nature are not diminished. Where Goodman laments over changes in the form, Hakewill denies any depreciation in the matter. Hakewill asserts that nature was impervious to decay at the beginning and that it has not been affected by man's sin. The perfect world, the direct work of God's hand, could not have been created corruptible, he contends; the "springs" of nature are generative and provide for the preservation of nature. Any loss is eventually restored. Mutability is not decay, and barrenness is followed by fertility, misery by happiness, evil by good. Nor did the Fall of man in any sense change the fundamental operation of natural law. In opposition, therefore, to the apparent corruption which Goodman finds in nature, Hakewill denies its corruptibility—either in its original constitution or as the result of any subsequent natural change.

Another point at issue has to do with the possibility of proving the decay from the evidence of an approaching end of the world. Goodman believes that the whole universe, if God had not decided to stop the process of decay by a merciful annihilation, would wear out and dissolve as the result of its natural corruptibility. The gradual, step-by-step beginning of the world, he indicates, implies a similarly gradual destruction at the end. Hakewill answers that a supernatural beginning can imply only a supernatural end and that no natural law or exterior agent can impair the work of God's hand. The fact that the world will end by fire precludes its decay, for God would not plan both a natural and a supernatural dissolution. Hakewill, agreeing that the world is now in its old age, contends that it has nevertheless lost none of the strength or integrity of its youth. Thus Goodman discovers in the miseries of the world many signs of its impending termination, whereas Hakewill holds that there can be no natural signs of a supernatural end, the date of which God does not wish us to know.

The controversy engages, further, a series of arguments whereby decay is established by characterizing the whole from its parts. According to Goodman, death of the individual proves death of the species, and the misery of man betokens the corruption of the world. Hakewill, denying the progression from part to whole, raises an objection of his own, i.e., that a continuous decay operating since the Fall of man would have completely worn out the world by now. The analogy of the microcosm and the macrocosm—most elaborate and most eloquent of the part-whole arguments and heavily relied upon by Goodman—provides the best single clue to the intellectual and imaginative environment in which this controversy is fought. The vicissitudes of man can more easily be extended to a world made for and epitomized in man than to a world of which man is but a minute and incidental part; and Hakewill argues, first, that man's sin will not be punished in nature, for only man is guilty, and, second, that there is nothing in the microcosm corresponding to the immutable heavens of the macrocosm.

Finally, there is the proof of decay from the actual material evidence, from the manifestations of corruption in the heavens, in the earth, and in man. Writers who present this argument may be concerned exclusively with the fall from original perfection to present decay, or, like Goodman, they may believe also in the progressive

deterioration of nature. They may find the decay only in the sublunary world, or, again like Goodman, they may include the heavens within the realm of corruption. The focus of interest in all
cases, however, is the sin and misery of man, from which the corruption of the whole may be known. These and other variations in
the method of interpreting the external signs of decay, therefore,
are based upon the same cosmology and the same philosophy of an
organic and unified world, in the parts of which the whole is revealed. Hakewill, of course, denies that the signs constitute valid
evidence of corruption, and he accounts for the mutability in terms
of other principles. It may be recalled, in conclusion, that, however
fully some who argue about the world's decay seem ostensibly to
rely upon the evidence of the senses, as they simply describe the
manifestations of decay or of constancy, most writers of the period,
including Goodman and Hakewill, actually make these manifestations not so much the basis as the verification of their argument.

Chapter IV

DEVELOPMENT OF THE CONTROVERSY

O F THE five regions of conflict defined in chapter iii, perhaps
the fifth affords the best means of introducing the principal
variations and affirmations of this belief in the decay of the world.
For one thing, almost all the defenders of the doctrine express
themselves in terms of the physical signs of corruption, and some
dwell upon these physical signs to such extent as to suggest that
their belief in decay is based upon what they see. On the other hand,
it will be remembered that Goodman, while professing to appeal
to the natural or rational man, bases his arguments on assumptions
that would have been untenable without faith in the supernatural;
and even Hakewill, with the weight of natural evidence on his side,
is less interested in the observations of scientists and historians than
in the prerogatives of God's honor.

Yet the physical signs of decay, without the additional proof of
revelation, are often sufficient to support the belief in decay; and,
what is probably more important, the actual and palpable evidence
of corruption, even where it does not serve to establish the decay
of the world on natural grounds, has a tremendous emotional
effect. For many others, as for Goodman, the signs of decay are actually presented not so much to prove as to exhort. Convinced by other
means that these are manifestations of a decaying world, men are
then deeply moved by consideration of spots upon the sun, the barrenness of the soil, the wickedness of society, and all the other
symbols of our mortality.

In continuing, therefore, by examining the signs of decay, predominantly in terms of the uses to which the evidence is put, we
get a detailed description of the natural and moral universe in

which these men lived. By presenting this exposition in more or less chronological order, we may also be able to follow the association between the belief in decay and other significant and related ideas of the period. The other four arguments listed in chapter iii (those from the purpose of creation, the natural processes whereby the world was created and is now sustained, the approach of the end, and the relation of part to whole) are discussed in this chapter wherever they are particularly pertinent or wherever their importance may be most clearly anticipated, but they are, on the whole, reserved for more complete study in the next and final chapter.

Excluding, for the moment, isolated appearances of the belief in decay, as well as classical and medieval sources of the idea, we shall find a general concern over the corruption of nature first growing around the middle of the sixteenth century, rising to an extensive and continuous excitement from the 1570's into the 1630's, and subsiding sharply from then on. The peak of this interest comes during the years immediately preceding and following the publication of Goodman's monumental work in 1616. Opposition to the doctrine of decay follows another course, as we shall see later; but most variants of the idea do not have a history which is significantly different.

I. SIXTEENTH-CENTURY COMMONPLACE

At the beginning of the sixteenth century, when there is little active concern over the corruption of the world, the occasional references to decay nevertheless indicate that the idea is not new or strange or dangerous and that it apparently needs no apology or explanation. Polydore Vergil, for example, Italian humanist, English archdeacon, and apologist in many ways for modern discoveries, shows in his *De rerum inventoribus* (1499) that belief in "an ende by putrifaction" is the conventional Christian position and opposes this belief to the notion, ascribed here to Pythagoras, Aristotle, and others and invariably refuted in the writings of the period, that the world is eternal.[1]

Since the doctrine of the world's decay did not become a subject for extended treatment or for debate until many years later, it often becomes difficult to determine the exact scope of the idea or the range of evidence as presented by particular writers. Vergil, in the passage just cited, refers to the "world" in general, without specifying whether the heavens are to be included or not. During the sixteenth century the evidence supporting nature's corruption seldom relies heavily upon signs of corruption in the heavens, and the Aristotelian distinction between mutable earth and immutable heavens, though not often made explicit in this context, is usually implied. Marcellus Palingenius, scholar and encyclopedist in the early part of the century, makes this distinction, whereas his contemporary, Pedro Mexia, Spanish poet and historiographer, does not.

In his popular *Zodiacus vitae* (*ca*. 1531), Palingenius admits the decay of the world to be a tenet of Christian faith, and, though he includes the heavens in the final destruction of the universe, he specifically states that time alone cannot "harme the heavens state." Nor is there any principle of physical decay, according to Palingenius, even in the sublunar world, notwithstanding its transitory, corrupt, and mutable state; only in God's word can there be true evidence of a permanent decline of nature:

> Wherefore, if we to Reason sticke then must we surely say,
> That this same world hath euer beene and neuer shal decay.
> But if that God sayd otherwyse long since, and then did giue
> To Moyses knowledge of his workes, we Moyses must belieue.

Mexia, on the other hand, developing his belief that this is the last, old age of the world, in which the fertility of the earth and the span of man's days are alike impaired, is inclined to regard the heavens as also corrupted, though only to the extent that in their influence upon the earth they were once "far more beneficiall, then they presently now are." Whether we reckon by the six ages of the historians or the four of the poets, the present times are the last and worst. The soil of the earth is now "worne, wasted, weryed and consumed." Man's life was once much longer, so that the earth might become populated, but "by the chaunge of Ages (whose propertie is to alter and to impair all things) yᵉ state of man began to weaken, yeelding his dayes in number fewer then before."²

The works of Vergil, Palingenius, and Mexia discussed here are all descriptive and instructional documents, not essentially original but widely read in their time; and what they say about the corruption of nature seems to be representative of the form in which the doctrine of decay appears before it becomes the popular vehicle of warning and exhortation. Other secular works of the immediate period reveal a similar disposition to accept the thesis that the world is wearing down, with even less concern over the implications of this thesis, among such works being the Lanquet-Cooper *Chronicle,* Richard Eden's Preface to his translation of Peter Martyr (1555), and Vincent Cartari's survey of mythology (1556).* In the mid-sixteenth century it is rather among the more specifically religious writings that we find the doctrine of decay expressed at greater length and directed toward the ends which motivate so many of the statements of the following period: the world's corruption is related definitely to man's sin, or it is a sign of the approaching day of judgment, or it is used to persuade sinners to seek salvation.

These traditional interests are evident, for example, in the expositions of William Tyndale (d. 1536), who does not, however, actually embrace the doctrine of a physical decay of nature. In his Prologue to II Peter, Tyndale discusses the decline of faith from "the tyme of the pure and true Gospell" until "at the last men shoulde beleue nothyng, nor feare God at all." In "A Pathway into the Holy Scripture" he emphasizes the fact that all our corruption is

---

* The history begun by Thomas Lanquet (1521–45) and completed by Thomas Cooper in 1565 indicates that the earth still suffers from man's Fall, and addresses its historical perspective to "the troublous and mutable state of theis dayes" (*Coopers Chronicle,* sig. aiii, fol. 1ᵛ). Richard Eden, affirming that "antiquitie had neuer such knowledge of the worlde ... as we haue at this presente," still is able to see himself living in a "declinynge worlde" (*The First Three English Books on America,* pp. 56, 247). Peter Martyr himself, in the first *Decade* (1511), describes the newly found savages in terms of the "goulden worlde" of the past (see Eden's trans., p. 71). Cartari indicates that "the canckred rust of effeminate desires hath so deeply eaten into this our yron age" that we are farther than ever from the gods and heroes of ancient times (*The Fovntaine of Ancient Fiction,* sig. Qᵛ).

the result of Adam's sin, and in the commentary on I John, he indicates that the corrupt times of the Antichrist have long been upon us, so that the end of the world cannot be far off.[3]

Much more explicit in his description of external nature is Martin Luther, who describes at some length the corruption of the world brought about by man's sin. In his commentary on Genesis, begun in 1535 and completed in 1545, Luther explains how the whole creation was cursed, how the full effect of that curse was not felt until the Flood, and how all things seem to grow constantly worse as time goes on and our sins increase.[4] In the beginning the world was "innocent and pure, because man was innocent and pure," he writes. "But now, as man is no longer the same being, so the world is no longer the same world. Upon the fall of man followed corruption and upon this corruption the curse of the now corrupt creation."[5]

Thus the whole creation reflects the sin and Fall. Man's judgment is impaired, his reason and his will fallen. His life is shorter, his body weaker, the diseases that oppress him more numerous. Death itself is the consequence of sin. The other creatures rebel against man's dominion. The earth has become barren, bringing forth briars and thistles. The sun is not so bright, the water not so wholesome, the air not so pure, as before the Fall of man.[6]

The process of corruption operated not only at the occasion of man's Fall; Luther finds it to have been even more fully manifested at the time of the Flood. The punishment imposed at the Fall was not completely realized until the Flood, which "destroyed paradise and the whole human race, and swept them from the face of the earth." The original curse "was afterwards greatly increased by the Deluge, when all the good trees were rooted up and destroyed, barren sands accumulated and both noxious herbs and beasts multiplied."[7]

The Fall and the Flood are the two principal stages, but time itself becomes a party to the decay; "the nearer the world approaches its end the worse men become," and the heavier their punishment. There is no doubt, too, that the end is near; Luther once predicts that the world will not last a hundred years longer, and on another occasion he sets the date closer still. "The end is at hand, at the very threshold," he says. "The joys of the world are played out."[8] The decay of nature is thus used by Luther, as by Goodman, to prove man's sin and warn of the world's end. The fire and flood, thorns and thistles, are messengers which preach to us.

The German scholar, Kaspar Peucer, is another who finds nature corrupted because of sin: it is God's curse *"sur le peché de l'homme"* which is the cause *"du desordre & de la foiblesse qu'on void en Nature."* The curse has not completely destroyed nature,

"mais elle a troublé l'ordre qui estoit si bien estably, a dissouls l'accord, brisé & ecrasé la force & la perfection [*text:* perfefection] des choses. De là est procedé ce discord entre les choses creées, suiui incontinent des antipathies & dissensions des corps celestes & elementaires, les discords des actions partie repugnantes, partie languissantes & imparfaites en la nature corrompue de l'homme. Le peché attirant la malediction de Dieu esclos tout ce qu'il y a de confusion, de desordre, de mutilé, de vicieux, d'enorme, de languissant & de deprau&é au monde. Il a tellement alteré & afoibli la matiere, qu'vne impuissance s'en est ensuiuie dont s'ensuiuent des agitations & mouuemens vagues, glissans, & qui n'ont point d'arrest."

The order of nature is thus confused and disrupted, though *"il n'est pas renuersé,"* for God "corrige & reforme beaucoup de choses." The sphere of corruption, furthermore, is limited; for the celestial bodies "ne viellissent, ni ne chāgent, ni ne se corrōpent," and the heaven itself, lacking contrary qualities, *"n'est suiet a meslinge ni a changement."*[9] On the whole, however, though he is especially concerned over the inconsistency of fortune in human affairs and includes all the sublunar world as subject to change and corruption, Peucer fails to find in this corruption of nature an incremental decay of nature.

A similar view of nature is to be found in *Ane Dialog betuix Experience and ane Courteour,* by the Scottish poet, David Lyndsay. Fortune is fleeting and inconstant, he says, the world itself is corrupted by man's sin and further damaged by the Flood, the final destruction cannot be far off, and the total misery increases "frome day to day." As a punishment for man's defection, the earth was cursed and made barren; by "the Feindis perswasioun,"

> The hole warld, universalye,
> Corruptit was alluterlye.

What strength or virtue remained to the earth, after the Fall, was destroyed by the Flood. The present is the last age of the world, and everywhere about us are signs that the end is near; if there be doubt about the physical signs, the moral signs at least are known.*

Zacharias Ursinus, Calvinist author of the Heidelberg Catechism in 1562, extends the sphere of corruption to include the heavens, though with certain qualifications, and implies that there is a continuous process of deterioration now evident in the whole universe. He recognizes a decline in the heavens but insists that there is no *natural* corruption, since the celestial matter is incapable of assuming a new form. The present is the "doting old age of the world," and these are the "last times"; "we are fallen into the last dayes, and daily see the signes which were fore-told concerning the judgement." The corruption of nature is indicated in *"The age of man decreasing;* which sheweth that there was greater strength in nature at the first, and that not without some first cause it hath decreased hitherto."[10]

The doting old age of the world is described also by Henri Estienne in *L'Introdvction au traité de la conformité des merveilles anciennes avec les modernes* (1566), a work designed to show that modern wonders are as strange as those of the ancient world, but developing into a violent satire against contemporary morals and

* The "fickle and brickle state of mans lyfe" is a principal concern also of Pierre Boaistuau, in his *Theatrum mundi* (1558). This work is developed in a manner much like that used by Goodman, by elaborating upon man's miseries as the results of his sin; the ends and the emotional attitudes are those which later serve so many others as a basis for belief in the physical decay of nature, but Boaistuau himself here says nothing about the external world (*Theatrum mundi,* sig. ¶v^v; pp. 44 ff., 73–122, 178, 179–204, etc.).

particularly against the immorality of the clergy. The sins of the past "were but sugar ... in comparison of the villanies of these [times] wherein we liue," and, in general, we may recognize that "the world waxeth daily worse and worse." Estienne's evidence is limited to the moral decline, but by analogy he draws in the macrocosm as well:

"... certaine it is that such dissolute demeanour and loosenesse of life, such riot and excesse, such swearing and swaggering, was neuer heard of in the prime and infancy of the world as afterward towards the middle Age, and as now in the decrepit Age thereof; in the decrepite Age (I say) if we may beleeue our eyes, or iudge by the course and cariage of things.... I am of opinion that it fareth with the vniuerse or great world, as with man the litle world; in that *The older it waxeth, the more it doteth.* For he that shall seriously consider the guise of the world at this day, cannot but say that it doteth extreamely, and that it resembles the age of our good grandsire, gray-bearded Saturne."[11]

II. DECAY AND MUTABILITY IN THE 1570's

Descriptions of a decaying world become more detailed and more intensive in the 1570's. More frequently now the change that is recorded is not simply a fall from original perfection but a daily process of deterioration. The evidence for decay is not so often limited to man's virtue or even his body but is more regularly broadened to include the material universe, heavens and all. This is not to imply that the decay of morals is no longer lamented; for it remains the starting-point of the argument, as in Goodman, and it must remain the starting-point as long as the decay of nature is the result of man's sin. But the Christian doctrine of the Fall of man now more often explicitly extends to the progressive decay of the entire universe, and there is a growing inclination to think that the corruption has taken root in nature and is there daily aggravated.

The awakening interest in the physical universe in general helps to explain the spectacular increase, through the next forty or fifty years, of the belief in the decay of nature. In the last quarter of the sixteenth century the Copernican theory is often discussed as a physical, rather than as a mathematical, hypothesis. Leonard Digges and John Dee use telescopes for terrestrial observations in the sixties and seventies, and Thomas Heriot makes new observations of the heavens in the eighties. In addition, Thomas Digges had probably devised a microscope before the end of the century.[12]

The explorations carried out for many years past had encouraged the study of the earth and of its properties. Gilbert publishes his investigations of magnetic principles in 1600. Perhaps the scientific development most affecting the belief in decay at this time is the realization that the "new" star in Cassiopeia in 1572 is in the realm of the heavens, hitherto usually considered immutable. There is now no part of the material world which is not subject to decay; the signs of corruption may be read everywhere in nature.

Yet we should not attribute to these discoveries more significance than they merit. The scientists themselves do not find in their new knowledge any indications of decay. The divines and the poets and the popular scientists who write about decay are still likely to take their astronomy from Ptolemy and their zoölogy from Pliny. When conflicting ways of thought begin to converge in the seventeenth century, whether in the poetic images of Donne or in the literal descriptions of Carpenter and Swan, the belief in decay unquestionably shows the influence of contemporary science, but it remains the old belief and simply invokes the new discoveries as confirmation.

The increased interest in the world's decay may, on the other hand, be recognized as a reflection of renewed interest in man's sin and in his need for salvation. Man's immorality is more apparent than ever in the busy, secular society of the Renaissance. The Reformation tends to sharpen the edge of religious endeavor and makes doctrinal controversies the subjects of popular debates. The six thousand years commonly allotted the world are now nearing an end, and divines are eager for new evidence with which to oppose the arguments for an eternal universe.

The early seventeenth century sees an overlapping of two great philosophies: the teleological Christian vision of a moral universe and the scientist's vision of mathematical order unfolding before the instruments and the theorems of man's devising. The doctrine of decay derives not from the second philosophy but from the first, in terms of which the controversy between Goodman and Hakewill is carried on. Hakewill offers a consistent philosophy in opposition to the belief in decay; but men like Bacon, Descartes, John Wilkins, and Hobbes make the repudiation of this belief even more necessary and complete.

In the 1570's the *Physica Christiana* of Lambert Daneau provides a good example of the natural world examined from the religious point of view.[13] Here Daneau portrays the old, worn universe as undergoing a daily deterioration, specifically as the result of man's sin. The opposition which he recognizes is not one between the "New Philosophy" and the old, but that between two forms of the old—the Christian and the heathen. He attacks both the Aristotelian notion of a world without beginning or end and the Epicurean notion of a world governed by chance, and reaffirms his conviction that the only truth is the truth of revelation.

God created a world that was perfect, Daneau writes, "and not as it is nowe, weake, sicke, and wounded," in its "crooked old age." All natural bodies are "weake and imperfect, scarce able to susteine themselues, or to doe theyr duety and function." The "wounderfull order" of the universe is destroyed. Because of sin, the universe is discordant instead of harmonious. Because of sin, "the strength and plentifulnes of the earth, and of all other thinges decreaseth dayly," and the whole world is "a confused mist."

Daneau thus sees decay increasing both in the heavens and in the earth. He suggests, however, that sin did not destroy the essence and nature of created things but only "impaired the integritie and perfection of them." Without sin, though the world was always

[95]

subject to alteration, there would have been no "euill thinges," the plenitude of nature implying that nothing is "absolute and in all respectes poyson."[14]*

The physical deterioration of the world is recognized also by Antonio de Torquemada in his treatises on natural wonders, published in 1570 as the *Jardin de flores curiosas*. The world, he says, steadily grows weaker in its old age; the diminished strength of nature causes a decrease in man's stature, so that giants, once very common, are now rarely found. Although the Flood represents an important step in the process of decay (and some even affirm "that the whole world before the time of the flood was plaine and leuell, without any hill or valley at all"), actually this process is continuous and cumulative: "as the world waxeth old, so al things draw to be lesser." After much travail, "the vvorld through wearines and long course of generation, ceaseth to breed men of so large and puissant statures as it wonted."[15]

In the sermons of Edwin Sandys, archbishop of York, written during the seventies and eighties and published in 1585, there is a similar concept of the world's old age, though without such specific indication of its attendant debility. The corrupt world is shown to be suffering because of man's sin, and particular emphasis is laid upon the corruption as proof and sign of the impending end: "all creatures now wax old with the aged world. This is even the last hour: the world cannot continue long." If the days of Peter were the "latter times," "surely these are the last times, the very end of the end." One sign of the times is that man's life is shorter than it once was.[16] But Sandys' interest is primarily in the moral decay, and he even translates the literal signs of the end into allegorical ones: the sun (Christ's teaching) is already darkened, and the stars (teachers of the gospel) are fallen.[17]

The old age and the wickedness of the world are again presented

---

* A similar view, though without the emphasis upon the increasing decay, is maintained in Daneau's *A Frvitfvll Commentarie vpon the Twelue Small Prophets* (1578). Here Daneau again discredits reason or the observation of nature as a final authority and describes the corruption of the world as the result of man's sin (pp. 316–17, 488, 1107, etc.).

in relation to its approaching end, in George Gascoigne's *Drum of Doomsday* (1576).* According to this work, man's life has daily been "more and more shortned." His miseries extend to all classes and all ages; his nakedness and the pains of childbirth are among the punishments he must endure. "So frō day to day, more & more, the nature of man is corrupted and made weaker." And in his weakness we may see also the daily decay of the whole material world, for both microcosm and macrocosm grow older and more corrupt with the passing years.[18]

Another widely read work which shows a world daily more enveloped in corruption is Pierre de la Primaudaye's *L'Académie française,* an encyclopedic study of man, the world, moral philosophy, and Christian philosophy, published in four parts (1577–94). Here again all natural phenomena are presented in terms of the ends for which they were created. Aristotle, Lucretius, and other ancient authorities are attacked freely, but with little understanding of contemporary science. The world is old, the end approaches, and all the corruption results from man's sin rather than from natural causes. Original sin has left its stamp in the ever increasing wickedness and misery of man. Because of sin, the "goodly agreement, harmony and concord which ought to be betweene God and man, is wholly peruerted and ouerthrowne." La Primaudaye compares the "sobriety of old time" with the corruption of this age, "wherein so many Epicures and Atheists liue," wherein men are worse than beasts, wherein "impietie and malice are come in the place of ancient innocency," "wherein store of false prophets are arisen, and haue seduced many, wherein all iniquity is increased, and charity

---

* The *Drum of Doomsday* is in part a translation of the *De contemptu mundi* of Pope Innocent III, a popular source for the kind of *memento mori* which we have been examining. In the *De contemptu* there is a great deal on the vanity, brevity, and misery of man's life and on the torments he must suffer; but not much attention is given to the increase of corruption or to the physical creation in general. The work was translated by Humphrey Kirton in 1576 as *The Mirror of Mans Lyfe,* and republished in 1577 and 1586. Other editions, translations, and borrowings attest the sustained interest in a popular medieval theme.

In his *Steel Glass,* also published in 1576, Gascoigne reflects the same concern over this weak and wretched world, from which a better age has long since vanished, though this is here expressed almost entirely in terms of the decay of man.

altogether frozen." Man's wickedness and his excesses cause his infirmities and his early death.[19]

These details are the very ones used later by Goodman, and the progression from man's sin to the world's corruption is similar also—the same argument from part to whole, the same analogy between the ages of man's life and the ages of the world. All things, the great world as well as the little, continually grow worse as they approach their end. It is sin "which hath infected the heauen, the earth, and all things contained therein, and put the world into disorder and confusion," which is, indeed, "the cause of all the discord in the world." The world is "altogether euill," and "we daily see it corrupt and approching to the ende," making man always more miserable. The decay has already become inbred in nature, as may be seen from "Mildew in wheat, rottennesse i[n] wood, rust in brasse and iron: yea euery thing is corrupted by it[s] owne euill, howsoeuer it escapeth all outward harmes."[20]

Whether or not the decay extends specifically to the heavens is a question which does not deeply disturb La Primaudaye. In Part II of *L'Académie,* for example, he finds the celestial bodies immutable when compared with the earth, remaining "alwaies intire and in their first forme," "neither do they weare or consume away." In Part III this statement is repeated (the heavens are "no whit changed," "neither are they more wearied, worne, or corrupted") and then qualified: "it is one thing to speake of the heauens comparing their nature with that of other visible and corporall creatures; and another thing, when we compare them with the nature of God." Before God, indeed, "this visible frame, both celestiall and terrestriall, is nothing else, but as a vesture which weareth, waxeth old & is cleane done, after that it is worne all out."[21]

This way of resolving the ambiguity obviously satisfies La Primaudaye, and his belief in the general corruption does not depend upon the evidence for decay of the heavens. He dismisses the problem, finally, by returning (as Goodman does a generation later) to his foremost interest—the frailty and insecurity of man's estate. We may leave to the astronomers, he says, the question of whether or not the motions of heavenly bodies "are somewhat different from those which they haue had from the beginning" or whether the heavens "waxe weary, are worne, and become old in their function, like to other creatures." Instead, we see how unstable is man's place when we remember that "all other creatures must receiue a change, & haue an end, yea the very heauens themselues."[22]

A contemporary whose world is in many ways like that of La Primaudaye is Guillaume du Bartas, author of the bombastic epic, *Le Semaine ou création du monde* (1578),[23] an encyclopedic work which reviews the current popular knowledge of the world. In it Du Bartas describes the creation and argues God's providence in sustaining the world. In so doing, he, too, like Daneau and La Primaudaye, refutes the Peripatetic doctrine of the world's eternity and the Epicurean doctrine of its accidental formation. But Du Bartas is concerned less with the continuous decline of nature than with its mutability, and he specifically excludes the heavens from the realm of change or corruption.

His interest in nature is primarily the interest in its mutability and in the contrast between present corruption and original perfection. Man is overcome by his miseries: the diseases of both body and soul are more virulent now than in former ages; creatures revolt against man's domination; the world which should have served him, now punishes him; and death itself is the result of sin. The elements are mutable and impermanent, and, although the heavens are not subject to alteration, they, too, will have an end. Damage caused by the Flood is added to the original effects of the Fall, and there is no recovery from either. The earth groans with its poisons, its weeds, its storms, and all the other ills it now engenders.[24]

Du Bartas does not, however, actually consider nature to be in the process of decaying. He describes many of the symptoms of decay but does not pursue the diagnosis. What gets his attention is the mutability of the elements as contrasted with the eternity of God's truth. His position may perhaps be illuminated by the use

[99]

that he makes of the Lucretian cosmology. Lucretius, often cited in the sixteenth and seventeenth centuries as an authority for both the idea of decay and the idea of progress, depicts a world which came into being by chance only, a world in which matter is indestructible but in which all forms must eventually disintegrate. Du Bartas accepts both the mutability of the forms and the permanence of matter, and the physical composition of his universe seems to be taken directly out of Epicurean philosophy.

But he does not, of course, accept the Lucretian principle of an accidental creation, and his entire performance may even be interpreted as a monumental refutation of just this principle.[25] Du Bartas and Spenser, Bruno and Bacon, owe much to the natural philosophy of Lucretius, without subscribing to its antiteleological basis. The cosmology of Lucretius is usually incorporated into the Christian frame of knowledge in much the same way as are the new scientific discoveries: the variety and complexity of things in the world show the greatness of God's creation; the mutability is evidence of material frailty when compared with God's eternal perfection. It is this frame of knowledge in which the belief in the decay of nature flourishes.

A similar kind of interest in the idea of mutability, though addressed to very different ends, is found in the work of other writers of this period, particularly Jean Bodin and Louis Leroy. Bodin, both in the *République* (1576) and the *Methodus ad facilem historiarum cognitionem* (1566), admits all worldly things to be unstable and attempts to arrive at the causes of the decay and downfall of states, but the changes that he records are changes only within the society of men. The decay of nature is excluded, and the morality of Bodin's state is political rather than divine; nature itself remains unchanged, and the growth or fall of a state is due to the will of the men who live in it.[26] The burden of the *Methodus* is that human history in general is a record of progress rather than of deterioration. Bodin specifically refutes the idea of the golden age, and in so doing attests to the popularily of such a notion, even among the learned men of his day. Offering the explanation later used by Bacon, Hakewill, and most others who attack the idea, he suggests that it is the natural inclination of old men to dream fondly about the greatness of the past.

Actually, men do not decay either in strength or in virtue, Bodin writes: Charles the Great accomplished more than did Alexander and other ancient heroes; we have improved upon the Romans in many ways; and our inventions—particularly printing, the compass, and gunpowder—surpass the discoveries of all former ages.[27] The same pattern of progress is not necessarily extended into the future, for all states and societies must some day perish, and an age of ignorance and chaos may well follow an age of achievement. But a new time of enlightenment will come, in turn, and the net result of the change is rather a gain than a loss.

Louis Leroy, French classicist and Bodin's contemporary, is similarly interested in the humanistic study of man's achievements and potentialities in this world. In his *Douze livres de la vicissitude ou variété des choses de l'univers,* he discusses "the successiue, or rather alternatiue changes of the whole world, aswell in the higher or superiour, as lower and inferiour part thereof," emphasizing, however, not decay and destruction but the permanence of a mutable world, the balance between generation and corruption, and the infinite possibilities of human progress.[28] Like the works of Daneau, La Primaudaye, and Du Bartas, Leroy's *De la vicissitude* is a storehouse of contemporary information and theories, but it is directed to the glorification of man's learning and not, as are the others, to the glorification of God's power over miserable and humble man. Like Bodin's *Methodus,* it is a secular (though not an irreligious) document, a forerunner of Bacon's *Advancement* as well as of Hakewill's *Apologie.*

Leroy admits that the belief in decay is current but ascribes it to the old men who "wish againe for the pleasures of youth."[29] Actually, he contends, the decay is only in our endeavor, not in the heavens, the elements, or the material part of man. The "perpetuall" bodies of the heavens remain "constantly alwaies in one selfe same estate." The mutable creatures and plants "participate of eternity ... by the meanes of generation." Thus even corruptible things, "tempered by alternatiue chaunges, and maintayned by contraries," are not subject to any final state of decay or disintegration.[30]

Yet, although the heavens are constant and immutable by contrast with the mercurial affairs of men or with the metamorphosis of the elements, Leroy does not hesitate, when he considers the universe as a whole, to include the heavens also as subject to the great cycles which periodically mark the course of the world. The end of such a cycle is now at hand: "Neuer were the Sunne and Moone eclipsed more apparantly; neuer were seene so many Comets"; and the signs of disruption are everywhere evident. Not only are there more earthquakes and monsters and more violent rivers and seas, but the "course of the sunne is no more such as it was wont to be in old time, neither are there the same points of the Solstices and Equinoxes," and, since Ptolemy, the sun has declined twelve degrees nearer the earth. Heaven itself must some day return to its "auncient Chaos, and former darknes," for, "since it hath a body, it can not wholy warrant or preserue it selfe from alteration & chaunge."[31]

The whole universe, therefore, is subject to corruption, the return to chaos, the loss of form; only divine providence, operating through the "agreement, and sympathie of heauen, and earth" and eventually through the process of generation, renews incessantly "the corruptible things in this sensible world." Finally, in a description so spirited in its prophetic melancholy as to be on the surface indistinguishable from a statement by Goodman, Leroy includes human affairs and the natural world in an inspired view of the cycle's end:

"I foresee warres arising in all Countries, both ciuile and foreine; factions, and diuisions springing, which will profane both diuine and humane whatsoeuer; famines, and pestilences threatning mortall men; the order of nature, the rules of the celestiall motions, and the agreement of the elements breaking off; deluges, and inundations comming on the one side; and excessiue heates, and

violent earthquakes on the other: and the world drawing towards
an end; bringing with it a confusion of all thinges, and reducing
them againe to their auncient and former *Chaos.*"[32]

The evidence which Leroy offers is thus in many ways the same
as that commonly employed in support of the world's decay, to
which Leroy is specifically opposed. What is important is not the
evidence but what is done with the evidence, what prior assumption the evidence is made to sustain. Though his natural philosophy
permits him to recognize the continuous threat of corruption, of
mutability, that is, which leads to an eventual dissolution, yet he
can envisage (still in the Lucretian pattern) the indefinite improvement of the arts and man's society. The vicissitudes and variety of
the world do not necessarily imply its mortality, and Leroy is not
primarily interested in that relationship of man to God which
would insure its mortality. Instead, Leroy proposes to write about
man's powers and his achievements, about the bright promise in
the new inventions and the new learning.

This is not to say that the cycles are not operative in "armes,
learning, languages, arts, estates, lawes, and maners." The periods
of prosperity and misfortune are not the same for all peoples because the various nations are honored and cast down at different
times, and, even in its greatest glory, each age or nation has its
share of troubles and vices. But, on the whole, Leroy's contemplation of the cycles brings him hope rather than despair. The present
age is superior in many respects: we have "recouered within these
two hundred yeares, the excellency of *Learning,*" and compare favorably with the greatest eras of the past in our mastery of the
sciences, of mathematics, grammar, poesy, history, rhetoric, logic,
and many other fields of inquiry.* The printing press, the compass,
and guns are to be listed among modern inventions. We are greater
in riches and empire and stronger in battle. Considering the vast
achievements of this age and the even greater hopes which are justi-

* George Best makes a similar statement supporting the superiority of modern
times, praising particularly the recent deveolpments in learning (*A Trve Discovrse*
[1578] in *The Three Voyages of Martin Frobisher*, I, [13]–14).

fied, Leroy has little patience with those who are "so affectionate to antiquitie, that they are ignorant . . . of the Countrie, and time wherein they liue."[33]

Leroy is not alone in stressing the world's mutability without preaching its permanent decay as the result of sin, though not for some time do we again find the doctrine of mutability converted into such a bright and positive promise of future glories. Giordano Bruno, for example, holds that all matter is mutable and in flux, the heavens as well as the earth; decay is physically possible, for the forms of all things are susceptible to destruction and the atoms will be scattered. But the cosmology of Lucretius, which Bruno incorporates into his own scheme, is not superimposed upon a world condemned a priori for man's sin, and consequently it does not necessarily involve the conventional implications about the decay and corruption of the world. This world and all other worlds are simply larger and more complex bodies than are the creatures: "You may say if you will that the worlds change and decay in old age, or that the earth seems to grow grey with years, and that all the great animals of the universe perish like the small, for they change, decay, dissolve."[34] The change and dissolution, however, are not the ends of Bruno's discourse, and he may be said to contribute to the spread of the doctrine of decay only some details of evidence and not any interest in or convictions about the idea.*

Still another who is concerned with the world's mutability, though not with its decay, is the Belgian scholar and antiquarian,

---

* R. F. Jones regards the scientific influence as more significant than the religious in establishing form and occasion for the doctrine of decay, and consequently he discusses Bruno from a different point of view.

It may be pointed out here that Montaigne similarly recognizes a change and even a wearing-down of the world, without projecting a metaphysics of sin and corruption. Identifying the first ages with the best and happiest, and accepting the common belief that the world is near its end, still he does not lament the world's mortality or despair of future ages.

Nor is the English surgeon, John Banister, interested in the decay of the world when he describes time as "the generall rust of the world, which weareth, eateth, consumeth, and perforateth all thynges"; his evidence is restricted to the size and age of man's body, and he investigates current differences in man's physical equipment throughout the world rather than any decline from past perfection.[35]

Justus Lipsius. Enlarging upon the weaknesses and the mutability of the entire universe, he attempts, in *De constantia* (1583), to seek out *"consolations against publick evils"* and to show that the alterations in the world are neither new nor harmful. The mutability exists in the heavens as well as on the earth, for "it is the Nature of all created beings, to hasten unto their change and fall, from a certain inward proneness, vvhich they have thereunto." The sun is eclipsed, the moon wanes, meteors fall; "There arose a Starr in this very year, vvhose increment and decreases vvere throughly observ'd; and we then saw (vvhat will scarcely be believ'd) that in Heaven it self, there may be something Born and Dye." The earth "totters, and is shaken into a palsy fit," or "it is corrupted by Waters or Fires." The changes imply the end; "the vvonderful and incomprehensible Law of Necessity" provides that nothing can be eternal: *"The Heavens and Elements change, and shall pass away."*[36]

But necessity is subservient to providence, which preserves the world, Lipsius goes on to show. We may fortify ourselves against necessity by remembering that the variations, meanwhile, are useful and beautiful: "I apprehend no beauty any where in this great frame without variety, and a distinct succession and change of things." Though the world now grows old, we may take comfort in knowing that whatever is lost in one place will be restored in another. Even if we find "many visible signes of an approaching ruine," so that "all sorts of Calamities seem to Centre in this Age," this age is really no worse than any other. "It is an old complaint; I know your Gransier said the same, and so likewise your Father; I know also your posterity vvill have the same complaint." The trouble is that we forget our better fortunes; but we love to contemplate our miseries. Actually, the misfortunes of past ages were greater than those of the present, and all the "Calamities do daily move in a Circle, and in a kind of round pass through this round World."[37]

Thus, though the evidence that Lipsius cites may be associated with belief in the decay of the world, his conclusions in many ways anticipate the position of Hakewill. Both Lipsius and Hakewill, furthermore, direct their treatises to the improvement of man's endeavor; both find the good in the world balancing the bad and God's providence preserving the whole. For Lipsius, however, constancy of mind is to be sought through the cultivation of wisdom, whereas for Hakewill the end of man's endeavor is religious and moral virtue.[38] And where Hakewill regards the world principally in terms of man's relationship to God, Lipsius emphasizes also the natural and historical explanation of universal mutability and urges the stoical constancy of man in the face of real or apparent evils.

III. END OF CENTURY, END OF WORLD

With the work of Francis Shakelton, "Minister and preacher of the worde of God," we return to the conventional pulpit lament over the sin of man and the approaching end of the world. *A Blazyng Starre* (1580) is Shakelton's effort to admonish *"of the finall dissolution of the Engine of this worlde"* and to demonstrate the world's mortality in opposition to the arguments of Aristotle, Galen, and Pliny.[39] His concern over the decay of the world is very much like that found in Luther, Daneau, La Primaudaye, or Goodman, in what may be considered the main line of interest in the doctrine: the dissolution of this old, decrepit universe as a symbol of man's frailty, a result of his sin, and a warning that man must look to his salvation.

Evidences of decay are presented as signs of the end rather than as indications of any natural process. These tokens, Shakelton says, are "the Ulcers, and Biles, naie I maie saie plainlie, the blaines of the whole worlde: and doe verie notablie prognosticate, and foreshewe vnto vs, the vniuersall dissolution, and destruction of the same." The world "doeth waxe old, and euery part thereof doeth feele some debilitie and weakenesse." Foremost among the signs of decay and the end is the fact that the sun is 9,976 German miles closer to the earth now than it was in the time of Ptolemy. Comets and meteors are also to be taken as omens of disaster, particularly when they appear in the realm of the fixed stars. The blazing star which gives Shakelton his title is the one which appeared in 1580, and others—notably the famous star in Cassiopeia in 1572—are listed.[40]

The corruption extends, of course, to the realm of the elements: "if there be so greate alteration in the superior worlde, what shall wee saie of the inferiour." Herbs and other plants are less useful, creatures are weaker, man's life is shorter, mountains wear down, monsters are found more frequently, and all these signs foreshadow the final destruction. The world is old and feeble and its end must be expected soon.[41]

A similar close association between the mortality of the world and its general physical disorders is found also in the work of several of Shakelton's contemporaries. Phillip Stubbes, for example, warns his readers in *The Anatomie of Abuses* (1583) that their wickedness and the universal disruption of nature are signs that the end is near and the time for repentance short. "The day of the Lord cannot be farre of,"

"For what wonderfull portents, strang miracles, fearful signes, and dreadfull Iudgements hath he sente of late daies, as Preachers & fortellers of his wrath, due vnto vs for our impenitence & wickedness of life ... haue we not seene Commets, blasing starres, firie Drakes, men feighting in the ayre, most fearfully to behold? Hath not dame Nature her selfe denied vnto vs her operation in sending foorth abortiues, vntimely births, vgglesome monsters and fearfull mishapen Creatures, both in man & beast? So that it seemeth all the Creatures of God are angrie with vs, and threaten vs with destruction, and yet we are nothing at all amended: (alas) what shal become of vs!"[42]

The physical signs of the dissolution are all given, but Stubbes is interested less in decay than in the end, and more in the corruption of morals than in either: "reformation of maners and amendement of lyfe was neuer more needfull, for was pride (the chiefest argument of this Booke) euer so rype?" We are more like "nice dames and yonge gyrles than puissante agents or manlie men, as our Forefathers haue bene." This is "the thirde and last age," "the yron or leaden age." The end must be near at hand.[43]

Thomas Twyne, a physician famous in his day for his translation of Virgil, is another who sees in natural phenomena the results of man's sin and the promise of the world's end. In his discourse on the earthquake of 1580 he urges repentance for the sins which cause earthquakes and other disruptions of nature and warns that "in these the later times of the worlde" we must return finally to the ways of God. Thomas Rogers, Protestant divine, also known for his miscellaneous translations, reflects a similar concern over the Fall and corruption in relation to the end of the world. In *The General Session* (1581), he argues that our wickedness is a sign that the world will have an end. Although the date cannot be known and there is no suggestion that the corruption grows steadily worse, we are being judged even now. We are being punished for our sins, in order that we may be moved to repent.[44]

Corruption of the world as evidence of the world's mortality is argued again in Philippe de Mornay's *Traité de la vérité de la religion chrétienne* (1581), where once more it is man's sin which is responsible for the world's decay. The whole world is mutable, since its parts are mutable; but Mornay's concern is primarily with the sin itself and with its immediate effect upon man, whose nature "is strangely defiled & corrupted" and much "digressed from the first originall." The time of Christ was the perfect age of the world, which declines now with the constant increase of sin.[45]

Corruption as the result of man's sin is introduced in a somewhat different light in *A Defensative against the Poyson of Supposed Prophecies,* first published in 1583, by Henry Howard, earl of Northampton. This work, like Peucer's *Les Devins,* is an attack upon astrological predictions; in it Northampton denies that the disposition of the heavens can be taken as signs or portents; for, he asserts, the vicissitudes upon the corrupted earth are not reflected in the immutable heavens, which alone did not suffer from God's curse. The elements are corruptible and subject to change, the earth has lost its fertility, and the whole world beneath the moon becomes more decayed as it grows older. There is no more specific indication of a belief in a continued and progressive decay, however, and the emphasis of the work is upon the inviolability of the heavens rather than upon the corruption of the earth.[46]

A very good summary of this conventional distinction between the mutable earth and the immutable heavens is found in Stephen Batman's modernized and augmented version (1582) of the *De proprietatibus rerum* of Bartholomaeus Anglicus.* Batman accepts the Aristotelian principle that corruption results from contrary qualities in the elements and that therefore all sublunar bodies are corruptible, whereas the heavens, actually composed of a fifth element, are unchanging.[47] But Bartholomaeus and Batman after him are more interested in describing the physical universe than in relating it to the moral or supernatural universe; there is in their work, consequently, no interest in the Fall of man, no indication of the effect of sin upon nature, and no inclination to find in the natural processes of change any progressive decay of the world.

The rising concern over man's place in the world and over the fate of the world itself is more clearly indicated in the work of men like Shakelton, Stubbes, and Mornay, men who have complaints to register and solutions to recommend: the complaint is regularly about immorality or irreligion, and the solution is regularly repentance. More and more, from the 1580's through the first half of the seventeenth century, the encyclopedic or expository *regard* gives over to the work with a thesis, in which the explanation of man's miseries is directed to the improvement of his morals. It is in this climate that the idea of the decay of nature flourishes, the corruption of man's morals usually providing the means whereby the corruption of the entire world is proved. For this reason the interest in the original Fall of man and in the constant decline of virtue is pertinent to a study of the idea of decay, even where such

---

* The original work, popular both in Latin and in the English translations of John of Trevisa (published 1495? and 1535), is here completely reorganized and brought up to date by extensive use of such authorities as Conrad Gesner, Paracelsus, Sebastian Münster, Abraham Ortelius, and many others.

interest is not explicitly extended to include decay of the physical universe.

It is important to remember, also, that the concept of moral decay, although almost invariably present whenever the decay of nature is argued, is often expressed independently as well. In other words, the corruption that began with original sin and which increases in actual sin is the object of growing concern as men search for ultimate truths amid the uncertainties and confusions of the new science and the new social order; in many instances the appeal for reform and redemption is based almost entirely on evidence of this moral corruption; in other contexts and with other men the appeal is broadened by citing the signs of physical corruption also, though even in such cases the proof of moral decay is very often the starting-point of the whole demonstration.*

A scholar who combines the expository purpose of Batman with an active interest in the moral and physical corruption is Simon

---

* There are many writers of this period who, primarily interested in the moral or religious universe, introduce physical details in a form too fragmentary to assure us that such details are part of an ordered, organic picture of man's relation to nature. William Perkins, for example, though he finds corruption in the whole "deformed substance" of the world, is more concerned with man's miseries as punishments of his sin; and, in recounting signs of the approaching end, he cites the corruption of manners and morals rather than the evidence for degeneration of the material world.[48]

The Jesuit, Robert Southwell, also grieves over the miserable estate of mankind, stressing the mutability of all things in the world, but not indicating specifically the physical decay.[49]

Andrew Willet emphasizes particularly man's participation in the guilt and his share in the punishment of original sin, which causes, among other things, "the deprauation and deformitie of nature, wherein there dwelleth no good thing"; and, though Willet does not accept the usual indications that these are the last days, he defends the mortality of the world.[50]

Bishop Gervase Babington actually indicates that the earth was corrupted by the Flood "and euer since still more and more," but his incidental description of the process appears simply as a conventional explanation of the longer lives of the patriarchs, and Babington is far more seriously concerned with the corruption that took place at the Fall.[51]

Thomas Beard is another who explains *"the Corruption and Peruersitie of this World, how great it is,"* by showing that "the world euery day groweth worse & worse." But the decline is only in virtue, and the "great and horrible punishments" designed to "terrifie and somewhat curbe" the wicked do not seem to extend to the sensible decay of the external world.[52]

Goulart, a Protestant divine known particularly for his commentaries on Du Bartas. According to Goulart, this is the last, corrupt age of the world's existence, wherein heaven and earth alike show signs of decay, although these signs can in no way indicate the date of the end. Man's sin, and that alone, brought the corruption upon the world, and "ouerturned all the order of nature," thus infecting, "by the venome of his reuolt, all the moueables and necessaries of his house."[53]

The heavens have therefore become subject to this corruption, and the influences of the planets are now "malignant, and sinister very often, by reason of sinne." Goulart reflects some of the wonder occasioned by the discovery of the new star in Cassiopeia and indicates that the classification of "fixed" stars is now in question. The earth, too, is decayed, for "man in falling from Gods grace, drew all creatures which were made for him, into ruine, especially the earth." The elements and the creatures rebel against man and help to punish him; without God's active providence the warring factions would bring about a confusion even more complete than that of the Flood, which itself contributed markedly to the total decay of the earth.[54]

Man's body is weaker, his life shorter; his illnesses and other miseries are "certaine testimonies, and set vpon vs as seales of *Adams* fall, of originall sin, and Hereditary corruption." His judgment is perverted, and his learning has declined since the time of the patriarchs. Most important of all is the decay of virtue. This is the age "which spetteth in the face of diuine and humane sciences. Each one runneth after dishonest gaine, or seruilely subiecteth himselfe to infamous passions; and in ouer-many places there is no other God to be found but the belly."[55]

It may be seen that the whole notion of decay, moral and physical alike, is somewhat more significant for the commentator than for Du Bartas himself, though Goulart's own position is far from extreme. Goulart specifically extends the realm of corruption to include the heavens, and, in general, he interprets the changes throughout the universe as a direct punishment for man's sin and not simply (as is often the case for Du Bartas) as evidence of the frailty and mutability of the material world. On the other hand, Goulart, though he digresses frequently to describe the miseries and weaknesses of the present age, adheres to Du Bartas' basic distinction between the perfect creation and the corruption that followed sin and does not develop in full the idea that the decay is getting progressively worse. Finally, Goulart, in doing his work as scholar and editor, is not essentially a preacher; he recognizes the evil in the world and ascribes it to sin; but his principal intent is discovery and explanation rather than the kind of exhortation which is often kindled by the idea of a decaying world.   .

Joseph Hall, bishop of Exeter and Norwich, offers no such elaborate view of nature as we find in Goulart, but he defends (by analogy with man) the approaching dissolution of the whole corrupted world, he finds a certain deterioration from the perfection of earlier and better ages, and we have Fuller's word that Hall, while at Cambridge, maintained "with a *Flourishing* wit ... *That the World groweth Old*."[56] In *Virgidemiarum* (1597) he compares modern senile corruption with the simpler life in the golden age: the world is now "Thriving in ill as it in age decays." "Our sinnes tainted the whole creation, and brought shame vpon all the frame of heauen, and earth," he tells us elsewhere, though it is "Not the frame of the world, but the corruption of that frame," which must ultimately be destroyed. The death of this corrupt world is implied in the death of man:

"Who can grieue to see a Familie dissolued, that considers the world must bee dissolued? This little world of ours, first, whereof this day [commemorating the death of Prince Henry] giues vs an image: for as our seruice, so our life must away; and then that great one, whose dissolution is represented in these."[57]

The decay of religion and virtue gets first attention also in *Times Lamentation* (1599), by the preacher and naturalist, Edward Topsell; and here, too, "the whole course of nature" is shown to suffer for man's sin. Once more we meet the familiar theme that the creation is frail and perishable when compared with the immutable

Creator: "All thinges come to an ende, but the lawe of God is exceeding large: The heauens waxe olde, the earth groweth barren, the golde is but dust." There is nothing in the world which God will not destroy because of man's sin.[58]

The misery of man himself "groweth so great and incurable euery day more & more," writes Topsell, that there seems to be little hope for his rescue. The decline of piety and religion is the most grievous sign of the corruption. Men would "rather goe with musicke to the gallowes, then with mourning to a sermon: they choose rather to goe singing to hell, then weeping to heauen." All preaching now is in vain, the Sabbath is polluted, and divinity is not the most honored but the meanest of professions. If man repents, however, the effects of the curse will be erased; and Topsell shows more concern over man's current sins than over original sin itself.[59]*

Closer still to the exhortations of Goodman is Sir Richard Barckley's *The Felicitie of Man,* first published in 1598, a work in which the continuous decay of virtue is lamented at great length and in which also the sensible world, rapidly coming to an end, is shown to be corrupted. Man's sin is the sole cause of corruption and death, and his wickedness "doth presage the destruction of the world to be at hand." It is sin which destroys the harmony of creation, corrupts the world, and renders it hostile to man. The universe, heavens and all, "resembleth a chaine rent in peeces, whose links are many lost and broken, and the rest so slightly fastened as they will hardly hang together." The elementary world feels directly the effects of man's sin; although the heavens are inviolate, their benign influences are blocked by the corruption below, and "turne to evill."[61]

---

* For another view of the effects of sin see Thomas Wright, *The Passions of the Minde,* in which nature's corruption is seen in the "many diseases, plagues, & pestilences" which beset man, in "the disconsorted courses of the heauens, with their influences, tempests and stormes, contrary to the generation and increase of fruits of the earth," but most particularly in the discord between man's passions and his reason (pp. 327, 344, etc.). Similarly, in the writings of Christopher Heydon, in which mutability of the heavens is established, man's sin is once more offered as explanation for the universal corruption.[60]

For Barckley, however, any consideration of the physical world is incidental to his treatment of the decline in virtue. We are so far corrupted from the golden age that we do not deserve even to place ourselves in the iron age, unless we say, indeed, that this is the golden age because honor now is bought with gold. We can see virtue declining "daily from evill to worse." If the same rate of change should continue for another forty years, it would be hard to find a single honest man. Human affairs are "unstable and uncertaine," "variable and uncertaine, void of all constancy," because our nature is "degenerate from his first perfection and estate to wickednesse and corruption." "Our manners are so contrary to those of former ages, that the world seemeth to bee turned upside downe," and "this generall and unnaturall eclipse of Christian manners, doth presage the destruction of the world to be at hand." We are lascivious, effeminate, and given over to affectation:

"But now wives and maides will not onely accompany men in their carowsing, but men in perfumes labour to exceede women, and be more carefull to smell sweet than to live well: And what can·be more lothsome than for a man to have his garments perfumed with sweete savours, and himselfe polluted with stinking vices and foule conditions?"[62]

Thus Barckley, like Goodman and so many others, attributes the corruption first to man's Fall and emphasizes the wickedness and miseries of this age, though his stress is more upon present sins than upon present miseries as the result of original sin. He uses the microcosm-macrocosm analogy, but only to prove the world's mortality; he is less extensively concerned with the decay of the natural world than is Goodman, and he specifically exempts the heavens from any actual corruption. His work is important less for cogent argument or for any serious contribution to contemporary thought than as a mirror of popular and conventional ideas. *"I desire rather to be taken for a Relator of other mens sayings and opinions, than to arrogate such sufficiency as to be Author of any thing my selfe,"* he is first to admit, as he rests upon the authority of ancients and moderns alike, protesting that he has *"simply collected and ap-*

plyed" to his purpose the most widely accepted judgments about man's place in the created universe.[63]

One of these widely accepted judgments, as we have seen, is that which links the idea of the world's decay with the fear of an early end of the world. The pages of such diverse thinkers of the last generation as Daneau, Sandys, Gascoigne, La Primaudaye, Du Bartas, Stubbes, and Shakelton all show this immediate apprehension over the final destruction; and now, at the turn of the century, the writings of Barckley, Robert Pont, John Case, and many others reveal, if possible, an even more acute realization that the remaining time is short and the need for repentance great. In these texts the decay of nature is customarily presented as evidence of the approaching end.

Robert Pont, also known as Kynpont or Kylpont, was an obscure Scottish reformer, who in his old age presented to posterity one of the most curious documents of the period, *A Newe Treatise of the Right Reckoning of Yeares* (1599). In it, by setting up an elaborate scheme of sabbatical years for calculating the world's age, he attempts to discredit the Roman Catholic year of jubilee in 1600 and to dissuade those who had thought they would journey to Rome for its celebration. The year 1600, he shows, far from being a true year of jubilee, is "the 60 yeare of the blast of the seaventh & last trumpet," and one which may justly be called "a yeare of the decaying and fading age of the world." The end is normally to be expected in the year 1785, but for the sake of the elect it will probably come earlier. We know this age is one of decay and corruption, "not onely because it appeareth to approche neere vnto the worlds end, but also by reason greater mutatiōs, & alteratiōs are likely to fal out therein, both in the visible heavens, the earth, & other elements, then in other ages before."[64]

The corruption is thus apparent in all nature, and even *"the signes and revolutions of the heauen, are changed and remooved from the olde accustomed places."* Comets and eclipses confirm our belief that the end is near. The new star of 1572 is "a signe of the approching of the Lord to judgemente." We still suffer from the effects of the great solar eclipse of 1598. And the future promises even more mutations than we saw in the past: "so manie and so greate Eclipses, namelie, of the Sunne, haue not bene seene, these manie yeares by-gane, as shall be within sixe yeares to come." All these signs indicate both the old age and the decay of the world, and "the age of the Worlde, betokeneth the decaying parte thereof, as the eeld or age of a man, is called the latter parte of his life. And indeed it may well be saide now, that we be come to the decaying parte, and latter age of the World."[65]

Pont concludes his treatise by returning to the corruption of morals and religion, urging his readers to redeem the time before it is too late. Like Barckley and unlike Goodman, he speaks more of actual sins than of original sin; and, like both Barckley and Goodman, he believes that the evidence of decay should move us to repentance. Because all the signs threaten "the hastie cumming of the Lord to judgment, it becōmeth vs now not to neglect the occasion offred vnto vs," the opportunity to return to virtuous living. There is an "abundance of all impietie" in the world "in these latter dayes," when the need for religion is greatest. "Surely," he pleads, "if ever there was any time since the beginning of the world, or any age where-into such corruptions and maners of men abounded: this may bee holden the principall, wherevnto charitie is waxed could, and all kinde of iniquity waxed hote."[66]

John Case indicates his belief in physical corruption in a similar attempt to prove the mortality of the world. In his commentary on Aristotle's *Physics* he presents the mutability of heaven and earth as evidence of their ultimate destruction. The world is old and declining; nature itself has grown weary and effete and cannot long endure. The sun loses its strength, and its influence upon the earth is less than it once was. New comets, new and terrible conjunctions of the planets, irregular eclipses—all prove the world to be approaching destruction. In addition, Case shows that the mutability of earthly institutions, as well as of the earth itself, is paralleled in the mutability of the whole universe, and in its eventual mortality:

"Porro, ascende in theatrum & Olympum mundi, circumspice, dic vbi imperia Assyriorum, Persarum, Graecorum, Romanorum? nonne iam seges est vbi Troia fuit?

"An imperia & regna suas aetates & periodos habent? cur non habet mundus? certe causam non video cur non haberet, cum omnia illius sydera propemodum ceciderint. Cecidit Babylon, cecidit Hierusalem, populi, nationes, imperia ceciderūt ēse, fame, peste cōcussa, exhausta, infecta omnia vbique cadūt: si omnia mūdus diu stare non potest."[67]

Pierre du Moulin is another popular theological writer whose interest in decay is largely worry over the corruption of morals; but he also recognizes that all the created universe, by contrast with God's perfection, is corrupt and mutable, and he accepts certain physical signs that the world is approaching its end. The pole star has declined some nine degrees since Ptolemy's time; within five or six hundred years more it may be touching the pole and unable to move farther. Then it seems that "there shall be a great change of *things, and that this time is the period which God hath prefixed to nature."*[68]

Lewis Bayly, later bishop of Bangor, once more implies the same kind of gradual decrease for nature as that which prevails in the life of man, holding that, just as man's body shows signs of his impending death, so shall the *"dissolution* of the vniu[e]rsall frame of the *great World"* be foreseen in the darkened sun, the bloody moon, and the falling of the stars. And though he does not explicitly say that the signs of the world's end are now visible, there is no doubt that these days are *"the* dregges of Time, *which being the* last *must needes bee the* worst *dayes."*[69]

An even more direct statement that the world's corruption is a sign of its impending destruction is to be found in John Dove's *Confvtation of Atheisme* (1605). The moon grows paler, the planets less favorable, the stars "more weake & suspicious"; the sun "now waxeth weary" and "shineth more dimly" than in the past; "what is this but an argument that shortly the high Arch of heauen which is erected ouer our heads, will fall & dissolue it selfe?" We may expect the world to end, furthermore, because it had a beginning, because as macrocosm it will suffer the same declination and death to which the microcosm is subject, and because the end is implied in the "irregular & threatning Eclipses," the "vn-vsuall aspects of the starres," the "fearfull Coniunctions of Planets," and the "prodigious apparitions of Comets." The decay is thus visible in the heavens and earth alike, the decline in man's body being especially great, what with his "lower stature, lesser bones and strength, and shorter life" than were enjoyed by his forefathers.[70]*

IV. AS POETIC IMAGE, SPENSER TO DONNE

Throughout the sixteenth century the belief in the world's decay is rarely expressed in a predominantly literary fashion but is rather asserted in philosophical, theological, or scientific terms. The idea of a corrupt universe, to be sure, is significant for Gascoigne, Lyndsay, and even more essential for Du Bartas; not until very near the end of the century, however, does the image of a decaying

---

* Indications that the present is the very last age and that the various natural disorders constitute signs of the end are common throughout the period. One "I. D.," translator of Leroy's translation of Aristotle's *Politics*, in his Dedication describes his own times as the "last age of the declining and degenerating vvorld." William Vaughan attributes the modern decline of virtue to "the corruption of the whole world: for now are *the abominations of desolation. These be daies of vengeāce to fulfill al things that are written.*" This is the "last rotten world"; the day is already come in which "the Heauens must passe away with a noyse, and the Element must melt with heate, and the earth with the workes therein must bee burnt vp." Henry Cuff's *The Differences of the Ages of Mans Life* is refuted by Hakewill (*Apologie*, p. 251) for its argument that the end is foreseen in the physical corruption. Arthur Dent indicates that in this worst of ages there is good reason to fear the immediate judgment of God. Christopher Sutton's *Disce vivere* (1602) shows the world to be in its sinful old age; signs of the approaching end include false prophets, wars, pestilences, and earthquakes; the principal concern of the work is with the "general decay of this Christian course" and with the warnings which we may discern in "these sinful days."

Philip Camerarius, in his *Operae horarum subcisiuarum* (1602–6), pictures the transitory estate of man's life and agrees that the signs of the end are everywhere apparent in these the last days of the world. According to the sermons of Samuel Hieron, the world is unstable and mutable at best, and God, who "hath a speciall controuersie with these times," will take his vengeance soon. For Anthony Stafford, to whom this is the "worst of ages" and who sees man as living "in those later dangerous daies, wherein euery thing hath lost his first puritie," the corruption is also inseparable from the imminent end of the world.[71]

world become a common property (or even a common device) of the imagination. Though at times, as may be expected, it is a mere conceit and its importance simply decorative, yet it is an idea which also animates and informs much of the poetry of the next twenty years, whether as part of the poetic idiom in the hands of Spenser or the grave reality which elevates Donne's hydroptic melancholy.

Spenser is the earliest of the English poets of this period to make much use of the concept that the world grows old and weary. From the first conventional laments over the lost golden age and the fluctuations of fortune in the *Complaints,* however, to Constancy's artificial triumph in the Mutability Cantos, the whole idea of decay, whatever its rich implications for a man with Spenser's understanding of a romantic past and an immoral present, is never fully exploited. The world, in its old age, is losing its strength:

> Me seemes the world is runne quite out of square
> From the first point of his appointed sourse,
> And being once amisse, growes daily wourse and wourse.

The heavens themselves are corrupted: the sun has declined almost thirty minutes and promises to disappear altogether, and the planets have moved from their accustomed places. Justice and truth are gone, and we live in a stony age instead of in the "first flowring youth" of the antique world.[72]

Mutability claims the heavens and the gods themselves, as well as the elements, for her own. But Nature rules that all things maintain themselves in the end, so that Constancy may be said to rule over Change, and the conflict is resolved by a balance of generation and corruption.[73] This balancing of generation and corruption is, of course, not unusual; it is the common argument used a generation earlier by Leroy and a generation later by Hakewill. But Spenser has neither the optimism of Leroy nor the doctrinal self-sufficiency of Hakewill. Temperamentally, he belongs with those who look backward instead of forward. Without a more intense concern over the relation of man's evil to the physical world, however, his feeling about the fate of that world does not go beyond an uneasy and poetic melancholy over the lost glories of a heroic age.

A belief in the physical decay appears again in the works of John Norden, poet and devotional writer, toward the end of Elizabeth's reign. These are the "latter" days, he writes, in which "the whole world was polluted and defiled with sin" and in which we see around us the false prophets and the corruption that have been foretold.[74] *Vicissitudo rerum,* a poem in imitation of Leroy's *De la vicissitude,* describes the change and inconstancy of all things in the world, but without the faith in man's achievements which characterizes Leroy. Manners, laws, and religion, according to Norden, were never held in such low esteem as at this very time.

Similarly, the whole earth trembles with tides and floods never before equaled:

> *The* Elements *and elementall things*
> *Do change, and by silent degrees decay.*

Nor are the heavens exempt, in spite of the balance achieved among their contrary motions: the sun and moon were never so much eclipsed, nor were there so many comets and "strange *impressions*" in the air. Notwithstanding the obvious debt to Leroy, the entire work, overcast as it is by a note of personal melancholy, retains nothing of the vigorous challenge to man's potentialities which so distinguishes Leroy himself.[75]

The world's old age and its declining estate are described again, though often in incidental references and without details, in a number of poems throughout the following decade. Sir John Davies, for example, takes the position we recognized in La Primaudaye, that by contrast with the spiritual world all the physical world is corrupt and impermanent. In the *Nosce teipsum* (1599), when stressing the immortality of the soul, Davies points out that all else, including the heavens, becomes old and must die. In the *Hymnes of Astraea* (1599), he manages a graceful and conventional tribute to Elizabeth, who brings back the golden age to these fallen times; and in *A New Post* he reaffirms his belief that man and world suffered from God's curse at the time of the Fall. Samuel

Daniel, complaining about contemporary evils in *A Queenes Arcadia* (1605), finds "our very aire" to be less wholesome, with "New Feuers" and "new Catarres" oppressing us all. Giles Fletcher also writes about the decline from the golden age in such terms as to indicate the present old age and corruption of the world: now when "that beauteous frame" has become deformed and ruined with age, only God's mercy arrests the decay.[76]*

The years immediately following 1610 perhaps show the idea of decay at its greatest popularity as a poetic formula, and we see the pattern recurring in the work of such men as John Davies of Hereford, Heywood, Alexander, and, of course, John Donne. After that, the doctrine of decay, though reappearing in Drayton's *Polyolbion* and Phineas Fletcher's *Purple Island* and used extensively by Drummond of Hawthornden, may be said, in general, to pass once more out of the realm of imaginative experience and to return almost exclusively to the area of theological and scientific dispute.

The image of universal decay is important for Davies of Hereford, especially in *The Muses Sacrifice* (1612). Again it is man's sin which has ruined the world, so that the decline which we see is more than temporary change:

> Our *Sinnes* haue so the *Elements* defil'd
>   that they with *Fire* must needes refinèd be:
> Nay, more; our *sins* the *Heau'ns* themselues haue soild;
>   then melt they must, from soile to set them free.

---

* Charles Fitzgeffrey is another who makes use of the idea that we are now in the iron age, the "dying worlds twise-infant-waxen dotage." Similarly, the *Chrestoleros* (1598) of Thomas Bastard paints the present time as the iron age by comparison with the "first and riper world." John Lane, referring particularly to contemporary morals, finds "the world much worse than twas before." Francis Thynne adds the detail that man must now work harder and undergo more hardships than during the golden age.

In Thomas Dekker's *Old Fortunatus* (1600), the sun is old and the world, which went on crutches yesterday, is now "bed-rid," aged, and decaying.

Finally, Robert Tofte, in a dull prose romance based on the French of Nicolas de Montreux, holds that man's sin is the cause of evil, including the evil influence of the heavens, and that all things are mutable in this world. Man has now lost God's mercy, for he has in this age divorced himself from virtue and piety. The golden world of our forefathers is gone, and in its place we have iron and steel, the *"causers"* of *"worlds and mans decay."*[77]

These are the last days of the old, decrepit world; the fruit of sin is ripe, and the *"end* is neere." The decay itself is a sign of the approaching catastrophe, decay in the heavens as well as on the earth: "the totall Frame of *Nature*'s out of frame." The mountains are wearing down, the sea encroaches upon the land, men are smaller and weaker than before, plants have lost their virtue. The stars themselves are less powerful, and "the *Sunne* in's *course* is out of course":

> For, since the dayes of *Ptolomey* it's found
>   many *degrees* more nigh the *Earth* he stoupes:
> So, like an agèd *Drunkard,* runneth round,
>   till flat he fall: for, more and more he droupes.[78]

Thomas Heywood, whose poems on the four ages (*The Golden Age* [1611]; *The Silver Age* [1613]; *The Brazen Age* [1613]; and *The Iron Age* [1632]) allow him to develop his interest in the idea of decay, is another who subscribes to the pattern of a corrupt world approaching its end. In the Prologue to *The Brazen Age* he explains the process largely in terms of moral deterioration:

> *AS the world growes in yeares ('tis the Heauens curse)*
> *Mens sinnes increase; the pristine times were best:*
> *The Ages in their growth wax worse & worse.*

Some of the details reappear in the Γυναικεῖον (1624), in which he explains that the first age was best "because the nature of man was then most potent and vigorous, as may appeare by their longeuitie, liuing so many hundred yeares." Then, in *The Hierarchie of the Blessed Angells* (1635), he expresses further implications of the doctrine of natural corruption, once more finding this age to be the last, with the end of the world not far away. Though the heavens are immutable, the sublunar realm is subject to great alterations, and the world itself grows old and barren.[79]

George Wither is another contemporary poet much interested in the corruption of society, and, although he does not concern himself with physical corruption, he finds these the last and worst times of the world, with signs of the end apparent around us. The corruption was caused by man's Fall, the plague is punishment for his present sins, and altogether this age is, as Wither sees it, the "worst that euer yet was knowne to be."[80]

In William Alexander's *Doomes-Day* (1614) the idea of natural decay is fully developed. Alexander pictures an aged, worn, corrupted world which is nearing an end. The decay is apparent in the heavens; the sun and moon grow pale and weak, and all the heavenly bodies are less strong than they were. New stars are seen, and old ones are not to be found in their accustomed places. The earth, made into an "odious masse" by the sin of man, is "weake through age and drunk with bloud." While "both heaven and earth doe shake," men's hearts remain closed to repentance, and vice is greater than ever among the "dregs of *Adams* race." One of the signs, indeed, of man's damnation is the failure of some doubters, disregarding the signs and warnings, to admit that the world decays and the end approaches.[81]*

For several decades, now, the poets as well as the preachers have been finding in the idea of a decaying world a symbol and an inspiration for the discontent which prefaced the great intellectual changes of the seventeenth century. John Donne, both poet and preacher, illuminates more effectively than anyone else the literal cosmology of corruption. Later in the century, with few exceptions, the poets who make use of the image of a declining universe do so without in any sense relying upon such an image. The preachers for at least another generation continue to find evidence as well as rhetoric in the signs of decay and destruction; but, as the century moves into its second quarter, the urgent excitement of discovery is

---

* *Doomes-Day*, written apparently in part to demonstrate to these skeptics the approach of the world's end as seen particularly in the visible corruption of nature, shows most explicitly Alexander's interest in the problem of decay; but some of his poems and plays, written a decade earlier, anticipate the position that he takes here. The tragedies composed around the misfortunes of Croesus and of Darius both stress the change, the insecurity, the transient mortality of man's miserable life. In *The Alexandraean Tragedy* (1607), a good deal is made of the falling-off from the perfection of the golden age, to the point where *"all good decayes"* and ills abound, although the corrupt society is not reflected in actual physical disruption of the world. Similarly, the sonnet sequence *Aurora* contains, woven into conventional conceits, several references to the corrupt and evil world so different from that of the golden age.[82]

gradually replaced by the kind of justification (still urgent but more doctrinal than personal) already found in Alexander and Goodman.

Donne's interest in the problem of decay develops in his middle and later years and is documented principally by the two *Anniversaries* and by many passages throughout his sermons. In the *Juvenilia,* or *Paradoxes and Problemes,* he even defends the thesis that "*Good* is as ever it was, more plenteous, and must of necessity be *more common than Evil,*" professing himself to be "pittifully tired" of the vanity of "silly" old men who find the present age in a state of decline: "Alas! they betray themselves, for if the *times* be *changed,* their manners have changed them." In the first *Paradox,* Donne praises inconstancy—particularly in women but also in the world as a whole. Change, in whatever terms described, is not to be confused with change for the worse.[83]

Even in a work as serious as his *Biathanatos,* in which Donne indulges in morbid reflections on the futility of life, he does not develop the obvious opportunity of describing in detail the decline and corruption of the universe. He does, however, quote Cyprian to show that men are born old, and he offers the authority of modern astronomers to prove that mutability extends to the heavens as well as to the earth. Nor does the very different spirit which prevails in *Ignatius His Conclave* reveal any more explicit interest in the doctrine of decay, though here Donne shows once more that he has followed, in an amateur fashion, recent discoveries in science. On the other hand, if Donne has not yet, in either of these works, turned to the decay of the world as a focus for his intellectual and personal troubles, he nevertheless indicates how pressing already are those problems which he later resolves in the kind of philosophy which admits and nurtures his speculations on the decaying world.

Similarly, such references to decay as are found in his early poetry are often restricted to a conventional phrase or two describing present decline from the golden times, as in *Satyre V,* with its allusion to the "Age of rusty iron," and *Elegie XVII,*

wherein the poet regrets the passing of an earlier day with its freedom of amorous expression. The concept of decay is still not central to the poem even in *Satyre III,* where the world is measured on
a grander scale and the fate of the whole derived from the decay of
the parts:

> as
> The worlds all parts wither away and passe,
> So the worlds selfe, thy other lov'd foe, is
> In her decrepit wayne....[84]

Donne's first extended use of this material occurs in *The Progresse of the Soule* (1601). In the opening stanza of this work he
indicates his plan to follow the world from "infant morne, through
manly noone," "to his aged evening." In the youth of the world
things ripened sooner and lasted longer. The decay now evident, he
says, is the result of man's original sin; it is apparent principally in
man's wickedness but also in the general frame of nature.[85]

Donne develops the full implications of universal decay for the
first time in *An Anatomie of the World,* or *The First Anniversary.*
Here, in a strange mixture of conventional hyperbole and apparently intense personal conviction, he laments the decay of all the
world's beauty and, in so doing, anatomizes his own doubt and
despair. Because the death of young Elizabeth Drury proves too
slight a basis to support or justify the image of universal corruption, the elegy is not always artistically valid and is at times even
grotesque; but the picture of total desolation and decay remains
a moving one. Donne describes the world as sick, "yea, dead, yea
putrified," or as a lame cripple, now that "she" is dead. Its beauty,
which Donne sees as harmony and color, is destroyed:

> 'Tis all in peeces, all cohaerence gone;
> All just supply, and all Relation:

it is "rotten at the heart," an ugly monster.[86]

The explanation for all the decay rests not only in the poetic
image of Elizabeth Drury's death, however; for Donne as for
others, when the belief in decay becomes much more than a figure

of speech it is anchored in some understanding of man's original
sin as the ultimate cause of corruption in the physical universe.

> The world did in her cradle take a fall,
> And turn'd her braines, and tooke a generall maime,
> Wronging each joynt of th'universall frame.
> The noblest part, man, felt it first; and than
> Both beasts and plants, curst in the curse of man.
> So did the world from the first houre decay,
> That evening was beginning of the day,
> And now the Springs and Sommers which we see,
> Like sonnes of women after fiftie bee.[87]

This is not to imply that Donne accepts the entire pattern of decay
in a literal sense, though there are passages in the sermons where
no other interpretation is permissible; it is enough to observe here
that the poetic quality of *The First Anniversary* is sustained by a
sense of disquietude and even of urgency, springing not from the
death of his patron's daughter but from the projection of his own
intense disillusionment into the image of a world without harmony
and without beauty.

Specific signs of decay are seen in the heavens as well as on the
earth. The sun is weary and declines nearer to the earth; the stars
do not keep their courses. Man's feeling of insecurity is heightened
when he sees new stars appearing and old ones vanishing. Bereft
of the beneficial influence of the heavens, the earth becomes barren:

> Th'Ayre doth not motherly sit on the earth,
> To hatch her seasons, and give all things birth;
> Spring-times were common cradles, but are tombes;
> And false-conceptions fill the generall wombes.

Men, too, are not now what they once were. Our lives are short, our
bodies small;

> We'are scarce our Fathers shadowes cast at noone.

All our pretenses are worthless:

> This man, so great, that all that is, is his,
> Oh what a trifle, and poore thing he is!

Not the least convincing sign of man's corruption is his refusal to
recognize the world's decline and his own doom therein. Neverthe-

less, it is Donne's one hope, helping to motivate the whole poem
(as it inspires Goodman and so many others who despair of the
decay of the world), that man can yet be saved if only he will
realize his own weaknesses, the frailty of all his systems, and the
mutability of the world. We may be better off when we recognize
our "dangers and diseases,"

> For with due temper men doe then forgoe,
> Or covet things, when they their true worth know.[88]

The First Anniversary is the only poem in which Donne develops the whole pattern of a decaying world: the Fall of man,
the curse upon nature, the cumulative stages of corruption, the impending death of all. But he refers to one or another aspect of the
problem often enough throughout these years to indicate his continued interest in the idea. In "A Funerall Elegie," anticipating the
idiom of the *Anatomie,* he expands on the notion that Elizabeth
Drury's death is the final blow struck at the old, decrepit world.
Of the Progresse of the Soule, written for the second anniversary
of Miss Drury's death, is less specifically concerned with the decay
of the world than with its mutability. True enough, the world is
"rotten," a "carkasse," "fragmentary rubbidge," corrupt, and as
good as dead. But Donne goes on to find his resolution in the distinction between body and soul, between temporary and permanent; there is no longer, as there was in *The First Anniversary,*
any doubt about, or even any great interest in, this world's estate.
As Mr. Grierson has pointed out, the work is "a *De Contemptu
Mundi,* and a contemplation of the Glories of Paradise." "What
essentiall joy can'st thou expect," Donne asks his soul,

> Here upon earth? what permanent effect
> Of transitory causes?
>
> .   .   .   .
>
> Next day repaires, (but ill) last dayes decay.
> Nor are, (although the river keepe the name)
> Yesterdaies waters, and to daies the same.

Finally, there is a minor reference to the world's decay in his letter

"To the Countesse of Huntingdon"—minor, that is, in its importance to the poem but significant because it is specific and at the same time so casually included. Even though the decline of the sun toward the earth, he writes, argues well the world's age and death, virtue, resident in the countess, is not dead but exalted.[89]

In the final and wholly religious period in Donne's life the concept of universal decay recurs many times, heightened in the eloquent exhortation of the sermons. He finishes the first of the *Devotions,* for example, by lamenting the lightnings, the eclipses, the blazing stars, the rivers of blood which the little world—man—must endure within himself: "O perplex'd discomposition, O ridling distemper, O miserable condition of Man!" And later he draws the whole world into this sphere of misery and decay: "THIS is *Natures nest of Boxes;* The Heavens containe the *Earth,* the *Earth, Cities, Cities, Men.* And all these are *Concentrique;* the common *center* to them all, is *decay, ruine."*[90]

In the sermons we find, developed and repeated, the philosophy that sees corruption in every part of this old and ailing world: "this is the last time, and the Apostle hath told us, that the last times are the worst." In the decay and death of all the parts—man, earth, and the heavens themselves—we have ample proof of the whole world's mortality:

"As the world is the whole frame of the world, God hath put into it a reproofe, a rebuke, lest it should seem eternall, which is, a sensible decay and age in the whole frame of the world, and every piece thereof. The seasons of the yeare irregular and distempered; the Sun fainter, and languishing; men lesse in stature, and shorter-lived. No addition, but only every yeare, new sorts, new species of wormes, and flies, and sicknesses, which argue more and more putrefaction of which they are engendred."*

* Mr. Coffin (*John Donne and the New Philosophy,* p. 274) notes that this description of the world's mortality "is for obvious reasons of edification" and need not be Donne's actual belief. It is, of course, always difficult to prove intent in instances of this sort, and he may be right. But, in the absence of any evidence to the contrary in Donne's own work and in the light of his consistent adherence to the principles involved, it seems no less probable that such statements adequately represent Donne's position.

Cyprian ascribes all the calamities of his time *"Ad senescentem mundum,"* and we must learn the lesson that he learned. In such a world nothing can be permanent: everything is "fluid, and transitory, and sandy, and all dependance, all assurance built upon this world, is but a building upon sand; all will change." Nor does he need the Copernican astronomy, Donne assures his listeners, to discover the mutability of all creation; that "nothing upon Earth is permanent" is known without proof that even the earth itself is in motion.[91]

The whole world is thus repeatedly included in the sphere of mortality and decay, though the corruption of man, "sour'd in the whole lump, poysoned in the fountain, perished at the chore, withered in the root, in the fall of *Adam,*" gets his particular attention. Death itself is the result of man's sin, for without sin "we had had our transmigration from this to the other world, without any mortality, any corruption at all." Death and destruction are not all, however, for the punishments are directed to our repentance, and the evils of this world are resolved in the glories of the next; the whole belief in decay is made possible by this hope, less obviously for Donne, perhaps, than for Goodman, but no less eloquently:

"Gods first intention even when he destroyes is to preserve, as a Physitians first intention, in the most distastfull physick, is health; even Gods demolitions are super-edifications, his Anatomies, his dissections are so many re-compactings, so many resurrections; God windes us off the Skein, that he may weave us up into the whole peece, and he cuts us out of the whole peece into peeces, that he may make us up into a whole garment."[92]

V. BACON'S REVOLT FROM AUTHORITY

The belief that the world is decaying, that man has reached the lowest point in his corrupt and sinful history, that the end of all is at hand, is almost universally accepted by the second or third decade of the seventeenth century. It is the traditional historical perspective of the age. Opposition to the concept of universal decay, such as that indicated earlier by Bodin and Leroy and fully developed later by Hakewill, is largely quiescent through the intervening half-century. There are signs, however, of the objections which the next generation, if it persists in its belief in the world's corruption, will have to meet. Conventional solutions to old problems are being challenged, and new problems are beginning to attract restless minds. It is this uncertainty, this anticipation of the denial, which helps to make Donne's arguments so urgent and which compels Goodman to elaborate so assiduously his defense of of a doctrine not yet widely attacked.

In the work of Francis Bacon we find expressed the one idea which, perhaps more than any other, is to render untenable the doctrine of decay, so long believed and so passionately asserted. Hakewill's arguments certainly weaken the hold of this doctrine, but the great change which finally disposes of it is the separation of the whole world into its disparate parts; the new emphasis upon the secular, natural world; the discovery in nature of an order which does not have man for its center, its climax, and its little world.

It was man's desire for knowledge which caused his Fall and the corruption of the world. To believe this is to discredit Bacon's kind of natural philosophy, in spite of Bacon's efforts to attribute the Fall to the search for moral rather than natural knowledge. The theory of decay, deriving natural laws from the divine law, is dependent upon the authority of the ancients and more particularly upon the divine authority of the Scriptures. In his opposition to the belief in decay, Hakewill attacks the subservience to antiquity, without challenging the basic argument from authority; but Bacon holds that eventually the two must go or stay together. It is the "reverence for antiquity, and the authority of men who have been esteemed great in philosophy, and general unanimity," he says in the *Novum organum,* which "have retarded men from advancing in science, and almost enchanted them." In the same passage in which he suggests that "the old age and increasing years of the world should in reality be considered as antiquity," he develops his point that time is the only guide, for "truth is rightly named the daughter of time, not of authority."[93]

If the particular authority is religious, Bacon goes on to say, so much the worse, for it then becomes sanctioned by a "blind and immoderate zeal." Some divines, in their simplicity, are fearful of prying into divine secrets. Others assume that only our ignorance of second causes (laws of nature) is consonant with religion or that any change in philosophy must weaken religious sanction. Arguing that God could not wish to be gratified by means of falsehood, Bacon insists on freeing knowledge from a restraining and traditional decorum.[94]

Bacon's opposition to the idea of decay is thus not addressed so much to the details of physical change, for he does not actually present the evidence against the common belief, as to the methods and ideas by which the belief is justified. He quotes Heraclitus, who saw that " 'Men seek for truth in their own little worlds, and not in the great world without them' "; and he goes on to condemn men who "compel their own genius to divine and deliver oracles, whereby they are deservedly deluded." If only we do not despair of our ability to discover truth in the world itself, our success will be the full measure of progress. "And indeed," he says,

"when I set before me the present state of the times, wherein learning makes her third visit to mankind; and carefully reflect how well she finds us prepared and furnished with all kinds of helps, the sublimity and penetration of many geniuses of the age, those excellent monuments of the ancient writings which shine as so many great lights before us; the art of printing, which largely supplies men of all fortunes with books; the open traffic of the globe, both by sea and land, ... we cannot but be raised into a persuasion that this third period of learning may far exceed the two former of the Greeks and Romans, provided only that men would well and prudently understand their own powers and the defects thereof; receive from each other the lamps of invention, and not the firebrands of contradiction...."[95]

[131]

In his own work, he hopes to surpass the efforts of the past, as he wishes his own discoveries to be transcended by those of posterity.* Even the idea of cycles is to be rejected in favor of the idea of progress, for infinite harm has been caused by those who think "that in the revolutions of ages and of the world there are certain floods and ebbs of the sciences, and that they grow and flourish at one time, and wither and fall off at another, that when they have attained a certain degree and condition they can proceed no further."[97] Because the world is not old or ailing and thoughts of the end must not vitiate man's effort, man's hope and the promise of his achievement are almost without limit.

VI. UNIVERSAL, VULGAR, AND LEARNED BELIEF IN DECAY

In spite of these hopes, however, and the arguments with which he supports them, Bacon is almost alone in the early decades of the century in his opposition to the belief in decay. The idea of decay reaches emotional and symbolic maturity with Donne and receives its ultimate doctrinal justification with Goodman; until Hakewill focuses attention on the subject and actually precipitates the controversy, the theory of universal and incremental corruption as the result of man's sin remains one of the dominant intellectual patterns of the age. Hakewill, it will be remembered, complains that in his attack on the belief in decay he must run counter to the common opinion both of the vulgar and of the learned and that he walks an untrodden path in his search for truth. In the twenty-odd years between Donne's *Anatomie* and the third edition of the *Apologie,* we find recurring in the work of preachers and satirists,

* Contemporary evaluations of Bacon's addition to past learning may be found in two testimonies included in Gilbert Wats's 1640 translation of the *De augmentis.* The first is Wats's own address to the reader, in which we learn that Bacon has *"gone beyond all Antiquity, yet upon their grounds; wherein he can never be outgone, unlesse followed, by Posterity."* The second is Pierre D'Ambois's advertisement to Bacon's *Natural History,* reprinted as a testimony in the Wats volume. Here we are told that it is not D'Ambois's intention *"to raise the reputation of this* Author *upon the ruins of* Antiquity," but that *"in this present Argument he hath some advantage of them."*[96]

of poets and scientists, this pattern which discovers a sensible decay in the old and ailing world.

During this period, for example, were published the major works of Samuel Purchas, who, because of his interest in the explorations which gave such impetus to man's new hopes, might be expected to oppose any notion that the world is old and decrepit.[98] Yet Purchas, too, thinks of the present as the last, worst age of a corrupt world and accounts for the new discoveries by ascribing them to some exceptional work of God, who pities us in our misery. Created whole and perfect for man's use, the world is now corrupt because of man's sin. Nature, infected by this sin, in turn reinfects man, whose corruption is particularly apparent.[99]

In 1614, a year after Purchas' *Pilgrimage* was published, Sir Walter Ralegh in his *History of the World* gives a similar picture of nature's senility. The strength of the world runs down as does a clock, Ralegh says; time is the measure of universal decay, not, as for Bacon, a principle of progress. As all things under the sun have their rise and their fall, "so Time it selfe (vnder the deathfull shade of whose winges all things decay and wither) hath wasted and worne out that liuely vertue of Nature in Man, and Beasts, and Plants." Even the heavens wax old and decay. Although the changes may be so gradual in the heavens as to be scarcely discernible, yet changes have actually taken place: *"wee haue reason to thinke, that the Sunne, by whose helpe all Creatures are generate, doth not in these latter Ages assist Nature, as here-to-fore."* No part of the universe will be spared, for *"why should heauenly bodies liue for euer; and the bodies of Men rotte and die?"* The decay of the sublunar world is more obvious: "as in all other kindes the Earth (before that Sinne had increased the curse and corruption) brought forth her young ones more strong and beautifull then it did in after-ages"; in that early time, in fact, "the earth it selfe was then much lesse corrupt, which yeelded her increase, and brought forth fruit and foode for man, without any such mixture of harmefull qualitie, as since that time the curse of God for the crueltie of mans heart brought on it and mankinde."[100]

Man, the microcosm and cause of decay in all the rest, is the most corrupted part of creation, Ralegh shows. The giants of past ages, the long lives of the patriarchs, furnish evidence of man's deterioration. We see the old age of the world reflected in the decay of our morals and manners; in the practice, for example, of hasty marriages in tender years; in the custom of bringing in strange nurses for our children; and, above all, in the exceeding luxuriousness of this gluttonous age, wherein we press nature with overweighty burdens, and, finding her strength defective, we take the work out of her hands and commit it to the artificial help of strong waters, hot spices, and provoking sauces.* Most important of all is the defection from religion, for the "grosse and blinde Idolaters euery age after other descend lower and lower, and shrinke and slide downewards from the knowledge of one true and very God."[102]

The fact that Ralegh's *History* begins with the Creation accounts in part for its detailed treatment of the corruption which has since come about. The work, however, remains a chronicle and does not become a vehicle for lament or exhortation; Ralegh does not here reveal himself as a man of melancholy temperament, moved by the implications of the doctrines which he accepts. At one point he makes clear that the golden age is not necessarily limited to the past, for "good and golden Kings make good and golden Ages: and all times haue brought forth of both sorts." He is, on the other hand, a sufficiently important figure in the dissemination of the belief in decay to warrant specific refutation by Hakewill, who marvels that "a man of that piercing wit and cleare judgment" should be so mistaken, unless it were that "as others, he tooke it up upon trust, without bringing it to the touchstone."[103]

The idea of the golden age appears in another work in 1614, Barnabe Rich's *The Honestie of This Age,* in which the present era is satirized as "golden" because of its avarice and as "honest"

* This passage is later used (without credit) almost verbatim by Hakewill, though Hakewill's point is that man's life is shortened by his soft living rather than by the decay of nature or the old age of the world.[101]

in its open acceptance of all sins. The whole world, too, which once was said to run smoothly on wheels, now goes on crutches, "for it is waxen old, blind, decrepit and lame, a lymping world God knowes," feeble and childish, beyond amendment. "If men should degenerate as fast the next age as they haue done but within the compasse of our owne memory, it will be a madde world to liue in."[104]*

In 1614 there also appeared the first English edition, *"newly corrected and inlarged, to almost as much more,"* of Sir Michael Scott's *Philosophers Banqvet,* first published in 1530 as *Mensa philosophica.* This work is a question-and-answer treatment of contemporary problems, ranging from points of conduct and manners to the most general scientific and philosophical issues; in it we discover the conventional description of a world infected by man's sin and now showing signs of age and decay. This is the evening of the world, we learn, and the spread of the Gospels shows "the end of the world not to be farre off." Morals are decayed today, and the present, just as for Barnabe Rich, is the golden age, "for now all things are put to sale"; drunkenness and gluttony are greater now than they were even two generations ago. Men's bodies are equally corrupt, and twice the author describes the decline of modern man by quoting Donne's figure, *"We are scarce our fathers shadowes cast at noone."* Finally, in the corruption of man we may

---

* That the modern age has declined from the virtues of earlier times is now a commonplace. In *Britannia's Pastorals* (1613), for example, William Browne praises the simplicity mixed with wisdom which he finds characteristic of the golden age, a time when pure and plain foods, perfect contentment, golden slumbers, healthy bodies, and open hearts did everywhere prevail. Similar material is found in *Conceyted Letters Newly Layde Open,*[105] in which the present becomes the rusty iron age, and sin is triumphant over friendship, love, and piety; "the misery of Time is such," in fact, "as puts Patience to the vtmost tryall of her strength," and the almanac-makers cannot tell what will become of the world. Several works by Richard Brathwaite also show this age to be the leaden age, wicked and depraved. Modern habits are frivolous and vain, judgment is decayed, the golden age is dead, and man "degenerates from his nature primitive." And, once more, John Reynolds, bewailing "the Iniquity of these last and worst dayes of the world," finds, in *The Triumphs of Gods Revenge,* only thorns and brambles, bloody and barbarous acts, infirm judgment, weak faith, and the general "corruption of our depraved Natures" in our present "Iron or flintie age."[106]

observe the full decay of the earth. "The first man did infect nature, but now nature infects man-kinde, the whole lumpe being poysoned," he reasons:

"...now in these barren and declining times of ours, as our old men want their reverence, so are they shortned in their age; our young men soone ripe, conclude, our old men soone rotten. For as the earth decayes in her fertility and power, not yeelding that vigor, vertue, and strength that formerly it hath to plants, hearbs, and vegetables, depriuing us thereby of many of our former benefits of health: all conspiring our brevity and ruine."[107]

Another who in these years helped spread the doctrine of nature's decay is Thomas Adams, Puritan vicar of Wingrave and highly eloquent preacher against man's sinful ways. Among his earliest published works is *Mystical Bedlam* (1615), made up of two sermons revealing man's miseries as the results of his sin. Man "is growne lesse," Adams says, "and as his body in size, his soule in vigour, so himselfe in all vertue is abated." Man is more fragile and brittle than the sun or the stars, less firm than the earth. "Man is a little world, the world a great man: if the great man must die, how shall the little one scape?"[108]

The same general pattern, with even more interest in the decline of the physical universe, may be found throughout Adams' work. This is the old, worn period of the world's duration, and all signs promise the end:

"...wee are those vpon *Whom the latter ends of the world are come. The World groweth olde,* and we grow olde with it: the bodies of men in olde age, waxe cold, and want the heate of nature; the soules of men in this decrepite age, grow cold in zeale...you see the Sunne of this World ready to set, and the Night drawing on: the declination of Goodnesse, the fainting of Religion, sayes, that the World lyes bed-rid, drawing on, looking for the good houre (to some,) and fetching a thicke, sicke, and short breath.... *Who shall say the Euening will not follow, or our Sunne is without setting?*"

The corruption of man is always the basis of Adams' view of

universal corruption, and the figure of the microcosm recurs often: "As the *little world* thus decaies in the great, so the *great* decaies in it selfe." Because of our sins, the world, created for our use, has become our enemy; it is man who turns all things to corruption: "We are sicke of sinne, and therefore the world is sicke of vs."[109]

The decay which Adams recognizes in the world itself is continuous and obvious. It is a "brittle" world and a "tired" one, "lame," "out of ioynt," and "the older it waxeth, the more maimedly it halteth." It fell sick when man sinned, early in the morning, and now languishes in "a lingring lethargy, till the euening of dissolution is at hand." The "dotage of the whole" is seen in the decay of the parts: mountains wear down, the sea encroaches upon the land, earthquakes increase, the sun "stoopes" and is weary, the planets fail, comets threaten our destruction; the world's sickness is promise of its death.[110]

The corruption reaches upward, Adams asserts, from man to the very heavens. Our lives, which once were cut on a folio scale, are now scarcely octavo. "The Elements are more mixed, drossie, and confused: the ayres are infected.... Our great Landlord hath let vs a faire house, and we suffer it quickly to runne to ruine." The splendor of the whole world is abated and impaired: the "skye lookes dusky," the sun looks old, the moon is pale, the stars are dimmer, the rainbow is faded. The corruption of the entire world must be our warning that the end is near at hand. Christ's almanac, the Scriptures, foretells "by *signes* in the Sunne, Moone, Starres, in the vniuersall decay of *nature,* and sicknesse of the *world,* what will happen in this olde yeare, what in the new-yeare, which is the *world* to come."[111]

A similar idea of the general corruption, though without the continuous decay, is found in the work of another Puritan divine, Nicholas Byfield. In his commentary on Colossians, which first appeared in 1615, there is considerable discussion of the corruption of man, the little world.[112] The relationship of man's sin to the physical world is presented in *The Principles or, the Patterne of Wholesome Words,* a popular synthesis of formal doctrine which was published a few years later. Man is called "the olde man" because he has been infected with sin; we have become miserable, deformed, imbecile. The eclipses and the uncertain seasons show that "the powers of Heauen are shaken." Because of man the earth was cursed, and in the whole universe may be read the signs of God's ultimate punishment, the end of the world.[113]

Robert Anton, in *The Philosophers Satyrs* (1616), gives yet another description of the decaying world, here primarily from the point of view of the contemporary decline in virtue. In this iron age all the vices flourish, while learning and scholars are neglected. Men are smaller in stature, and they die sooner, than in past ages. What is true in the microcosm is true also in the macrocosm: "all *parts* of this great world *decline*." The sun is nearer the earth than it was formerly, and the heavens themselves are corrupted. This is the last age, Anton asserts, refuting Aristotle and contending for the mortality of the world. We cannot doubt the end,

> VVhen by the state of *starres* we may discrie,
> The *world's* firme *ruin* and *mortalitie*.[114]

Another popular work which first appeared about this time, and which offers further evidence that a belief in the decay of nature was generally accepted, is *A Help to Discourse,* a combination almanac, cookbook, and guide to meditation, which reached sixteen editions in the next fifty years. We discover therein that this is the last age of the world, "infeebled," "weak and sickly," with the end to be expected soon. Men were stronger in the past, they were subject to fewer diseases, and their span of life was longer. Their knowledge was greater, and they were more continent in their conduct. Since man is a microcosm, it is not surprising that the whole world should also grow old and eventually die. Decay in the fruitfulness of the earth is daily evident. Variations in the heavens, too, are more apparent. Planets are less effective in their influences; innumerable defects proceed from the increase in meteors, comets, and eclipses. Man, the cause, is also the sufferer.[115]

Robert Burton uses many of the same gloomy details in yet a different context in *The Anatomy of Melancholy* (1621). He is particularly concerned over the present wickedness of man, whose Fall is the greater because he was created a *"Microcosmus,* a little world, a modell of the World, Soveraigne Lord of the Earth, Viceroy of the World, sole Commander and Governour of all the creatures in it." In this iron age of ours, we have lost our noblest faculties; we are more miserable than beasts; we are covetous; and, cultivating "so much Science, so little Conscience, so much knowledge, so many Preachers, so little practice," we turn our religion into superstition and madness.[116]

Burton is sufficiently detached from the manifestations of decay, however, to admit that the hope for improvement is not dead; he goes so far as to quote the Baconian figure which settles the modern dwarf upon the shoulders of the ancient giant. This objectivity is maintained also when he wonders whether the heavens actually are subject to generation and corruption or whether possibly the newly discovered stars are caused by regular motions not fully observable in a short period of time. In general, though, he seems to accept the common opinion that because the "fixed starres are remoued since *Ptolomies* time 26. *grad.* from the first of *Aries,"* and "the *Exentricity* of the Sunne is come neerer to the Earth, then in *Ptolomies* time, the vertue therefore of all the vegetals is decayed, men grow lesse, &c."[117]*

Both the universal decay and the final destruction are reflected in the world's mutability, according to William Drummond of Hawthornden. Men are wicked and unhappy in this doting old age of the world; signs of the end may be found in the heavens as well as in the inferior bodies. These are "vnhappie Times, and dying

---

* The notion that the world is "growne Aged" and that the "Light of Nature is put out by time" appears also in Henry Parrot's *The Mastiue.* John Hagthorpe develops the point that all created things are mutable: the planets change; the earth, though frugal, is apparently using up her store of metal; material bodies are all subject to the same fluctuations.

Patrick Hannay, on the other hand, in his two *Elegies on the Death of Our Late Soueraigne Qveene Anne* (1619) protests that a decaying world could never have produced perfection so great as that of the lamented queen:

"*They* are deceiu'd, who say the *world* decaies,
And still grows worse and worse, as old with daies."[118]

Dayes," when virtue is scorned and good is lost. Time not only destroys whatever man creates but causes change in the heavens themselves.[119]

Drummond's most sustained view of the frailty of the world is expressed in *Flowers of Zion* and *The Cypresse Grove* (1623). In the former the instability of the created universe is stressed throughout:

> All onely constant is in constant Change,
> What done is, is vndone, and when vndone,
> Into some other figure doeth it range;
> Thus moues the restlesse World beneath the Moone.

Here, too, mutability is not excluded from the heavens: new worlds are thought to exist, new stars appear above the eighth heaven, heavenly bodies approach nearer to the earth, comets blaze, "false" stars decline, and all this disruption works upon the earth. Though the Resurrection restored the *"pure Age,"* relieving *"the World, that wanning late and faint did lie,"* the decay is once more dominant, and the shadow of the final judgment is already upon us.[120]

In *The Cypresse Grove,* mutability is again extended to the whole universe. Empires have their periods, great cities lie buried in the dust, arts and sciences have their eclipses and even their death. Moreover, some stars, or "Lights aboue (deseruing to bee intitled Starres) are loosed and neuer more seene of vs." In fact, "the excellent fabrike of this Vniuerse it selfe shall one day suffer ruine, or a change like a ruine." "Who can bee great on so small a Round as is this Earth," Drummond asks, "and bounded with so short a course of time?" The entire estate of the world undergoes "an impetuous Vicissitude." Echoing Donne, he exclaims that "The Element of Fire is quite put out, the Aire is but Water rarified, the Earth is found to moue, and is no more the Center of the Vniuerse." The fixed stars are no longer fixed but "swimme in the etheriall Spaces," and comets appear in the realm of the stars. Spots are now seen in the sun itself, and some even affirm that there is another whole world in addition to our own.[121]

The mutability of the aging world is stressed once more in the

Resolves of Owen Feltham, who holds that the world and all its parts daily grow weaker as the end approaches. *"Change,"* he asserts, "is the great *Lord* of the *World; Time* is his *Agent,* that brings in all things, to suffer his *unstaid Dominion."* Man is most inconstant of all, but plants and the elements are subject to the same vicissitudes.[122] The thesis, developed in full by Goodman, that a gradual growth implies a gradual decline, appears here as well: "All things come to their height by *degrees;* there they stay the least of time; then they *decline* as they *rose."* The *"fulnesse of time"* was reached with Christ's descent to the earth; the degeneration has been steady and cumulative ever since. The downward process is accelerated by the fact that importunate mischief can ruin in a moment "what *Nature* hath beene long a rearing."

Feltham might have borrowed from Goodman almost without a change his argument that *"Man* may be *kil'd* in an instant; [though] he cannot be made to *liue,* but by space of time in *conception."* The inclination of the world is toward corruption, the visible process of decay is demonstrable, and the rapid decline of the universe is proof that its ultimate destruction, though we cannot know the exact date, cannot be far off. The whole world, like its parts, decays faster than it grows. The world's infancy and youth are already gone; its old age is a sign that the end is approaching.[123]

The instability of the universe, heaven and earth alike, is asserted also by Nathanael Carpenter, briefly in his *Achitophel* (1629) and in considerable detail in the *Geography* (1625). He believes that the world, now in its old age, suffers a total corruption. Man's sins "inuaded" "natures vniuersall Monarchy," so that "the Heauens, Elements, Plants, and Beasts" groan "vnder their tedious burthen, and desire to bee at liberty." To the contention that the heavens are unchanged and therefore incorruptible, Carpenter replies that sufficient refutation is provided by "the last *Comet,* which Mathematicians by the *parallax* found to be in the heauens."[124]

The decay is most easily discerned on the earth, which, because of the Fall and the Flood, has "degenerated, & proued more unfit

[141]

for humane habitation then in former times." We may thus note "a generall defect and weaknesse of the Creatures, still more and more declining from their originall perfection granted in the first creation." The shortened lives of men in the present age is one of the direct results of this universal Deluge, "which caused a generall defect and decay of nature in the whole earth, the like whereof hath not since bin found." Other specific signs of nature's decay are found in the wearing-down of mountains, the disappearance of forests, and the formation of islands by the breaking-up of a whole and perfect world.[125]

Though this belief in decay seems to be unequivocal as here stated, at times Carpenter so qualifies his position out of a kind of overscrupulosity that he very nearly seems to take the opposite side.* He consistently shows nature's first intent to be its perfection and conservation, both as to its parts and as a harmonious whole. The earth as a whole, for example, is "ransom'd" from such mutability as may cause any "dissolution and separation of the parts one from the other," and neither the earth nor any of the heavenly bodies can actually disintegrate by natural means alone; "howeuer the parts interchangeably corrupt and ingender daylie, yet the whole Globe will apparently remaine the same." We cannot deny, but neither can we accept without reservation, the fact that this corruption exists. The gradual decline from original perfection is certainly obvious; many great philosophers, therefore, have reasonably conjectured

"that the world from the first creation hath suffered the change of ages sensibly, and this wherein we liue to bee the last and decrepite age, wherein Nature lieth languishing, as ready to breath out her last. But this opinion seemes to be controled by reason; forasmuch as we finde not a proportional decrement and defect of naturall vigour in things, as well in man as other creatures."[127]†

* He does something of the sort also in dealing with the Ptolemaic-Copernican controversy, though in this case he is fortunate enough to find in Tycho's compromise a satisfactory middle ground.[126]

† It should be noted that, although the belief in decay generally is derived from a belief in man's Fall and the curse upon nature, by no means all expositions on the

Nor is Carpenter's position the only compromise met with in this period. There is the very common opinion, for example, that the world was stronger in its youth but that men are more moral, more prosperous, or more judicious now in the world's maturity. Among the many documents in which this view is maintained is *The Treasvrie of Avncient and Moderne Times,* a collection of "Iudicious Readings, and Memorable Obseruations," gathered and translated by Thomas Milles largely from the work of Pedro Mexia. Milles accepts and elaborates upon Mexia's position on the world's decay. We live "in the last age," and "smal time of passing hence remaineth." The whole of nature was stronger in the earlier period, but the natural harmony of the elements has since been steadily diminishing. Decayed at the root, man's life "became abridged and shortned dayly more and more." The heavens, too, were "farre more beneficiall and auspicious then, then now they are." The decay of the world does not mean, however, that our virtue or our achievements need be less than in the past. In a sense, there is "No defect in the time, but in our selues." Old men are always too ready to praise the time of their youth, at the expense of the modern age. Actually, the moderns are better in their buildings, their food, garments, armor, battles, and in many other respects.[129]*

Fall are made to carry (as they do for Goodman, Adams, Carpenter, and so many others) the implications of a decaying universe. Stephen Jerome, for example, shows sin to have been the cause of man's death but says no more about nature than that it is "corrupted." Thomas Peyton, in *The Glasse of Time,* a history of the world's early ages, sees vice greater now than in the earth's infancy and stops with saying that the very womb of earth suffers because of this "baneful breath" of sin. Léonard Marandé, who published his *Jugement des actions humaines* in 1624, merely deplores "the vniuersall iniquity of our times, & the generall deprauation and corruption of our liues and manners." The exhortations of Arthur Lake and William Whately also lament the sin, Fall, and present wickedness of man, but say little about the fate of the world.[128]

*Drayton also inclines toward such a pattern when, in *Noah's Flood* (1630), he describes the wickedness of the early ages, at which time man and earth alike were young, strong, and fruitful. In general, however, and throughout his other works he presents the view that the present age is sinful and corrupt by contrast with the greater virtue of the past.[130] Peter Heylyn, describing in his *Cosmography* "the

The full picture of a decaying world, in which all bodies and all virtues decline as the end approaches, is found again in the work of Samuel Rowlands, particularly in his *Heavens Glory* (1628). His earlier productions are primarily satires on the wickedness of the age and show only incidentally any concern over the physical universe. *The Letting of Hvmovrs Blood in the Head-Vaine* (1600), for example, is such a satire, with an indication that the world grows worse while it nears its end. *The Melancholie Knight* (1615) also refers to the passing of the golden age; and *A Paire of Spy-Knaves* (probably 1620) shows that the present is the "worst of wicked dayes," in which the world grows old. Only in *Heavens Glory* is the interest in the actual corruption of the world more definitely expressed; and here we have it that the whole strength of nature, heavens and all, is constantly decreasing:

"The heauens shall perish, and they shall waxe old as doth a garment, and the Lord shall change them as a vesture, and they shall be changed. As a garment the older it waxeth, the lesse comely it is, the lesse able to warme him that weares it: so the materiall heauens by continuance of yeares decrease in beauty and vertue. The neerer the Sunne drawes to the end of his daily course, the lesse is his strength; in the euening we feele the Sunne to decay in his heat, and he waxeth alway the weaker. Now if those superiour bodies, then much more things inferiour and sublunary, are included within the compasse of vanity."[133]

The decay of nature and the approach of the world's end are indicated again in Henry Reynolds' *Mythomystes* (1632?), as a

Infancy of the World, when the bodies of men were most perfect, and of greatest vigour," expresses a preference for the present age, with its higher morality and truer religion.[131]

Thomas Jackson, eminent Anglican divine, is another whose position constitutes a sort of compromise. Men are presumed to be wiser now than in the past, he says, but the world no longer bears so clearly the mark of God's hand: "The visible characters of this great booke of nature were of old more legible; the externall significations of divine power more sensible, and apter to imprint their meaning." It is not clear, however, if nature is less virtuous than before or simply more subtle. In any case, now that proof of God is not so apparent in the universe, men are more atheistic, in spite of the maturer judgment which should shield their faith.[132]

partial explanation for the decline of modern poetry.* It is not always clear, when Reynolds refers to "this declining state of the world," "the sordid and barbarous times wee liue in," or "the diseased world," whether he thinks solely (as he does customarily) in terms of moral and intellectual corruption or whether he would include the actual physical universe. We may conclude that the physical decay of nature is at least strongly implied, however, in his various descriptions of the world as "decrepit" or "doating," in the present "wracke and maime of Nature."[135]

The daily and sensible decay of the universe is envisioned more specifically by Thomas Taylor, Puritan divine, who wrote a number of doctrinal and meditational treatises during the 1620's. The world was created perfect, he asserts, but now suffers because of man's Fall. The creatures are punished for man's sin. Looking at his miseries, man sees "himselfe a masse of sinne, a lump of uncleannesse; and that no good thing is in his nature, which in no part is free from the running issues of that festred and inbred sinne."[136]

There is no doubt that the world will indeed have an end, Taylor reminds us, and that all nature, whether we proceed from part to whole or from whole to part, will decay and die. In the first place, the world's beginning implies its end; and, second, the fate of the whole world must be the same as the fate of its parts—of creatures and men. Conversely, since "the whole world is mutable and mortal, and falleth dayly from it selfe, and its estate," all the parts must necessarily "follow the reason of the whole." The strongest states are but "fraile and brittle," empires are as mortal as their princes, even the sun and moon are always changing, the world is "a kind of grave of things dead or dying," "a figure, a forme, a species or *Idea,* and that passing away too," and there is nothing constant but inconstancy.[137]

Both George Herbert and Phineas Fletcher also take occasion to

* Even Ben Jonson, who denies that the world is decaying, indulges in the conventional description of the golden age as a time of greater beauty and fruitfulness; sees a decline in poetry, effort, and studies; and concludes that, in general, "things daily fall, wits grow downward, and eloquence grows backward."[134]

say that the world is old and man's place in it less honored than once it was. God was closer to man in the sweet past than at present, Herbert shows, and, as the world grows old, the heat of God's love is driven out by sin.[138] When Fletcher, in *The Purple Island,* sees the aged world as mortally hurt, he possibly indicates thereby that the physical universe partakes of the decline, though the poem deals predominantly with moral qualities. Apart from the elaborate and grotesque allegory of the purple island itself, he shows little interest in external nature, disposing of it in the first stanza as "this wretched world" which "grows worse by age." The more surprising, he says, that in such a dying world we still make new discoveries. The present is the iron age, by contrast with the innocent virtue of "the worlds first infancie."[139]

More extended treatment of the idea of universal decay is found again in two relatively obscure works, both "scientific" encyclopedias published in 1635, the year of Hakewill's third edition; they are *Varieties,* by David Person, and *Speculum mundi,* by John Swan. Both Person and Swan are interested in man's relationship to the exterior world, both explain the decay as resulting from original sin, and both see the present times as the old age of the world. Where Person, however, exempts the heavens from the general corruption, Swan, though still conservative, insists that there is no difference between the heavenly and the elementary matter, adopts the Tychonian astronomy, and, in general, embraces a semimodern view comparable to that of Carpenter.

According to Person, the heavens are formed of an immutable "quintessence" and are therefore not subject to "corruption, which is peculiar to all other things." This corruption of the elementary bodies, whereby "some Countries, or rather Grounds, are become more barren than they were," and whereby "men are more weake, and lower of stature than they were," is at least partially caused by the natural processes of time, by "the decaying age of the World, as in plentifulnesse, so in vertue." Though there are limits beyond which even the sublunar corruption will not extend, because all things "in perpetuall revolution do observe the course prescribed

[146]

unto them by their Maker," yet within these limits the corruption is not doubted, either by Person or (according to him) by his contemporaries; "for my owne part," he says, "wheresoever I have beene, whatsoever I heare or reade," he can find "nothing but universall complaints of the Earths waxing worse and worse."[140]*

Swan, dealing more fully with laws of the physical universe, is more definite and detailed than Person in describing the general decay. The world, created for man, because of man's sin now suffers "a successive declination" and grows old. It must finally end "as being worn out, and little able to continue any longer." If man and all other parts of the world must die, then surely the whole world must be mortal. Its end, Aristotle notwithstanding, is inevitable and will come soon, though we cannot know the exact date. Current prophecies which suggest 1645 or 1657 are likely to be false. We know only that the last age is the present and that the signs of the end are always more apparent. When that time comes, the corruption of all things will be purged, and the great world, like the little world, will put on an incorruptible state.[141]

The corruption is manifest at all levels, from the lowest creature to the highest heavens: "as it is with Man who is the little world, so certainly it is with *Macrocosme* who is the greater world." Since man "changeth and declineth daily," it must follow that "the greater world doth also suffer change." Men today are of "lower stature, lesser bones and strength, and of shorter lives" than their forefathers were. The earth is less fruitful, its plants less nutritious. The heavenly bodies grow old in years, strength, and influence. "And indeed this must needs be a manifest proof, seeing lesse and weaker bodies are conceived every Age in the wombe of nature, that nature therefore waxeth old and weary of conceiving."[142]

Swan dwells particularly upon the signs of decay in the heavens. The strength of the heavenly bodies is steadily declining; the various planets are less rubicund, orient, and amiable, or more hypo-

---

* Person, by failing to mention the controversy over decay in a two-page list of current theological and metaphysical differences, does not grant Hakewill and his party even the courtesy of recognition (pp. 179–80 [sig. O2–O2ᵛ]).

critical, "and all the rest both of the wandring and fixed starres more weak and suspicious." The sun "waxeth wearie, as if he would stand still in heaven," and good authority has it that "he shineth more dimmely, and appeareth more seldome then before, being much nearer to the earth then of ancient times." The new stars which appeared and disappeared in modern times, proving the corruptibility of the heavens, were paralleled by a similar star which Hipparchus, "who had better skill in Astronomie then ever *Aristotle* had," fully described.[143]

It cannot be true, for all these reasons, that the heavens are created of a matter different from that comprising the earth, Swan contends. The heavenly matter may even be said to need "daily sustentation, like a lamp which can burn no longer then the oyl lasteth which ever feeds it." Such a fuel would be supplied by the waters that exist above the firmament, at the very outer shell of the universe. It is possible that the corruption of the heavens was accelerated at the time of the great Flood, when the waters passed through the heavens in falling to the earth; and it is most likely that "the daily wasting of these waters may be the cause that the world is perceived to have a successive declination." At any rate, there is no doubt whatsoever that this declination takes place, that the heavens and the earth both grow old, that "by little and little they are changed, tending so long to corruption till at last shall come the time of their dissolution."[144]

VII. AFTER 1635: THE PATTERN TENUOUS

The quarter-century from Purchas and Ralegh to Person and Swan—the period roughly covered by the Goodman-Hakewill controversy—may now be seen to be one in which the idea of nature's decay is more specifically expressed and, on the whole, more fully defended than ever before. The heavens are more regularly included in the area of corruption.* The belief in decay, despite modifications such as those adopted by Burton on one issue or

---

* Though some writers (Thomas Taylor, Feltham, Henry Reynolds, or Person, for example) do not so include them.

Carpenter on another, becomes more and more consistently like the conventional pattern developed by Goodman, with unequivocal acceptance of a general decline in the entire universe.

The decline is also more normally seen as a gradual and constant one, reaching into the present and future. In the earlier period a progressive deterioration is noted, especially by Spenser and Donne, as well as by minor figures such as Pont or Dove; but the decay, with all its implications of the world's old age and its imminent end, is often described as primarily the difference between the perfect creation and the corrupted present. In the 1620's and 1630's, on the other hand, one writer after another—Adams, Feltham, Carpenter, Taylor, Rowlands, Swan—recognizes a daily cumulative decay, a decay invariably caused by the Fall but ever increasing with man's actual sins and the inbred infection of nature. Perhaps the only pattern which remains unchanged from one period to another is the underlying emphasis upon these sins, actual and original, the constant concern over man's moral decline, the sustained search for salvation.

The work of many of the men under discussion here, including Rowlands, Henry Reynolds, Taylor, Person, and Swan, was published largely *after* Hakewill's *Apologie* had already reached two editions, in 1627 and 1630. It was not to be expected that Hakewill's attack upon the belief in decay, elaborate and cogent as his arguments are, should immediately cut short all expressions of a belief so firmly established and so long held. A third edition of Goodman's *Fall* had, after all, been published in 1629; and the doctrines there supported actually reappear in one form or another throughout the entire century. The *Apologie,* furthermore, receives our attention rather for the completeness of Hakewill's arguments than for the extent of his influence. Nevertheless, after 1635, when we get the final statements of the two protagonists and when, for the first time, those statements are so opposed as to constitute a specific, point-by-point debate, the popularity of the belief in natural decay suffers an immediate, considerable, and permanent drop.

After 1635 only rarely do we find the pattern that we have traced

[149]

from Daneau and La Primaudaye to Donne and Swan. Jean Francis Senault, for example, who gives a most detailed treatment of man's sin and the earth's corruption, fails to indicate that the corruption of nature is a cumulative, progressive decay, whereby the world, once cursed, grows steadily worse. In the 1640's, James Howell, Sir Thomas Browne, and Archbishop Ussher and, later in the century, George Wharton, William Bates, and Thomas Burnet, among them contributing what are, from now on, some of the more important statements justifying a belief in decay, are all men whose adherence to the belief is regularly qualified and often even tenuous. Open hostility is now not uncommon, being clearly established by John Wilkins and reaching something of a climax in the writings of Henry Power and John Spencer in the 1660's, after which time serious discussion of the matter largely disappears from the literature of the period. The remainder of this chapter proceeds, first, by considering briefly those writers who still profess, in whole or in part, their conviction that the world is less good now than it once was, and then by summarizing, in the work of several important antagonists, the principal grounds of opposition.

Senault presents a full account of the scope of God's curse, particularly upon man but also upon the entire creation. He does not see the corruption as incremental and denies that signs of the world's end are currently visible. Only in his description of the world's corrupted and miserable estate does he closely approach the position taken by the advocates of a regular process of decay. The face of the world, he says, "was changed when man altered his condition," "the earth lost his beauty when man lost his innocency," and "thorns were mingled with roses when concupiscence was mingled with nature." The creatures rebelled against man when he rebelled against God; the earth, when man grew sinful, grew barren and "lost the fertility which was naturall to it"; the very "Elements began to mutiny," "the Seasons grew unseasonable," and the whole order of nature was destroyed.[145]

The heavens also were affected by man's sin; "losing their

purity," they "suffered some change" and "alter'd their Influences."
Senault contends not only that "the Sun is sullied by giving light
unto the sinfull," a condition which may mean that the corruption
is entirely in man's ability to accept the sun's beneficial influence;
but he also says specifically that "the Sun gives not so much light
as he did before the sin of *Adam*." The earth, "being a neerer
neighbour to man then the Heavens," is "more changed." Man,
the cause of all the disorder, is, of course, most severely affected,
both in his own person and by the decay of nature.[146]

Senault does not recognize, however, any process of decay
which continues to operate in nature; the corruption described at
length above was a change which took place completely at the
time of the Fall, and no further deterioration is suggested. He insists also that the essence of nature, as distinguished from its present corrupt state, is entirely good; there was, in other words, no
principle in nature which would admit the possibility of decay
without sin. The world, he says, "doth still subsist, and seems not
to draw neerer it's end for all it's growing further off from it's
beginning. All it's principall parts are yet intire, and though they
be preserved by change, yet are they always like themselves." The
sun, sea, and earth are not weakened by the years. Though "the
world lost it's first purity, when man lost his innocence," though
"it be disordered in some of it's parts, though the elements whereof
it is composed do divide it, though the seasons which maintain the
variety thereof cause it's confusion," yet, Senault asserts, there
remains "enough of beauty," it is easy "to observe the worlds ad-
vantages amidst it's defaults," the elements "are lodged according
to their deserts," and, finally, "Nature repaires the havock made
by death."[147]*

* There are many other spokesmen for this generation and the next who adopt,
though without developing it so fully, Senault's general position. Occasionally, they
imply something more, but the usual view is that the present stage of the world's
corruption dates from the Fall of man. The Anglican minister, Daniel Featley, for
example, holds to the conventional formula that the world, heavens and all, was
cursed because of sin and that the earth, particularly, is not now so fruitful or
healthful as it was in former times. But Featley is more interested in the Fall than

One of the important distinctions between Senault and Goodman is Senault's detached view of the world's end. A more pressing
concern over this end, together with something of the earlier ex-
hortative spirit and even a suggestion that the corruption increases,
appears in the volume of funeral sermons prepared by Martin Day,
Richard Sibbs, Daniel Featley, Thomas Taylor, and others, which
was published in 1640 as *Threnoikos*. Here we learn again that
men's lives grow shorter ("now, more die before ten, then after
sixtie"), "reason is decaied in man by sinne," "there is a generall
corruption in the manners of men," and, on the whole, the world
grows worse as the end approaches. Though we cannot know the
exact date of that end, these are surely the last days, and "there is a
day that will be the last of all those last dayes. And me-thinkes it
will not be long before that last day of all come: me-thinkes I see
the day broke already, it is breake of day alreadie."[149]

It is a very similar concern over the world's imminent end which
here brings Sir Thomas Browne into this history, for, although he
specifically denies the decay of nature, he is temperamentally
disposed toward a melancholy contemplation of human frailties
and of the death of man and world alike. He thus represents
a considerable deviation from the pattern of lament which prevailed earlier, while still reflecting the spirit of the old philosophy; the world he is so anxious to investigate remains a world to
die in, not to live in. His debt to Bacon is obvious when in the
Pseudodoxia he exclaims against giving too much credence to
antiquity. We should seek truth in nature itself rather than in the
authority of the past. We should separate the province of reason
from that of faith. We need not attempt to relate supernatural
causes and natural means.[150] Browne makes these distinctions,

---

in any possible decline since that time, and in any case the whole question gets only
minute consideration in the large body of his ecclesiastical discourses.

Richard Overton similarly shows how death and destruction date from the Fall.
Moïse Amyraut, in an orthodox attack upon deism, atheism, and Epicureanism, also
makes sin the cause of corruption both in man and in the earth. Even in expressions
as popular as the London pageants, we learn that nature has been confused and
disordered ever since man's transgression introduced conflicts not known in the
first age.[148]

however, not to free science from the restrictions of dogma, as Bacon did, but to preserve religion from the corrosive influence of the new philosophy.

Browne has no doubt that a process of degeneration operates for man, who will be worse in the future than he is at present. He points out "how widely we are fallen from the pure exemplar and idea of our nature" until "we are almost lost in degeneration; and ADAM hath not only fallen from his CREATOR, but we ourselves from ADAM, our Tycho and primary generator." The earth was cursed "in the first days of the first man" and drowned "in the tenth generation after." But "there is a general beauty in the works of God, and therefore no deformity" in any species; and, though the world nears its end, it is "neither old nor decayed, nor will ever perish upon the ruins of its own principles." On the one hand, Browne laments that "'tis too late to be ambitious," for the "great mutations" of the world are all over; yet, on the other hand, he insists, as Hakewill does, that changes of the parts do not alter the integrity of the whole.[151]

The unified Christian philosophy which operated for man and world alike has been split: the truth about man is still determined by the ends for which he was created, but the truth about nature is sought in nature itself. Browne's belief in the world's mortality, however, is derived not from observation of the world but from reflection upon the relation of man to God. It is the urgency of this belief in the world's end which makes the lament finally prevail in Browne's works. Our present generations "are ordained in this setting part of time," he says, so that we can turn our thoughts only to the next world. It is amazing that God's patience "hath permitted so long a continuance" of the world with its "corruption of manners, inhuman degenerations, and deluge of iniquities." The end cannot be far off, and "the greatest part of time being already wrapt up in things behind us; it's now somewhat late to bait after things before us."[152]*

* Bishop Jeremy Taylor, who also writes about man's corrupt and transitory life and not about the corruption of nature, insists upon the physical signs which will precede the end, these signs to include the darkening and disruption of the heavens as well as the disintegration of the earth.[153]

The approaching end of the corruptible world is of immediate concern also to two almanac-makers, the famous William Lilly and an obscure one who signs himself simply "Dove." In 1653 Dove prophesies that "the times are not like to be so good, quiet and prosperous," as men could wish. "But we are they upon whom the ends of the world are come," he reminds us; and we must expect "to heare of sects and heresies, warres and rumours of warres," and other tokens of the end. That final date, he says, is not likely to come for at least two more years.[154] Lilly writes more specifically of the mutations set in motion by the comet of 1572, indicates a general unrest to be prevalent in the heavens and earth alike, and suggests, as does Dove, that troublesome and vexatious times must be expected if this is the last age of the world.[155]

Still without focusing upon the gradual decay of the world, Henry Vaughan is another whose view of the world's corruption and final dissolution at least implies some process which relates that corruption and end. Amid a good deal of melancholy description of the world's vanity, he complains that the whole face of the world is changed because of our sins:

> Heaven's just displeasure & our unjust ways
> Change Natures course, bring plagues dearth and decays.
> This turns our lands to Dust, the skies to Brass,
> Makes old kind blessings into curses pass.
>
> . . . .
>
> The dregs and puddle of all ages now
> Like Rivers near their fall, on us do flow.[156]

The comparison of past and present is still more clearly indicated in *The Mount of Olives,* where the present age is shown to be weakest of all: "We have seen such vicissitudes and examples of humane frailty, as the former world (had they happened in those ages) would have judged prodigies." But even in this context, in which Vaughan proceeds to derive the mortality of the whole from the mutability of the parts, the principal problem is man's estate rather than the world's estate:

"And sure the ruine of the most goodly peeces seems to tell, that

[154]

the dissolution of the whole is not far off.... Vain therefore and deceitful is all the pomp of this world, which though it flatters us with a seeming permanency, will be sure to leave us even then, when we are most in chase of it."[157]

James Howell, writing somewhat earlier in the century, subscribes even more explicitly to the theory of decay, stopping, however, with the sublunary corruption. He is particularly interested in the corruption of man, who gets worse with each succeeding generation, but he recognizes that man's decay is a *"shrewd symptom"* that the world is also decaying. Howell derives the corruption of languages from the decay of all elementary things, which "by reason of the frailty of their principles, come by insensible degrees to alter and perish." The present is, moreover, the *"last doting and vertiginous Age of the World,"* our villainies proving this *"Hectically"* world to be near its "Fatal *Climacteric* year."[158]*

Sir George Wharton, the astrologer, also clings to the idea that man and his world are alike corrupt, though he approaches the question through his interest in the changes and mutations which the heavens effect upon the earth, and he does not lament over

---

* Such criticisms of contemporary society, often without explicitly drawing in the physical world, are common throughout the period. Henry Peacham, for example, defends the learning and inventions of the ancients as greater than those of the moderns and, in an incidental reference in another context, marvels at the "great Changes and Alterations" which may be observed in states "at the ende of every five hundred yeares." The similar views of Roger L'Estrange are indicated by his verse in the first collected edition of Beaumont and Fletcher:

> *"Mankinde* is *fall'n againe, shrunke* a *degree,*
> A *step* below his very *Apostacye.*
> *Nature* her *Selfe* is out of *Tune;* and *Sicke*
> Of *Tumult* and *Disorder, Lunatique."*

The successive stages of decline from golden age to iron age are set forth in detail in *The Four Ages of England* (1648), a poem commonly attributed to Abraham Cowley in spite of his denial that he wrote it. The work is a satire on the immoderate vices of these degenerate times and even repeats the conventional description of the earth's greater fertility in ages past. William Winstanley adds to the traditional four ages a fifth, baser than all the others: the present wooden age. Edmund Waller calls this an iron age, with greater extremes of climate adding to the other miseries that we bring upon ourselves. Our days, he says, are so evil and so few that we must be dwelling on the ruins of the world.[159]

such falling-away from perfection as he notices. He says that the
sublunary world is particularly subject to vicissitudes, but as an
astrologer he testifies that the heavens also are not spared:

> Nay, *Heav'n* it self grows *Old,* and will *away:*
> It had a *Birth,* and shall a *Dying-day.*
> All, all to *Change* and *Dissolution* tend.[160]

In the work of William Bates, a Presbyterian minister who wrote
in the last half of the century, we return to the old-fashioned, religious view of a world suffering for man's sin: "For the world being
made for man, the place of his residence, in his punishment it
hath felt the effects of God's displeasure. The whole course of
nature is set on fire."* Man is corrupt—his morals, his will, his very
soul—in this "winter of the world." The course of decay is not
generally distinguished from the corruption imposed at the Fall,
however, though the world will not be rescued or restored by any
natural means. Such an interpretation of history would presuppose
earlier degenerate periods like our own. Since our own times are
the worst that we know about, we can assume only that no ameli-
oration is in store for us.[162]

We come, finally, to a view of the world much like that of
Senault, but with the modification that the Flood is recognized as a
further stage in the corruption dating largely from the Fall. A great
many of the writers who explicitly trace a gradual process of decay
even to this day—and Goodman among them—regard the Flood
as a most important step in this process; but we see here that the
Flood becomes an additional cause and mark of physical corrup-

* The decline of virtue remains, of course, one of the most consistent interests of
the age, even in texts here examined from other points of view. For further manifestation of such interests see Sir John Suckling's *Account of Religion by Reason;*
showing that the Christian concept of a Fall from a golden age (or from a similar
period of early perfection) is shared by many religions, Suckling asserts that man's
sin has shortened man's life and deprived him of *"something Divine."* Anthony
Burgess defends the doctrine of original sin and identifies our miseries with the
punishments inflicted upon us. Benjamin Camfield is also worried about *"that
Atheistical and degenerate Age we live in."* By the time we get to Archbishop King,
in the beginning of the next century, only this consideration of man's morals remains
of the entire doctrine of decay: man's moral state is all that suffered at the Fall, and
since that time there has apparently been no further corruption of any sort.[161]

tion even with men who otherwise do not commit themselves to belief in an incremental change in nature. James Ussher, archbishop of Armagh, is one of these men.* The corruption, in so far as he is concerned with it at all, is principally a sublunary phenomenon. Man's sin, he says, caused the decay of his body and of "Gods glorious Image" in his soul. The creatures were also punished and are now harmful to man; the beauties of paradise were damaged partly at the time of the Fall and partly by the Flood, though the process of decay is not shown to be continuous from the time of the Deluge. The world's end will be preceded by signs, apparently not yet visible, in the heavens as well as upon the earth.[164]

A similar point is made by Thomas White in his *Theological Appendix of the Beginning of the World* (1656). Here White translates into physical terms the effect of God's curse upon the earth, the curse which disrupted the earth's motion, despoiled it of its beauty, upset it with the variety of seasons, and introduced death to its creatures:

"... the Sun, raising the Wind and the Flux of the Sea, turn'd the Earth aside, which before had its *Axes* direct and even with those of the *Ecliptick;* and spoil'd the Country where Man liv'd, of all its beauty: and introducing *colds,* brought in the *mortall state* of the World: and Man was forc'd to guard himself with Garments."

This corruption is not seen as a continuous process in nature at the present, although the Flood contributed to the further decline of man's body and his life. Even the Flood, however, for White, is a net gain because, in the more rarefied atmosphere that followed, man became "more subtile-spirited," more sharp-witted, and "more addicted to *Sciences* and *Arts.*"[165]

The importance of the Flood in determining the earth's condition is stressed again by Thomas Burnet. According to Burnet, it was the Flood which brought about the great and deleterious

---

* Ussher had read the *Apologie* and praised it as "artificially mixed" with "variety of learning and matter of delight." See also Hakewill's letter to Ussher, dated July 16, 1628: "YOur Lordship's favourable interpretation and acceptance of my poor Endeavours, beyond their desert, hath obliged me to improve them to the utmost in your good Lordship's Service."[163]

changes in the world's estate, though he recognizes that "the Earth was said to be curst long before the Deluge." Man's life is shorter now than before the Flood, the elements have more unequal and contrary motions, the soil is less fruitful, and the very stability of the world is now upset. The earth was "so broken and disorder'd" by the Flood,

"that it lost its equal Poise, and thereupon the Center of its Gravity changing, one Pole became more inclin'd towards the Sun, and the other more remov'd from it, and so its right and parallel Situation which it had before, to the Axis of the Ecliptick, was chang'd into an Oblique; in which skew Posture it hath stood ever since."[166]

Burnet qualifies his general position by indicating both that the heavens are exempt from the decay and that the process of disruption was largely halted, once the effects of the Flood had been felt. It is true that man's life-span continued to decline until it was "fixt at length before *David*'s Time"; but Burnet, relying more upon physical than upon doctrinal explanations, implies throughout that the present exhausted state of the world dates almost entirely from the last known natural cause, the Flood. The heavens, being immutable, are wholly removed from the effects of the Fall or the Flood. Only the planets are probably mutable, and even they are not subject to any decline. The supposed approach of the sun to the earth is simply a difference in calculation, as the methods of measurement are refined. Disturbances on earth may cause the heavens to appear changed, but the heavens themselves are not affected. Biblical references to a darkening of the sun are to be regarded as entirely figurative.[167]

For these two reasons—the heavens' permanence and the earth's arrested decline—the world's end will not be caused by a gradual deterioration or by any other natural means, according to Burnet. The final destruction will come about by fire, as all authorities agree, but there is no increased proximity of sun and earth to afford a natural explanation for that fire. All signs and prophecies of the final date are unreliable.[168]

VIII. NO DECAY IN NATURE

Thus we see in Burnet, as in most others after 1635, that the evidence of corruption is rarely directed to the ends that were so common earlier in the century. Even though we still find sympathy with the earlier attitudes, interest in the idea of the decay of nature dwindles so much that it is no longer a significant part of the contemporary intellectual apparatus. Some of the preachers and quasi-scientists still adhere to the views of Goodman; but by the end of the seventeenth century the belief in decay, as a sustained and general pattern in the minds of men, scarcely exists.

The belief in decay has disintegrated into its various subspecies, it has been refuted (part by part and in its entirety), and it has been stripped of its emotional significance. A detailed history of the ideas which replace it is not within the scope of this study, but some account of its reduction is necessary if the philosophy which we are examining is to be fully delineated. The principal grounds on which it is opposed have already been introduced: in the discussion of Bodin, Leroy, and others in the sixteenth century; in the consideration of Bacon; and, of course, in the analysis of Hakewill's *Apologie*.

A great deal about the nature of this opposition can be deduced also from the arguments of the proponents themselves, from the limitations that they recognize and the positions which they feel required to defend. The whole idea of a physical corruption of nature, as distinguished from a social or moral decline only, is less important than it was a generation before. There are few attempts to defend the decay on empirical grounds. From 1635 on, as we have seen, the heavens, though often regarded as mutable and as composed of the four basic elements, are not often drawn into the world of decay. There is very little inclination to argue that the corruption which took place at the Fall still remains a malignant process which eventually must destroy all nature.

The hypnosis induced by the grandiose analogy between microcosm and macrocosm is now scarcely operative. In addition, the scientists of the period show that mutability (terrestrial and celestial alike) is a fluctuation rather than a degeneration. The debate over decay is now often limited to the question of a possible decline in learning or in the arts, or it becomes merely a quarrel over the ancients and moderns. Even the teleological philosophy which in one way justifies condemning the world for man's sin is, as we shall soon see, now being challenged. The philosophy of the whole is being broken down into various philosophies of the parts: the law of man is no longer valid when inquiring into the mysteries of nature; the realm of reason and the realm of faith are separated; moral knowledge and natural knowledge are examined by different means and for different ends.

In the works of Milton we see the doctrine of decay in what we may call the process of liquidation. As do many of the men whose works we have just discussed, he accepts the corruption of man and world as a result of the Fall; but he is distinguished from these others by his interest in the secular, humanistic achievements and potentialities of man, as well as by his refusal to lament over the world's mortality. His first clear statement on this subject is found in the poem *Naturam non pati senium,* written in 1628 as his contribution to a formal Cambridge disputation on the issue of whether or not the world is decaying. That such a dispute was held the year after Hakewill's *Apologie* appeared is a further indication that the whole question was made more explicit in the debate between Hakewill and Goodman.*

* If we credit Fuller's statement that Hall, in the preceding generation, took the opposite side of a similar issue (that the world is growing old) (see p. 112, above), then we have evidence that the topic had been a debatable one for many years. But such evidence need not be weighed too heavily, for the university disputations were designed primarily as exercises in dialectic and were frequently on topics about which serious disagreement would be considered heretical. Other reasons for not accepting these disputes at their face value include the trivial or sophistic subjects often set (that dogs syllogize), the custom of assigning affirmative and negative sides without regard to actual conviction, and perhaps the very frequency with which the debates were held, in some colleges as often as several times each week.[169] Milton, incidentally, later complains that the universities by such means offer a poor training in the ministry, for "those theological disputations there held by professors and graduates are such, as tend least of all to the edification or capacity of the

In this poem Milton asserts that a perfect and permanent order prevails in all the realm of creation. Shall the face of nature, he asks,

"o'ergrown with furrowing wrinkles, wither, and shall the common mother of all things, her all-producing womb contracted, grow barren through the lapse of years? Shall she, confessing herself age-worn, move with uncertain steps, her starry head all a-tremble? Shall the loathsome lapse of time and the never-ending hunger of the years, and squalor, and mouldy decay harry the stars? And shall insatiable Time devour the skies, and whirl his own sire into his vitals?"

The answer is obvious. The sun and stars keep their same courses, without diminishing. The elements are unchanged; even the earth retains "that old-time vigour of a far-off age." There is no decay, therefore, and "the righteous series of all things will go on into endless time," until the final conflagration shall destroy the whole universe.[171]

Even if the *Naturam* be regarded as no more than a youthful exercise, the opinions there expressed may be confirmed in later works. In *Of Reformation in England,* Milton defends the present authority of the church as equal to its authority in ages past, and he belittles, in passing, the stories of ancient giants. More significantly, the *De doctrina Christiana* shows no adherence to the particular Christian doctrine that the world decays. In the detailed treatment that this treatise gives the Fall and punishment, the decay of nature plays no part. The matter of which the world was created, though it has now become mutable, "proceeded incorruptible from God; and even since the fall it remains incorruptible as far as concerns its essence."[172]

In *Paradise Lost,* however, though there is still no progressive decay of nature, we get the full story of a world corrupted by sin,

---

people, but rather perplex and leaven pure doctrine with scholastical trash, than enable any minister to the better preaching of the gospel."[170] On the other hand, Milton's obvious care in preparing his poem and his return to the same position in later, more serious works prevent us from altogether dismissing it as an exercise of his youth.

of moral decay that gets ever worse, and of despair in man's rescue until "this worlds dissolution shall be ripe." The corruption dates from man's sin:

> Earth trembl'd from her entrails, as again
> In pangs, and Nature gave a second groan,
> Skie lowr'd, and muttering Thunder, som sad drops
> Wept at compleating of the mortal Sin
> Original.

God's curse condemns heaven and earth along with man. Winter and summer become intolerable. The moon and plants are taught the aspects "Of noxious efficacie, and when to joyne In Synod unbenigne." Malignant winds and thunders strike the earth. Even the earth's axis is distorted, though here Milton admits some possibility of doubt:

> Some say he bid his Angels turne ascanse
> The Poles of Earth twice ten degrees and more
> From the Suns Axle; they with labour push'd
> Oblique the Centric Globe.

All these changes in the heavens bring about

> Like change on Sea and Land, sideral blast,
> Vapour, and Mist, and Exhalation hot,
> Corrupt and Pestilent.

The creatures fight among themselves and lose their awe of man. Adam's suffering is greater even than the outward corruption can show. "O miserable of happie!" he cries, "is this the end Of this new glorious World." And the misery will not end with the evil he already knows; all is "propagated curse."[173]

Now the world must go on "Under her own waight groaning," until the hour of vengeance brings "New Heav'ns, new Earth, Ages of endless date." Not until that last day shall the corrupt universe be reborn. But then evil will turn to good, light be brought out of darkness, grace abound over wrath.[174]

There is no true discrepancy between *Paradise Lost* and the earlier position, but only a difference in emphasis. In the poem Milton pictures the corruption instituted by the Fall; in the other

[162]

works he indicates similarly that no further deterioration of the physical world is apparent after the Fall. Actually, such a combination is a conventional one, often associated with laments over the approaching end of the world and despair over man's future. But Milton is not basically responsive to this pattern and clearly does not accept many of its implications. The corruption, both of man and of world, is established only in a poetic context, where it is effective for its imaginative and symbolic validity. Milton's assertions of doctrine, on the other hand, are, on this issue, always made to limit the area of corruption.

There are many of Milton's contemporaries who also contribute, in one way or another, to the new mode of thought.* John Wilkins is among those whose opposition provides, in the first half of the seventeenth century, the real challenge to Goodman's basic assumptions. For one thing, he takes the initial step required in order to free nature from the punishments directed against man: he questions whether the various works of nature, which according to Scriptures were made for man's use, could have been intended simply for man's use.[176] Furthermore, in *The Discovery of a World in the Moone* (1638), one of his earliest productions and the most important for this investigation, he insists, as did Bacon, that the solutions to "Philosophicall secrets" be sought through "humane reason" rather than by use of the Scriptures.[177]

Wilkins opposes also the Aristotelian thesis that the heavens are incorruptible; "witnesse," he says, "those comets which have beene seene above the Moone. As also those spots or clouds that encompasse the body of the Sun, amongst which, there is a frequent succession by a corruption of the old, and a generation of new." But he cites Hakewill to show that the heavens will not "weare away and grow worse," however long the time or great the changes. Nor

* The decay of nature is attacked in 1632 by John Johnstone, in his *Naturae constantia*, a work which Hakewill protests is "little else but a translation of mine." Johnstone testifies, as did Hakewill, to the enormous popularity of the belief in decay and is indebted to Hakewill particularly for his treatment of cycles and the principle of compensation, but presents his refutation more in scientific than in religious terms.[175]

does he find any signs of decay in the mountains, the seas, or any other features of the earth itself: "Certainly then such usefull parts were not the effect of mans sin, or produced by the Worlds curse, the Flood, but rather at the first created by the goodnesse and providence of the Almightie."[178] It is not surprising that with such views he should deny that modern learning or skill or mechanical power is less than in ancient times.[179]

The mutability and constancy of nature are reconciled again in the *Synopsis physicae* of Johann Amos Comenius, Czech theologian widely known for his works on education. "All things," he says, "grow up, increase, decrease, and perish again." Because comets move above the moon, we understand that mutations exist *"every where in this visible world."* This process of change may actually be called a corruption:

> *"Every body is liable to corruption.* Because compounded of a decaying matter, and an agitable spirit.... And hence perhaps every materiall thing is called CORPUS, as it were *corrupus,* because it is subject to corruption."

But the corruption of one part is always the generation of another. The vaporous, atomic matter, of which the whole world was created, changes, but it never dies. Therefore the world, potentially eternal, is a "meer harmony," without evil or decay.[180]*

In Henry Power's *Experimental Philosophy* (1664), one of the

---

* Other attempts to justify the integrity of the natural world are made a few years later by Nathaniel Culverwel and Walter Charleton. Culverwel, in his *Light of Nature* (1652), seeks to establish a proper balance between reason and faith, to that end discovering God's hand in the universal excellence of nature. Nature moves "not by its own weights," but more directly "by fresh influence" from God. Neither "defective nor parsimonious, nor yet sprouting and luxuriant," it is "that regular line" drawn and maintained by the Creator and is thus not likely to corrupt and wither away.[181]

Charleton's position is similar, though at one point, when deploring the current practice of attributing causes to fortune rather than to God's providence, he suggests that the world must be in "its *Dotage"* and "man sunk a whole sphear below that of his Ancestors simplicity and knowledge." But in arguing more directly to the point, he asserts that all things are compounded from the one eternal matter; and, on the whole, he considers the process of corruption balanced by the process of generation, thus leaving himself no natural grounds for a belief in decay.[182]

most illuminating documents relating to the subject, the belief in the decay of the world is disposed of with finality and authority. Power's purpose is the joint one of explaining current developments in science and defending the new learning in general. One principal "Impediment" or "Authentick discouragement to the promotion of the Arts and Sciences," is, he finds,

"... The Universal Exclamation of the World's decay and approximation to its period; That both the great and little World have long since pass'd the Meridian, and, That the Faculties of the one doe fade and decay, as well as the Fabricks and Materials of the other; which though it be a Conceit that hath possess'd all ages past, as nearly as ours, yet the Clamour was never so high as it is now: Something, therefore, I shall here offer, that will abate and qualifie the rigour of this Conception."[183]

Though he pays tribute to "the Learned *Hackwell*," whose "Apology shall be mine at present, for not treating any further of this Subject; he having long since perform'd that Task, to the conviction of Prejudice it self," actually Power goes well beyond the arguments presented by Hakewill. First, he undermines the imaginative as well as the philosophical basis for the belief in decay by arguing, as Wilkins does and Hakewill does not, that "though it may be a pious, and morally good conception, To think that the whole world was made for him [man], yet I am sure 'tis no real and Physical Truth." The earth and even the whole solar system are mere points in the entire creation, insignificant parts of the complete work.[184]

Furthermore, Power adds, "As for the Earth being the Centre of the World, 'tis now an opinion so generally exploded, that I need not trouble you nor my self with it." He also goes on to defend precisely the kind of inquiry into nature which Hakewill decries. A great enemy to our learning and our well-being, he says, is ignorance among scientists, many of whom "daily stuff our Libraries with their Philosophical Romances, and glut the Press with their Canting Loquacities." Where they could be enriching themselves and the world with their discoveries, they instead "wrangle out a vexatious dispute of some odd Peripatetick qualities."[185]

Power concludes with an expression of hope, in its eloquence comparable to the most moving laments of two and three generations ago. The world is not near its end; the future is longer than the past. To what extent "our Modern Wits have outdone the Ancient Sages, the parallel 'twixt the few Inventions of the one, and the rare Discoveries of the other, will easily determine." His challenge to despair is issued not in God's name but in man's. He does not take shelter behind the signs of God's providence but speaks with confidence based on man's strength:

"And this is the Age wherein all mens Souls are in a kind of fermentation, and the spirit of Wisdom and Learning begins to mount and free it self from those drossie and terrene Impediments wherewith it hath been so long clogg'd, and from the insipid phlegm and *Caput Mortuum* of useless Notions, in which it has endured so violent and long a fixation.

"This is the Age wherein (me-thinks) Philosophy comes in with a Spring-tide; and the Peripateticks may as well hope to stop the Current of the Tide, or (with *Xerxes*) to fetter the Ocean, as hinder the overflowing of free Philosophy: Me-thinks, I see how all the old Rubbish must be thrown away, and the rotten Buildings be overthrown, and carried away with so powerful an Inundation. These are the days that must lay a new Foundation of a more magnificent Philosophy."[186]

A similar hopefulness, based on similar grounds, is found in the writings of John Spencer, eminent Hebraist and student of comparative religion. In *A Discourse concerning Vulgar Prophecies* (1665), Spencer objects to the extensive current "talk of *terrible Signs, Revelations, new-lights, Prophecies and Visions*" and recommends what he considers a more reliable way to discover truth. The age of prophecy is not pictured as a golden age in which man walked hand in hand with God but rather as a time when the Scripture was "more dark and incompleat then now, the People were of a more weak and worldly temper, the Oeconomy more carnal."

Our own age, one "of Action and Expectation," is also "a time of improvement in all humane and divine knowledg,"

"and that happy day seems risen upon us to which God hath promised an increase of Knowledg: Nature begins now to be studied more then *Aristotle,* and men are resolved upon a Philosophy that bottoms not upon phancy but experience, a Philosophy that they can prove and use, not that which commenceth in faith and concludes in talk."[187]

In *A Discourse concerning Prodigies* Spencer denies that there is any decay of nature and specifically attacks two of the principles upon which the belief in decay rests: first, that man is "the *great measure* of things, that the greater World is but a larger Paraphrase upon the less," and, second, "that he is the *great End* of things." Though the whole of nature, including the heavens, is mutable, yet all the alterations, including earthquakes, comets, new stars, changes in the planets, and spots upon the sun, are variations within the *"general constancy and harmony of Nature."* Nature has been faithful *"to its Original laws of motion,"* all things continue now "as they were from the beginning of the Creation," and *"God never saw it necessary (as upon maturer thoughts) to correct and amend any thing in this great Volume of the Creation, since the first edition thereof."*[188]

If man did not think the whole world an expanded image of himself, he would be less likely to believe in signs, prodigies, and other myths and more inclined to accept the world for what it is. The soul, Spencer explains, is *"greatly impressive to a Perswasion of Parallels, Equalities, Similitudes, in the frame and Government of the World,"* particularly to the idea

"that there is a very rigid and strict analogy and conformity between the Macrocosm and the Microcosm, the World and Man, that he is a kind of *Terella,* containing lines, natures, conditions and necessities corespondent to those which display themselves in the World with greater pomp and observation, (a conceit as dear to some Ancient and Modern Writers as their very eyes:)...."[189]

[167]

Only our "fond valuation of our selves" causes us to see a direct relationship between man and nature:

"We first conceit Man the *great measure* of things, that the greater World is but a larger Paraphrase upon the less, carrying nothing but perpetual Analogies to some parts and faculties of his Body or Soul: and next, that he is the *great End* of things, and (though we are told *God made all things for himself*) we imagine all things were made for Man, but to minister some way or other to an humane benefit. Hence we easily fancy no New Star or Comet shines from Heaven, but we are extreamly concerned in the occasion. . . . And as we thus think our affairs great enough, so our selves valuable enough, for whose sake God should be continually altering of the *Ordinances of Heaven* which proceed upon such excellent and mysterious Wisdom."[190]

The attack on the idea of nature's decay, as anticipated by Bacon and made explicit by Wilkins and later by Spencer and Power, often accompanies the defense of modern learning; for the belief in decay is regarded as an impediment to that learning (Hakewill saw it as an impediment to moral endeavor) and the modern inquiry into nature has, in turn, on empirical grounds denied the decay of nature. This emphasis on man develops into a quarrel over his intellectual, moral, or social virtues. Hobbes, for example, opposes the idea that primitive man was happier or better than man in a more highly developed society. Skeptical of the images or myths which distort man's picture of his universe, he leaves no room for a golden age from which man declines to the present period of evil and contention. Nor can the decay of nature be explained as a punishment for man's sin; for Hobbes's naturalistic and even mechanistic philosophy separates the physical world from the moral or religious end for which it might have been designed.[191]*

In the works of Joseph Glanvill, though he is not unequivocal in

* Or, from a somewhat different point of view, one showing the influence of Bacon, we find Richard Whitlock, in his skeptical Ζωοτομία (1654), opposing subservience to antiquity or to any other authority, professing that, in general, our "*accusings* of the *Times,* is but *excusing* our *selves,*" and arguing that the learned man need not be disturbed by thoughts of any "Worlds Declination."[192]

his position, we find an attitude of confidence in the moderns, similar to Power's or Spencer's, with a specific interest in the actual physical universe. In *Lux orientalis* (1662) he refers to the renewal of the world's youth after the conflagration, at which time our souls may find shelter in "some pure *efflorescences* of *balmy* matter" which are not to be found now in the earth's "exhausted and decrepit *Age*." In *The Way of Happiness* he talks about how men's natures are depraved because of their sin.[193]

But in *The Vanity of Dogmatizing* (1661) he is outspoken in his defense of the modern world. We have been servile before antiquity and have dreamed of a golden age which never existed. What we considered the world's antiquity was really its nonage; the present age is its *"Grandaevity."* Though the telescope reveals impurities in the heavens, these impurities are not recent developments or signs of decay. No more evidence against decay is needed than we nave in the accomplishments of these wonderful times: "the sole Instances of those illustrious Heroes, *Cartes, Gassendus, Galilaeo, Tycho, Harvey, More, Digby;* will strike dead the opinion of the worlds decay, and conclude it, in its *Prime*." This attitude reappears in *Scepsis scientifica,* a 1665 restatement of the *Vanity,* and it serves as the basis for *Plus ultra* (1668), in which modern improvements are described at length.[194]

Bernard le Bovier, sieur de Fontenelle, illustrates the respect and appreciation for nature which usually accompanies a hope for man's future in this world. In his *Entretiens sur la pluralité des mondes* (1686) he expresses his "Glorious and Admirable Idea" of "the Fecundity, and Magnificence of Nature," which sustains life through incessant revolution and change. Again we find the notion that the world of nature was not intended solely or primarily for man and that therefore it remains independent of man's needs or actions. Man's own understanding and mastery of nature grow greater as the moderns add their achievements to those of the ancients. The size of the world is, in effect, increased by recent discoveries. It is not at all fantastic to suppose that man will some day fly, even unto the moon. The ancients, "in comparison of us," were mere boys.[195]

In the *Digression sur les anciens & les modernes* (1688) Fontenelle supports his defense of the moderns with an argument that the size of trees or of man's body has not changed since the time of Homer and that nature herself, in spite of her mutability, is constant. The moderns can equal the best performances of the earlier ages and will certainly surpass them in most things. We must turn from the authority of Aristotle and others among the ancients; we must be confident of our own abilities. Once more there is the familiar assertion that "Rien n'arreste tant le progrés des choses, rien ne borne tant les esprits, que l'admiration excessive des Anciens."[196]*

The gradual emergence of the moderns as victors in this conflict

---

* Francis Osborne also says that the progress of knowledge is obstructed by "the exorbitant veneration which *Tradition* rather then *Merit*, hath awarded *Antiquity*." He adds that men do not decline now from any supposed ancient state of wisdom, as we see from "*Contemplation* of the vast *Improvement* one *Age* makes of what went before, and how many *New* and more *usefull Arts* are now as it were daily *invented*."

Elias Ashmole, notwithstanding the antiquated stuff he collects for the *Theatrum chemicum Britannicum*, in his Preface to that work is another who defends and praises the discoveries of modern times. The prospect of man's improvement, especially in learning, is expressed also by John Hall.

Dryden defends modern poetry and modern learning by showing that the genius of every age is different and that there is no achievement of the past that cannot at least be equaled, for "good sense is the same in all or most ages; and course of time rather improves Nature, than impairs her."

As late as 1702, George Farquhar also feels required to protest against a "Superstitious Veneration for Antiquity" and against the notion "that we live in the decay of Time, and the Dotage of the World is fall'n to our Share." The world, he says, was "never more active or youthful, and true downright Sense was never more Universal than at this very Day."

Nor is the question entirely settled when Edward Young writes his *Conjectures on Original Composition*, a half-century later, in 1759. Young, like Farquhar, Dryden, and even Fontenelle, is not immediately concerned with the physical aspects of nature, but, assuming nature to offer no hindrance, he proceeds to examine man's opportunities, his hazards, and his hopes. Without subservience to the past, the moderns, "by the longevity of their labours, might, one day, become antients themselves." Modern powers are certainly "equal to those before them," and it must be asserted that "by the bounty of nature we are as strong as our predecessors; and by the favour of time (which is but another round in nature's scale) we stand on higher ground."[197]

over science and the arts follows the discrediting of the whole philosophical order which had prevailed earlier. It is a manifestation of the new approval that men give to change, heretofore a sign of corruption only. It is part (though no more than part) of the pattern which sees all authority challenged, all rational and dogmatic truths questioned. The belief in the sensible decay of the world, a significant tenet of the older philosophy, has but a slight hold on men's imaginations after the middle of the seventeenth century; and, although there is testimony that the popular assumption still persists, scholarly or serious defense of this assumption now rarely appears. John Webster, for example, indicates that the belief in decay is common for some time after Hakewill's attack; but that there is "no decay in Nature," he says, is "a truth now sufficiently known, and assented to." And Thomas Creech, annotating his translation of Lucretius in 1682, in one brief note disposes of the earlier tendency to take Lucretius as an authority for the world's decay. There is no need, Creech asserts, to discourse of the decay of the world, which is obviously as vigorous and as young in appearance as ever.[198]

Nevertheless, the old image of a decaying universe remains to be explained away also by John Ray, a leading biologist at the turn of the century. Ray testifies to its popularity even at this time, and he must dispose of it before going on with the rest of his argument. While attacking the concept of an imminent end of the world, he refutes the "old Argument for the Worlds Dissolution, and that is, its daily Consenescence and Decay: which, if it can be proved, will in process of time, necessarily infer a Dissolution." And, he adds, that all things "do succesively diminish and decay in all Natural Perfections and Qualities, as well as Moral, hath been the received Opinion, not only of the Vulgar, but even of Philosophers themselves from Antiquity down to our times."[199]

Though the heavens and all the world are subject to alterations and though the length of life decreased precipitately for some generations after the Flood, Ray maintains that there is actually no decay (as we know from Hakewill and other scholars) in the heavens, among the animals, or in mankind. Whereas Hakewill had contended that there is no decay because such a sensible decline might enable us to anticipate the exact time of the world's end, Ray argues that we cannot know this exact time because there is no decay by which to measure it. "And here it may be worth the observing," he notes, "that the longer the World stood, the further off generally have Christians set the day of Judgment, and end of it."[200]

The texts here listed in nature's defense, though by no means all which expressed such opinions during the last half of the seventeenth century, are representative; and among them they clearly define the principal grounds of opposition to the belief in decay. The opinion of the world's decay is refuted on empirical grounds or in defense of God's honor and providence. It is refuted because it sets too high a premium upon antiquity and authority. Even more significantly, the belief in decay is refuted because it depends upon a philosophical and natural system of which man is center and end, a system wherein the decay of the part can be extended to the decay of the whole. There is less talk now about an imminent end of the world, less exhortation over man's sinfulness, more interest in the secular society of man, and more study of the external world in which he lives.

In the course of this chapter, many of the major documents pertinent to the controversy over decay are introduced. The points of conflict are isolated and reviewed in the terms used by the individual authors. The material evidence offered for (or against) decay has generally served to characterize the works discussed and to delineate a background against which further analysis may be attempted. The changing form of the argument suggests a changing perspective. Other arguments, prior to the more obvious recital of signs, are suggested wherever it is necessary to do so in order to illuminate either the purpose of a particular work or the context in which it appears. Examination of these other arguments—actually, the broad principles underlying the doctrine of decay—has otherwise been reserved for the next and final chapter.

Chapter V

THE BASIC ARGUMENTS

THE argument establishing decay of the world from the material evidence of the senses, as developed in the preceding chapter, is supported by a series of even more important arguments, without which the supposed signs of decay would in themselves have little meaning for Goodman or for those who share his views. The controversy between Goodman and Hakewill is, of course, part of a complex pattern of conflict between contending philosophies, and the differences made explicit in their debate comprehend many of the most significant points at issue for the men of their generation.

Goodman and Hakewill are nearest to agreement in their understanding of man's relation to God, farthest apart in their interpretations of external nature—its relation to man and God alike. In the subsequent history of the controversy which they popularized, their agreements as well as their differences should be noted, for the theory of universal decay is finally disposed of by men who are as much removed in spirit from Hakewill as Hakewill is from Goodman. To define the problem primarily in terms of the argument over apparent signs of decay is thus to invite oversimplifications and the obscuring of important distinctions. The study of other basic differences between Goodman and Hakewill should provide a commentary necessary to the full understanding of the problem.

In addition to the debate over signs, there are four essential arguments, as isolated and described at the end of chapter iii, arguments which reveal the exact nature and extent of the disagreement between Goodman and Hakewill. As developed by Goodman and specifically opposed by Hakewill, these four are the arguments from the purpose of creation, from the natural processes by which the world is corrupted, from the necessary and natural destruction of the world, and, finally, from the analogy between microcosm and macrocosm.

In the first place, it is Goodman's position that the world's decay, by disclosing the world's frailty and turning man to the contemplation of God, operates to enhance God's glory—the end to which all creation is directed. Hakewill replies that this end is better served by a constant and inviolate universe which itself reflects the glory of God; and an even more complete refutation of Goodman is offered by Wilkins and others, who, denying that the world is created for man's use, indicate that the question of God's honor is irrelevant to a discussion of the world's decay.

Goodman's second argument is that the decay is a natural process, potential before the Fall and set in motion when man sinned. He explains this natural process in terms of contrary motions, which, because of privation, work an ultimate dissolution of all things. Hakewill insists that the contraries balance corruptive motions with generative, and he denies that privation or any similar principle can establish a permanent tendency toward decay. The form taken by the elements may be subject to change, but the forces of nature are not diminished.

The third basic disagreement then arises from Goodman's argument that the natural process of decay may be said to lead to the natural destruction of the world. The decay may thus be proved from the present signs of a necessary and approaching end. To this, Hakewill replies that the end, like the beginning, must be supernatural and will in no sense be indicated by natural signs or derived from natural causes.

All three of these arguments are combined and symbolized in a fourth and final one, in which the decay of the world is suggested by analogy with the natural corruption and death of its principal part—man—a figure strengthened by the idea that the world was created for man's use and condemned for his sin. The harmony that should have been found in the universe, as Goodman sees it, was destroyed by man's defection, and the corruption of the whole may be discovered in any part. Hakewill denies that the same principles prevail for microcosm and macrocosm, whereas Wilkins, striking at the very basis of the analogy, contends that the world is neither designed for man nor in any way bound by his actions.

I. FOR GOD'S GREATER GLORY

Goodman and Hakewill have a common concern for God's honor and a common interest in God's providence. In their debate the doctrine of providence is accommodated both to the belief in decay and to the opposition, Goodman finding the decay and Hakewill the constancy of the world more fully in accord with God's honor and the accepted ends of creation. The doctrine of providence is important to Goodman's belief in decay because God's divine justice punishes man by condemning the world also and because divine mercy permits the corruption to serve as a warning of sin and a preparation for grace.

According to Goodman, there is no progress in this world; our only progress is in leaving this world for a future and better world. The Augustinian concept of absolute dependence upon God accounts for both the Fall and the redemption, particularly in the sense that there could be no Fall unless a restoration of grace were ultimately promised also. God's providence is manifested both by natural and by supernatural means, Goodman asserts; it is both general and particular. Our miseries and corruption provide a further occasion for God to show his goodness, and, because he destroys only in order to preserve, both the destruction and the preservation depend upon his mercy. He turns sin into "a further manifestation of his owne glory" and holds the rebellious elements in check; the corrupt world, without his active providence, could thus no longer endure.[1]

Opposition to the belief in decay is ultimately identified with the modification or rejection of the doctrine of providence. A separation of the religious and natural worlds frees the natural world from any corruption imposed by sin. The seventeenth-century scientists who reject the belief in decay do so because it is incompatible with their empirical evidence and because it depends also upon a wholly teleological understanding of the universe. Hakewill, however, rejects it while defending this teleological, providential universe; his attack upon Goodman is an apology for God's providence.

In his use of empirical details, Hakewill's method is that of the scientists; but these details are concessions to the senses, to natural man, to the spirit of the times. His principal grounds of refutation are rather theological and metaphysical, depending upon demonstration that a provident God will sustain the world he created. He believes it more probable that a provident God will preserve than that he will destroy the universe. The world's constancy, he maintains, is more openly in accord with God's honor. Not only is God the first cause, but his unsleeping eyes watch continuously over the operation of all second causes. The "worlds preservation from decay best suiteth" the attributes of God; the world's decay cannot express God's power and beauty.[2]*

The doctrine of providence assumes a world designed for a particular end—man's sovereignty over all creation. Man, in turn, is designed for God's glory. Not only is God the efficient cause, but his glory is the final cause of the universe.† This teleological view is necessary to the belief in the general corruption which results from sin, for not unless nature is subordinated to man's destiny, and the whole natural order made subservient to the supernatural, can we find nature suffering for man's violation of his compact with God.‡

---

* Hakewill quotes a number of passages from the *Fall*, in which Goodman seems to agree that God is more honored in a constant than in a decaying world (VI, 247–48).

† A god without change or potentiality of change and thus one whose activity, once the world is created, can be only as final cause, is, of course, the Aristotelian concept dominant into the seventeenth century. With it may be compared the explanation of Galileo, that God is the efficient but not the final cause.[3]

‡ See Mosheim's note. The opinion that the world was made for man alone led the Church Fathers to "conclude that on the lapse of man into sin, created things also fell from the state in which they were first created by God, and became much deteriorated."[4]

In such a system a creation by a fortuitous concourse of atoms is excluded. The world and man, furthermore, must be perfect at the beginning; present imperfections are then sufficient proof of the Fall and corruption. The hierarchy of world-for-man-for-God is not seriously questioned through the sixteenth and early seventeenth centuries, and, like the doctrine of providence, it is accepted by Hakewill as well as by Goodman; even Bacon and Boyle and later the Cambridge Platonists, while making concessions to the natural order, defend this hierarchy. When the challenge does come, however, and opposing patterns are adopted, the theory of decay is finally and conclusively disposed of.[5]

This conventional ordering of the universe provides a natural world that is finite in time and space. It makes the realm of man greater than the realm of nature, though both, it is assumed, are part of a still larger whole. Man is the microcosm, the image of God and nature. The natural world is subservient to him and intelligible to him. The proper study of mankind is neither man nor world but God. It is not strange that man is reluctant to give up his place of eminence.[6] There are two steps in the refutation of this doctrine: denial that the world is created for man and denial that man is created for God. In order to dispose of the belief in the corruption of the world, it is enough to take the first step; the second step would also dispose of the belief in man's Fall.

The position that the world was made for man is reinforced by a geocentric astronomy. God "did square and proportion the heauens for the earth," says Goodman, with "the earth as the center." Or, as Donne puts it, "Man is but earth; Tis true; but earth is the center." The corruption can thus spread outward from man to all the world. In *"Natures nest of Boxes,"* the "Heavens containe the *Earth,* the *Earth, Cities, Cities, Men.* And all these are *Concentrique;* the common *center* to them all, is *decay, ruine."*[7]

Henry Power, when denying that the world was made for man, denies also that the earth is at the center of the universe.[8] The popularity of the Tychonic compromise was no doubt due in large measure to the fact that it salvaged man's dignity by retaining a geocentric order. The Copernican theory, held by few who believe in the world's decay, strains the teleological unity of the creation. Further implications of the new astronomy unfix the fixed stars, admit the possibility of many habitable worlds, and leave the universe with no center at all. It is hardly conceivable that such a universe was made for man or that it is punished for man's sin.

The mathematical view of the world makes man no longer the center and end of all creation. The real world is now removed outside man; man is no longer the microcosm. Galileo suggests that God's honor is not at stake in our quarrel over the world's mutability, nor need we think of God as wasteful when creating a world not designed specifically for us. Descartes separates completely the primary realm of the world from the secondary realm of man and finds it "not at all probable that all things have been created for us in such a manner that God has had no other end in creating them."[9] The new philosophers, not seeking final causes, ask how rather than why. If a qualitative understanding of the world made man supreme among created things (because only man is capable of determining values and ends), a quantitative system reduces him to insignificance, except, of course, in so far as he still does the measuring.

Wilkins accepts the idea that there may be other inhabitants on other worlds and points out that, although "Scripture doe tell us" that the works of nature "were made for our use, yet it do's not tell us, that this is their only end." John Spencer denies that man is "the *great End* of things" or that all the world is "made for Man, but to minister some way or other to an humane benefit." Power devotes an entire chapter to proving that *"the World was not made Primarily, nor Solely for the use of Man, nor in subserviency unto Him and his Faculties."*[10] The opposition of these men to the doctrine of decay has already been stated, with the grounds of their opposition.[11] The Fall of man may henceforth continue to be an unquestioned tenet of the church, for the sequestration of the spiritual world need not mean its elimination, and the idea that man was made for God remains widely accepted. But, when the world cannot be said to have been made for man, the *natural* basis for tracing the corruption and decay of the world is dissipated.

If Goodman had wished to avoid the controversial question of nature's decay, he might have been content to present the Fall simply as a revealed truth. Certainly, he would thereby have disarmed most of his opponents. But, not content with revelation alone, he is anxious to confirm faith by other means, to make his point with natural man. This further desire entails two procedures. First, he sets out to prove a perfect creation and infers from present corruption that there must have been a Fall. Second, he shows, from historical records and an examination of man and nature, that the process of corruption is even now operative; his appeal to natural man assumes that there has been a further or incremental decay in addition to the Fall.[12]

Turning for a moment to the second of these procedures, we recall that throughout this period the evidence for decay, as well as the evidence against it, is offered most generally as a series of "signs." These signs have at least the ostensible appearance of being derived from the senses. Goodman, in appealing to the natural man, proceeds from sense to spirit; the truth of nature leads inevitably to the truth of grace. Natural alterations, he maintains, need not always be apparent to the senses, but such changes as are apparent are enough to establish, without any other argument, the decay of the whole world.[13] This empirical evidence, of little value to Goodman in establishing the Fall of man or the corruption of nature, is heavily relied upon in confirming the incremental decay. Such evidence is, of course, important for Hakewill, whose long comparison of the ancient and modern worlds is presented by means of his own observations and the records of others, past and present, and whose contemporary influence and subsequent reputation are based primarily upon the efficacy of this method of defending his thesis.

Yet, as was pointed out in chapter iii,[14] this is but one of several ways by which Hakewill develops his argument, and a less significant one than it may at first appear. Nor is it much used by either Goodman or Hakewill in their long debate in Book V of the

Apologie. It should be remembered, also, that for both Goodman and Hakewill the use of empirical evidence is in large measure a matter of gathering and presenting proper authorities, though, as may be expected, it is Goodman who warns against opening *"a gap to all innovation and projecting"* and Hakewill who points out that "if you will give no way to the Reformation of old errors, you will thereby condemne not onely the reformed religion in regard of Poperie, but the very Christian religion it selfe in regard of Paganisme."[15]

Goodman's other and more fundamental procedure—the verification of faith by reason—is, of course, no new approach. The world which is Goodman's heritage is a full and perfect order, in which reason, though it cannot reach as high as faith, can confirm many principles of revealed truth and is contrary to none. Reason is thus particularly valuable in maintaining the essential principles of religion against those who might question them. "The light of naturall vnderstanding, wit and reason is from God," Hooker had written not long before. Reason and nature help man to understand things of the spirit and, though insufficient alone as a guide to salvation, reveal to man (exactly as Goodman later contends) "not onely that there is a God, but also what power, force, wisedome, and other properties that God hath and how all things depend on him."[16] It is not wholly improbable also that Goodman was meeting some specific challenge delivered in the language of natural man, though, in the absence of such evidence, we need understand only that Goodman's method does not represent, either to him or to his contemporaries, any deviation from accepted practices.*

Where Goodman thus defends the belief in decay because it is more in accord with reason, Hakewill denies that such a belief is more in accord with religion. Reason, he insists, neither enforces nor excludes faith and cannot extend to the articles of the Creed.

---

* Goodman's orthodoxy in this respect may be seen also in his praise of the scholastic philosophers as the lights and lamps of all true learning, in his often professed obligation to Aristotle, and in his long flirtation with, and final conversion to, Catholicism.[17]

The world's mortality, which Goodman derives by reason, is supernatural and can be known only in God's word. Revealed truth,
independent of reason, need not be confirmed by reason. Furthermore, in challenging the congruity of reason and faith, Hakewill
moves toward the separation of natural and religious knowledge
which Bacon had adumbrated. In Bacon's schematism the natural
world is removed from the unified whole which had been encompassed by traditional theology. And when man and nature are
divided, with the result that what is true of man need not be true
of the world, then the belief in nature's decay, at least in Goodman's terms, is no longer supportable. Bacon, in order to free natural
philosophy from what he regards as the restrictive bonds of prejudice and superstition, concludes that "sacred theology must be
drawn from the word and oracles of God; not from the light of
nature, or the dictates of reason"; the more incredible any tenet of
faith, the more we honor God by believing it, and the more noble
the victory of faith.[18]*

II. A DECAY ROOTED IN NATURE

The relation of religious to natural knowledge raises the question of whether natural decay may be proved from natural principles or whether it must be defended as wholly supernatural. The
possibility of natural decay—Goodman's second major argument as
made explicit in his appeal to natural man—depends on the original susceptibility of the world to decay. Before man's Fall, according to Goodman, God restrained the privative natural tendency
toward decay; but with man's sin the disruptive forces are released

---

* Browne makes a similar point when he professes to be glad that he saw none of
the miracles, for it is a higher act of faith to believe without seeing. Wilkins, developing his thesis that natural knowledge be made similarly independent of theology,
opposes the attempt "to confirme Philosophicall secrets from the letter of the Scripture, or by abusing some obscure text in it." Instead, he says, " 'tis the more naturall
way, and should be observed in all controversies, to apply unto every thing, the
proper proofes of it; and when wee deale with Philosophicall truths, to keepe our
selves within the bounds of humane reason and authority." This emphasis on the
limitations of reason is found in many other works of the period, though usually,
as in Hakewill, without any indication of a necessary conflict between reason and
faith.[19]

and are permitted, through contrary motions, to bring about the decay of the world.

The distinction between natural and supernatural decay involves knowing the extent to which the Fall has natural, as well as religious, consequences. The Fall is, of course, denied by none of the major parties to the controversy over decay. There is general agreement, too, that sin is alien to God's creation and that it was introduced not by man, nature, the stars, or God, but by Satan. Thus not even Goodman, who accounts for the decay in natural terms, defends any natural principles of evil or sin itself. But, once the evil in introduced, says Goodman, it acts through the agency of natural law. The disagreement between Goodman and Hakewill, then, occurs in measuring the effects of sin upon the world and in determining what, if any, natural means are used to bring about the corruption.[20]

God's curse may be variously thought of as a curse upon the soil only or upon the sublunary world or upon the entire material creation. Though the Scriptures themselves do not afford a clear authority either for or against any of these positions, the Old Testament apocryphal and rabbinical literature had, by the time of Paul, established a fairly strong tradition in favor of a general corruption resulting from sin. In the sixteenth and early seventeenth centuries the idea that nature suffers extensively for man's sin is rarely questioned. Again and again the disorders of the physical universe are explicitly charged to the Fall of man. The world, made for man, is punished for man's defection. The corruption is limited to the soil far less often than it is extended to the heavens.

The mutability, the uncertainty, and the imperfection of the sublunar world, and often of the celestial, are regularly explained as the direct and immediate consequences of God's curse. The world, in turn, is a further instrument for perpetuating the corruption: "The first man did infect nature," as Scott describes the process, "but now nature infects man-kinde." The Flood, another punishment of man's sins, is usually regarded as a stage in the corruption of nature; and again permanent natural corruption is shown to result from supernatural causes. The inundation "of so many waters," writes Goulart in a representative passage, has "curroded and putrified the seede" of the earth, so that "the signes of Gods displeasure seemed to haue remained there euidently in sencible manner."[21]

But to give the natural corruption a supernatural cause is not to deny natural means for bringing it about. It is argued also that natural principles, even without the Fall, are capable of effecting the corruption. Thus, for Goodman, man's sin, which is not in nature, releases the wholly natural process of decay. Most, though not all, advocates of a belief in decay hold that the world was so designed as to make possible a natural corruption in accord with natural laws.

Goodman indicates that the world's decay proceeded *"from the very principle of that corporeall nature, whereby out of her weakenesse shee is apt to bee worne out with use."* The impostume is "first bred in that radicall humour, which is the foundation of nature." Man and world were corruptible even before the Fall. Daneau believes that the world "was subiect to alteration, vnlesse GOD did susteine, and preserue it." Lipsius finds in all things an "inward proneness" to their change and fall, and Ralegh implies that the sin of man merely increased the corruption already to be found in nature. Citing Scaliger, Person also makes the law of nature, by which all things tend to ruin, the *causa agens* of decay.[22]

Senault, on the other hand, is one of the few to oppose directly the doctrine of the original potential weakness of nature. He warns us not to imagine, by confusing the corruption of nature with her essence, that there was "a bad *Principium*." Ursinus is another who points out that the corruption—of the heavens, at any rate—has no natural basis but is effected only by God's power. Even Goodman, denying the Manichean dualism of good and evil, admits that the actual malignity of nature "proceeds not from her first institution, but from some after accidentall corruption."[23]*

If an original propensity for decay can be denied even by some

---

* Though the malignity is subsequent to the Fall, the corruptibility of nature is still, for Goodman, the essence rather than the accident. Only because of God's direct care was the corruption stayed before the Fall, and only because of his care is the world now preserved from a complete return to chaos and confusion.[24]

of those who believe nature corrupt at present, certainly it will be denied by Hakewill. Hakewill holds that corruption was not in nature before the Fall, for God could not be the author of evil, or after the Fall, for any natural condition must have been introduced at the beginning. The first mold could only have been perfect. Nature, he concludes, "not onely before the fall, but since is kept inviolable, save only in men and Angels, who wilfully cast themselves away."[25]

What, then, are the natural explanations which Goodman and his partisans offer, in order to account for the world's corruption? Perhaps the simplest and commonest device is to show the world to be in its old age and, therefore, its substance wasted and its strength exhausted. This method has the recommendation of long tradition, classical and biblical alike, and an easy analogical effectiveness. Among the important authorities for the idea are Seneca, Pliny, and especially Lucretius, whose opposition is acknowledged by Hakewill to be of great weight.* The tradition is enforced by Psalm 102, in which the heavens and earth are said to "wax old like a garment," by the apocryphal Book of Esdras, and by the writings of St. Cyprian.[27]

In the literature of the sixteenth and seventeenth centuries the image of the world's old age is a common one, particularly where the world's decay also is argued. As Daneau puts it, "not so muche as the least part" of the world's perfection remains now "in this latter, and as it were, crooked old age of the worlde." Or, in Shakelton's words, the world "doeth waxe old, and euery part thereof doeth feele some debilitie and weakenesse." This is Alexander's picture:

* "E'en now the World's grown old," Lucretius writes; all things are worn by time and must end in death.

> "And *Nature* alters; this grows *weak*, this *strong*,
> This *dies*, this *newly* made is firm and *young*.
> Thus *altering* Age leads on the *World* to Fate,
> The Earth is *different* from her *former* state;
> And what in *former* times with ease she bore,
> Grown feeble now, and weak, she bears no more,
> And now doth that she could not do before."[26]

The Earth (ag'd Mother) loe, is barren growne,
Whose wombe oft worne, now torne, doth faile in brood,
And may (since staggering else) be soone o'rethrowne:
What wonder? weake through age, and drunk with bloud.

Giles and Phineas Fletcher both show the world growing more
and more deformed in its senescence. Writers as diverse as Swan
and Comenius describe the world's old age in terms of Psalm 102,
though, of these two, only Swan, as may be expected, sees the increasing corruption end naturally in dissolution. The world's age in
relation to its end is discussed also by Shakelton, Donne, Christopher Sutton, and George Wharton, among others. The comparison
of man's life and the world's, which underlies this entire aspect of
the belief in decay, is discussed in full later in this chapter; and it is
sufficient to say here that the world's old age is so generally admitted
that even Hakewill does not deny it, contenting himself with his
distinction between age and an actual decline of powers.[28]

The world's old age, however, provides at best a poetic
and analogical, rather than an analytical, approach to the problem.
More precise philosophical distinctions are to be found in other
ways of understanding the natural decay, particularly in the Aristotelian principle of privation, which had been adapted to the needs
of Christian theology. Privation is seen to be inherent in all things.
It is the force or potentiality by which form is drawn out of matter,
as well as "the want of that forme, of which this matter was capable." It explains the general corruption in physical terms by showing that the world was potentially decaying before the Fall, for all
things had (and have) in them the possibility of converting their
matter into some different form; it is this privation of the form
which constitutes chaos and destruction.[29]

The world did not decay before the Fall, but that was simply
because God did not permit it to. After the Fall privation becomes,
in effect, the force behind the process of decay. It is the impotency
which opposes every potency and is thus to be distinguished from
mere negation. In privation, "difference is present over and above
what is implied in negation; for negation means just the absence of

[185]

the thing in question, while in privation there is also employed an underlying nature of which the privation is asserted."[30] Whatever imperfections may exist in the soul, for example, are negative rather than privative, for "there is nothing wanting that *ought to be* in the soule."[31]

Privation is regarded in any of various senses, all based on distinctions set up by Aristotle. It may be the lack or removal—even the forcible removal—of some quality which had been or should be characteristic of whatever suffers the privation, as death of man is the privation of life. More often it is in one way or another simply a potentiality not realized and thus a possibility of (even an inclination toward) change. It is, in this sense, only "accidentally a naturall principle," required in order to provide continuity through generation and corruption, whereas matter and form are required essentially. It may thus be the mean between generation and corruption, "a vacuity, a *Nihil* or *non entity,* between two formalities." By this definition it need not incline more to corruption than to generation, and Hakewill insists on regarding it in this fashion, if it is to be accepted at all. Privation, he says, "implies an endlesse circle of corruptions and generations by turnes, in things generable and corruptible."[32]

A third, and for this study the most significant, way of defining privation is as an actual tendency to corruption or disintegration. According to this view, the world has always contained the seeds of possible corruption. Privation is the chaotic or decomposing principle in nature, the potentiality of not-being. In a universe already complete in its hierarchy of forms, it amounts to an accidental and hence a fragmentizing force. As Goodman puts it, nature, because of privation, *"stands not indifferently affected"* both to generation and corruption, *"but indeed* wholly inclines to corruption; *and thereby implies a generall decay."*[33]

Fludd contrasts privation, or the "decomposing nature," with form and matter, the constituting or composing principles of being. The "dark privative Principle" is "that which seemed before all beginnings to be without form, and therefore mortifieth and depriveth of life." John Abernethy distinguishes further between "a simple and naked priuation" and "a priuation potentiall, including a power and disposition to euill: like vnto rottennesse in an apple, which is not onely a priuation of the natiue heate thereof, but also a disposition to corruption." Every privation, says Drummond, is "abhorred of Nature and euill in it selfe." A century later Edmund Law, in the Preface to his translation of William King's *Essay on the Origin of Evil,* reflects the same view of privation when he says that such a principle, if admitted, must imply a *"Defect"* or *"Mixture of* NON-ENTITY *in the constitution of created Beings,"* and therefore a *"necessary Principle of all Natural Evils."*[34]*

Once the force implied in privation is released, as it is by man's sin, the contrary elements and qualities are free to bring about corruption, according to Goodman. Contraries are necessary to any process of change, for they are the attributes in respect of which things are capable of change.[36] The change, of course, need not be toward decay or dissolution unless, by the principle of priva-

---

* Original sin itself is seen either to be merely privative—that is, operating as a restraint upon the potential good in man—or to include also his positive corruption. The division on this point has to do rather with the attitude toward man's depravity than with that toward the decay of nature, and both interpretations permit us to understand that the world's decay, though not active before man sinned, is in accord with nature. Sin, thus, whether understood as merely privative or as positive also, may be said to release the natural privation and bring on the decay.

Goodman's idea that sin is "meere defect and priuation" is one which underlies many of the religious works of the period. For example, Barckley characterizes sin as "no efficient, but a deficient cause." "Evil is no substance nor nature," he says, "but an accident that commeth to the substance, when it is voyde of those good qualities that ought naturally to be in them, and supplieth the others absence with his presence." The same opinion is held by La Primaudaye, Perkins, Davies of Hereford, and Phineas Fletcher.

The other, severer view, generally traced back to Augustine, is probably more common throughout the Reformation. Opposing the stand of Bellarmine and other Catholics, who hold sin to be privation only, Willet contends that it is privation plus "an euill habite" or disposition. Du Moulin similarly sees it to be "not onely the want of righteousnesse, but also the inclinablenesse to vnrighteousnesse," or "the pronenesse to euill." Similarly, we find Bates writing that "in the depravation of nature there is not the mere want of holiness, but a strong proclivity to sin," and, in another context, "the corruption of nature is not a mere privation of holiness, as darkness is of light, but a contrary inherent quality." Adams and Burgess are also among those who describe sin in terms of both privative and positive evil.[35]

tion or some other natural or supernatural law, all change must be away from an original perfection and therefore toward imperfection. Corruption and generation may be thought of as balancing each other, or corruption may be considered greater.

Goodman's thesis that the general intent of nature is toward corruption is fully developed at the beginning of his treatise, affirmed at the end, and defended in the rebuttals. To destroy is easier than to build, he says; there is but one way to be born, many ways to die; all generation must lead to corruption, but not all corruption is followed, in turn, by generation. Hakewill, in his opposition, shows that any corruption of nature serves only to prepare for further generation, so that the world in no sense may be said to approach its natural end. The one way of birth, he adds, has more than kept pace with the many ways of death. The difference between Goodman and Hakewill on this point illuminates and grows out of a disagreement, very common in the period, about the meaning of contraries, and the area in which they prevail.[37]

The contrariety of elementary qualities is a necessary cause, and the only natural cause, of corruption, according to Goodman and many of his contemporaries. Mortality and corruption *are proper to the corporeall nature,* in that even before the Fall *both man and the world it selfe were corruptible, as subsisting of contrary qualities, which were ever active and opposing each other.* Whereas the soul cannot decay, "since nothing in the whole world is contrary to it," contrary qualities render the elementary bodies corruptible. The process of corruption may even be described as the disintegration of all bodies into the elements of which they were compounded. Prior to the Fall, the conflict of contraries was restrained by the direct intervention of God; natural oppositions were withheld in the supernatural perfection. At present the destruction would be more precipitous, and the chaos even upon us, if God did not retard the world's natural inclination to destroy itself. Whenever the contraries are fully released, all elementary forms and the elementary order itself will be dissolved, for the natural end imposed by the warring elements can be only mortality and dissolution.[38]

[188]

The principal objection to this view is the argument that the heavenly bodies have no contrary qualities. Natural corruptibility may be found below the moon, it is admitted, but the heavens are obviously seen to be exempt from elementary contraries and therefore from corruption. Or, even more directly opposed to Goodman, the mutability of the earth may be said to be moderated (and the limits of change in the elements established) by this immutability of the heavens. Such a view may be carried so far as to assert, as Leroy, for example, asserts, that contraries are the means of preserving the world. Hakewill argues that because the heavens are without conflict or alteration, without either generation or corruption, the heavens will restore any temporary or partial sublunar losses.

Though Goodman professedly borrows his argument from Aristotle, Hakewill is actually closer to the source on this issue, for Aristotle (admitting no ultimate dissolution in an eternal world) holds that contraries motivate generation as well as corruption, and makes the heavens free of elementary mutability. With these opposing views may be compared Galileo's challenge not only to the distinction between celestial and terrestrial natural law but also to the basic idea that corruption is in any way a product of supposed contraries. Galileo rejects the category of quality in favor of the category of quantity; as Aristotle himself makes clear, there are no contraries in quantity.[39]

The immutability of the heavens is supported, then, by the theory that there are no contrary motions above the moon. The presence or lack of contraries in the heavens depends, in turn, upon their material composition.* Normally, that is, those who believe the heavens corruptible would argue that all bodies are made of the

---

* It is usually assumed that God originally created a chaotic "first matter," from which the earth and possibly the heavens were compounded. From this first matter or original chaos was then created "a second particular matter: that is to say, a corporall, and naturall" body.[40] To return from the second matter, which has been invested with a definite form, to the amorphous first matter, is to partake of natural corruption. Both the progression from first to second matter (from the material to formal stages) and the regression from second to first are effected by means of privation, in the one instance as privation is understood to be the lack of a potential form, and in the other as it is considered a necessary inclination toward corruption.[41]

same matter, whereas those who restrict change or corruption to the earth would assume that the heavens are composed of a different substance. Yet actually these positions are often reversed. Goodman, for example, believes that the sublunary matter is compounded of the four base elements but that the celestial matter is *"a quintessence, a pure body without mixture."* Nevertheless, the heavens and the earth are alike corruptible, he goes on to argue, for the heavenly matter, while lacking in the gross "appetites" of the elements, shares the inbred weakness common to all material things.*[42]

Hakewill denies the existence of a double matter, insisting that the heavens were created either of the elements or of the matter of which the elements were created. The distinction between the heavens and the sublunar regions, he says, is not one of matter but of form: the lower bodies are mutable in form, whereas the form of the heavens so completely satisfies its matter that no natural change or mutability is possible. Hakewill insists that Goodman is inconsistent in defending both the double matter and the corruptible heavens.[43]

It is generally agreed that, if separate matters exist for the upper and lower regions, the heavens must be composed of some substance other than the four elements comprising the sublunar world. This substance may be described as a fifth element, differing in kind and in properties from the rest. The *"Schoole-men,"* Hakewill indicates, "following *Aristotle,* adhere to the *Quintessence,* and by no means vvill be beaten from it."[44] Increasing opposition to the fifth element, however—an opposition supported by Plato and the Church Fathers and reaffirmed by the discovery of change in the heavens—becomes so general in the seventeenth century that Wilkins, for example, can dismiss the Aristotelians without serious consideration.[45]

* Goodman actually distinguishes three levels of creation, two of them material and the third nonmaterial: the sublunary, the celestial, and the *"glorified,"* which exists above the heavens and *"beyond the reach of* Philosophie" and which consists of form without matter. Out of this division comes the distinction between the corruptible, material world, on the one hand, comprising both the heavenly and elementary matters, and the incorruptible, spiritual world, on the other.

The immutability of the heavens may thus be argued on many different grounds. The heavenly bodies may be exempt from corruption by God's special favor, perhaps because they are directly moved by angels or "intelligences" or simply because God intends to keep them inviolate for the preservation of the world or for the contemplation of man. When a natural explanation is offered, the heavens may be said to be composed of a second matter, a fifth element without contraries and wholly circular in its motion. Without privation, the heavens are already perfect in form and have no necessary inclination toward change. They have no need for the alternate movements of corruption and generation, retaining their original nature until such time as God shall by his direct and supernatural agency destroy the whole world.[46]*

The prestige of this idea—that the heavens are immutable—suffers from two principal influences. First is the Christian opposition to Aristotle's idea that the world is eternal. Because the world is mortal—heavens and earth alike, according to Goodman—the whole may well share in the common frailty. Decay of the heavens is a particularly convincing sign of this world's weakness and of the need for divine grace. If the end is imminent, it is not surprising that the entire framework of the world begins to disintegrate.

Second is the new astronomy, which reveals change in the highest regions of the heavens and which shows that the earth is in no respect different from other bodies and that therefore the same laws must apply to all. Mutability of the heavens, especially when it is supported for the second reason rather than the first, need not imply the decay of the world.[47] But it does make the decay more probable and more pressing for those who are already inclined to find the world corrupt and the shadows lengthening. When even the heavens are subject to alteration and diminution, restitution of local or temporary losses is prevented, a certain har-

* I repeat here that these circumstances need not all prevail in order to prove the heavens immutable, as we see by Hakewill's refusal to admit the fifth element. Nor does any one of these points in itself constitute adequate proof of the heavens' immutability, for Goodman's double matter is subject to privation, contrariety, and corruption.

mony of the universe is destroyed, and the whole material creation is seen to be of short duration and of little consequence.

The new science may thus have either of two opposite effects upon the belief in decay. It may affirm this belief, extending the area of decay to the heavens and disrupting the order by which the world had been thought to be preserved. Or, more often and more significantly, it may seriously weaken the belief in decay, discrediting the laws of motion which had accounted for privation and contraries, banishing man from the center of creation to the obscure and uncertain periphery, and thereby removing any likelihood that his sin will—by natural means, at any rate—destroy the whole universe.

To the stimulus which the new science gives the idea of mutability of the heavens may be added the influence of Lucretius, who also believes that the same conditions of change prevail in the heavens as on the earth. The Lucretian method of understanding the universe is in many ways like that of modern science, and it is not surprising that a serious revival of interest in the atomistic philosophy should develop in the sixteenth and seventeenth centuries. Nor is it extraordinary that the authority of Lucretius should be invoked both in defense of and in opposition to the belief in the world's decay. The Lucretian pattern supports the Christian concept of decay by confirming the world's mutability, old age, and mortality; but at the same time it also admits the possibility of human progress, indicates that the eternal atomic "seeds" insure an infinite number of worlds in an infinite universe, and—most important—denies the teleological creation and the hierarchic order of world, man, God.

Lucretius' intention is to dissolve the fear of invisible powers; his universe has no creator but is formed by an accidental conflux of atoms. Because of his atheism, he is more often attacked than quoted by those who believe in decay. The differences between the Lucretian material world with its infinite change, on the one hand, and the qualitative world with first and final causes, in terms of which the world's decay is regularly accounted for, on the other, should illuminate further the parallels between the atomic theory and the new science and show once more how the increased interest in Lucretius tends to dissipate the belief in decay as well as to support it. The Lucretian doctrine of plurality of worlds, for example, far from being a comfort to those who are troubled by the decay of this world, violates the fixed order indicated by the Aristotelian and Christian systems and is generally attacked by the advocates of these systems. The harmony of the atomic universe is not qualitative, and any philosophy of ends, such as that upon which the belief in the decay of nature rests, must imply some sort of qualitative hierarchy.[48]

The continuous mutability of forms, in the Lucretian pattern, may be regarded as merely a reminder of the eternity of matter, and it is by letting an ultimate permanence prevail over periodic change that men such as Leroy and Hakewill oppose the idea of decay, finding in each age its proper genius and in the whole a perfection lacking in the parts. Hakewill goes so far as to show mutability and decay to be incompatible.[49] As Lucretius sees it, the eternity need not be of this world, for other worlds will succeed this one: "*Death* dissolves, but not annihilates."[50]

But Lucretius, by showing that the world as we know it must some day come to a natural end, supports the belief that nature is now in process of decaying; he is actually recognized by Hakewill as among the most influential authorities for that belief. When the atoms rebel, Lucretius says, the world will return to the original seed; it is already crumbling to its first atomies. Nature is weary and exhausted; the process of disintegration, to which the heavens are also subject, has already begun. The whole world is mutable because the parts are mutable. Change is the great lord of the world, and time its agent. Age and decrepitude are here, and the end of all is inevitable:

> Now I must teach, the *World,* as *Years* prevail,
> Must die, this *noble* Frame must *sink* and *fail;*

> . . . .

> *One* fatal hour (dear Youth) must ruine all,
> This glorious Frame, that stood so long, must fall.

> . . . .

[193]

Perhaps thou soon shalt see the *sickning* World
With strong *Convulsions* to *Confusion* hurld;
When every *Rebel* Atom breaks the chain,
And all to *primitive Night* return again.[51]

III. NATURAL MEANS TO A NATURAL END

Thus the question of the world's natural corruption leads direct-ly to the debate over the possibility of the world's natural end, the debate upon which the entire controversy is focused in Book V of the *Apologie*. That the decay of the world is apparent in the signs of its necessary and imminent end, the approach of the end estab-lishing the corruption, hence becomes the third of Goodman's principal arguments. To Goodman's assertion that the decay would ultimately and inevitably have resulted in complete dissolution, unless by God's intervention the world had been preserved, Hake-will answers that only God's supernatural action will destroy an otherwise eternal creation.

If there were a natural end, both are agreed, it would be the logical extension of a natural principle of decay. Since that which is wholly natural may be established by observation and reason, Goodman by such means demonstrates the world's mortality, whereas Hakewill asserts that the end, being supernatural, can-not be recognized or anticipated in any natural signs and must be accepted on faith alone. Goodman's extensive argument that the creation is apparent to reason is meant to support the same thesis, that the end, too, is reasonable and natural. Hakewill, regularly supporting the *possibility* of eternity, is careful to insist that, though the potential eternity of the world will not be realized, no inbred or natural corruptibility will have any part in the destruction.[52]

On this issue the entire Christian society turns against Aristotle, opposing the eternity of this world with the vision of everlasting life in a world after death. The visible decay of the world becomes for many men a proof of its mortality and a reminder of the glories which await those who are saved. To deny the corruption is to deny the mortality and possibly to embrace the consolations of this world; and many of the texts in which the decay is most fully pro-

[194]

pounded are attempts to refute Aristotle, prove the imminent end
of the world, and move all Christians to repentance.

Conversely, to hold the world to be potentially eternal, as Hakewill does, is to deny that there can be any natural decay. The difference between those who concede the mutability of all created
things but not the decay and those for whom the mutability implies
also a progressive deterioration may thus very well be illuminated
by their attitudes toward the natural mortality of the world. Goodman, for example, characterizes Hakewill's attack upon decay as
an un-Christian defense of the world's eternity, and their long
debate over this point becomes a principal issue of the controversy.[53]

Another consideration which reinforces the association between
mortality and decay is the possibility of a renovation of the universe after its destruction. Swan states the issue most compactly
when he distinguishes between these two opinions regarding the
end of the world:

"1. If it [the world] be destroyed according to the substance,
then it must be so destroyed, as that nothing of it be remaining.

"2. If it be destroyed according to the qualities, then it shall onely
be purged, the substance still abiding."[54]

Like most of the others who believe in the world's decay, Swan
takes the second position, as though the decay, also a question of
quality rather than of substance, had anticipated the very manner
of the end. Those who agree with Swan hold, with Goodman and
in opposition to Hakewill, that the world is simply purified or
purged in the final conflagration; the renovated world will continue to be material, though without contrary qualities and thus
without corruption. When Burnet takes the same position later
in the century, however, he finds himself differing from the common sentiment, which by then, he says, has apparently given
up the idea of the renovation and has settled upon the complete
annihilation of the substance as well as the form of the world.[55]

But, whether natural or supernatural and with or without
promise of a material renovation, the end is inevitable and, accord-

ing to the usual Christian calculations, probably not far off. The world now nears the close of the six thousand years commonly allotted it, and, for the sake of the elect, even this period will be shortened. The expectation of an early destruction increases the concern over decay, whereby we may measure our approach to the end. A few, more daring than the rest, actually attempt to name the date, sometimes setting it only a year or two hence; Goodman conservatively anticipates the end within "a few hundred yeeres."[56]

The manifestations of decay are read as signs of the end. The prophecies of the Book of Revelation are realized in the present disorders of the world. Man's wickedness promises an early end and possibly hastens the day of its coming. Decay in the heavens affords eloquent proof of the whole world's impending destruction. It may be understood that these are, broadly speaking, the last days and that the age of Christ is the last age. The Christian emphasis upon the death of this world and upon the everlasting duration of the next is something that Hakewill, in attacking the doctrine of decay, finds it impossible completely to offset, the authority of the Scriptures and of the Fathers, Cyprian in particular, serving to neutralize his efforts. Though the machinery whereby the decay is explained may be Aristotelian, Lucretian, or even scientific, the motivation toward such a belief is at this time almost wholly Christian, and the ultimate dissolution of the world is inseparable from its present corruption.[57]*

The last age of the world is its old age, and from its old age its end is argued. "It remaineth therefore (of necessitie) that shortly there shall be an ende and consūmation of the worlde," Shakelton explains, "because it is (as it were) subiecte to olde age, and therefore feeble in euery parte." This consummation "cannot be mightily distant," according to Feltham, for we have seen "the *Infancie,* the *Youth,* the *Virility,* all past: Nay, wee haue seene it well stept into *yeeres,* and *declination,* the most infallible *premonitors* of a *dissolution.*"[58]

---

* Detailed references to the various signs of decay as anticipations of the world's end and to discussions of the date of the end are listed in n. 57.

When the world's mortality is made to follow in this fashion from its old age, the process implies a similarity between man's death and the world's death, a similarity often explicitly indicated. The world's end is epitomized and anticipated in man's death. Even the world's eventual renovation is represented in the resurrection of man. Mortality of the whole is thus established by the mortality of the part. If the particular is corruptible, the general must also be corruptible. If the part is mutable, the whole must die. As all things in the world "haue a certaine age and continuance of time, so the Worlde it selfe" has its allotted span. Lest the world "should seem eternall," God has given a warning sign, the "sensible decay and age in the whole frame of the world, and every piece thereof." The growth and decline of each individual only mirrors the life and death of the world itself:

"And that which we see in euery particular body, the same we perceiue to be in the whole frame and course of the world, & in al the estates thereof. For the world hath had his infancie, next his youth, then his mans estate, & now he is in his old-age. For we see how all things decline daily, and continually waxe worse and worse, as it were approching to their end."[59]

IV. THE GREAT WORLD DECAYS IN THE LITTLE

This analogy between whole and part, whereby the decay of the macrocosm is derived from the decay of the microcosm, provides Goodman with his fourth fundamental argument and is enormously important as a summary and epitome of all the others. In the image of microcosm and macrocosm, which does much to establish the doctrine of decay in its full imaginative fecundity, are combined the arguments from the world's purpose, from its natural processes of operation, and from its destruction. The analogy is the most felicitous extension of the argument from part to whole. It presents a pattern faithful to the philosophical and theological plenitude of the universe.

It is intelligible in terms of privation and contrary qualities but is none the less convincing without difficult or disputable metaphysical support. The ancient legends of the declining ages, once concerned almost exclusively with the decay of society, were first applied to the whole physical world by just such an analogy. Throughout the Renaissance, the image of man as microcosm remains a valid way of portraying the structure of the universe, and not simply "a pleasant trope of rhetoric." Once the figure is accepted, the suggestion is almost inescapable that the frailty of man's estate is reflected in the world at large.[60]

The image of the microcosm, furthermore, epitomizes better than any other single argument the Christian philosophy of the whole organism. The microcosm combines in man the corrupt and the incorruptible, the sensible and the rational, the elemental and the celestial, the discordant and the harmonious. Man is a little world, sharing his body with the elements, his soul with God. He is the "truest Mappe of the World, a summarie and compendious other World," "the quintessence, extracted from the Macrocosm." The seasons of his life are like the seasons of the world, his seven ages are the seven planets, and the complexions of his body are the elements of nature. *"All is in Man,* both Heaven and Earth, Stars, and Elements; and also the Number Three of the Deity." He may well be called

> Of the great world, the small epitomie,
> Of the dead world, the live, and quicke anatomie.

In him, in *"the Little-World, wherein the Great is show'n,"* we may best understand the world and God himself. "The world is a great Volume, and man the Index of that Booke; Even in the body of man, you may turne to the whole world; This body is an Illustration of all Nature; Gods recapitulation of all that he had said before, in his *Fiat lux,* and *Fiat firmamentum,* and in all the rest, said or done, in all the six dayes."[61]

Opposed to the use of such an analogy in argument, Hakewill protests that any inference drawn from man to nature is, of necessity, infirm and imperfect, for the microcosm and the macrocosm "subsist not of the same principles, nor are in all things alike."[62] Believing that the little and great worlds, so called, have none of the reciprocal or interlocking symmetry often attributed to them, Hakewill insists there is no way for man's sin to be transmitted to the external world. The decay of the individual, far from indicating the decay of the world, serves to maintain the world; loss in the elements is restored by a process of compensation, and decay of the parts is repaired in the great world but not in the little. The operation of cycles assures us that what is true at one time need not be true at another and that what is true of part is not true of the whole.*

Important in this connection is Hakewill's refusal to recognize any loss whatsoever in the heavens. Though the figure of the microcosm may not, in itself, do violence to common sense, yet, according to Hakewill, the immutability of the heavens, when contrasted with the mutability of man and earth, is sufficient to discredit the entire analogy. Hakewill's refutation, to the extent to which it is dependent in this fashion upon the perfection and inviolability of the heavens, thus places him in a position which will soon become untenable, as the heavens are almost universally recognized to be subject to change.

The pattern of the microcosm and the macrocosm is rejected on more substantial grounds, however, and in Hakewill's own day. When man is no longer the great end of things, neither can he remain the great measure of things; and writers such as Wilkins, Power, and Spencer, by denying the one, dispose also of the other. When man is removed from the center of the world, when other worlds—possibly with other inhabitants—compete for the dignity which had been man's alone, when he becomes simply one among the creatures and the world is no more directed to his use and pleasure, then the idea that man is a microcosm—the epitome and quintessence of the whole world—has lost its power to satisfy the mind and move the spirit.[64]

Once more it is apparent, in the debate between Goodman and Hakewill over the microcosm, that the order about which they are

* The idea of cycles, though used by Hakewill to refute the concept of decay, can be turned to an opposite end, as in William Temple's argument that cycles preclude progress.[63]

[199]

contending is a logical order. Their differences cannot be resolved, therefore, by what they see and measure. The signs of decay are sufficient to satisfy Goodman and the signs of constancy to satisfy Hakewill, though actually neither of them rests his argument upon the signs which he cites. Between them they present evidence enough to confirm both positions, but not enough to prove either. The signs of decay are offered in order to ensnare the natural man and awaken the sluggish and unrepentant heart, but the last stage of corruption, like the first and eternal vision of grace, is seen in all signs or in no signs.

Nor is Hakewill's refutation ever as effective as it might be, for whatever notion of progress or even of cycles develops as part of the Christian philosophy of history is circumscribed by the certainty of the world's mortality. The Christian philosophy of history is the Christian epic of creation and dissolution, for man and for world alike. Christian philosophy surrounds with a beginning and end the recovered segment of recorded time; the whole world is man's world, and its history can be reckoned only by the covenant between man and God. Life can be only a preparation for death. We cannot move in this world toward a fuller revelation of the truth, for the truth has already been long revealed. The vision either of progress or of cycles is foreshortened by the expectation of the end and is obscured by the realization that all achievements in this life are mean and trivial when seen in the light of future glories.

We see, then, in its refutation, how the image of the microcosm, like the belief in the decay of nature, gains strength from an assumption that man is center and end of the universe, "greater then the greater World," "*Lord* of the *World* Epitomiz'd." He is immortal in a world of mortality, and, though the great world dies in the little, yet shall the little outlive the great. His greatness will survive the death of all,

"for man subsisting, who is, and will then truly appear, a microcosm, the world cannot be said to be destroyed. For the eyes of God, and perhaps also of our glorified selves, shall as really behold and contemplate the world in its epitome or contracted essence, as now it doth at large and in its dilated substance."[65]

[200]

Though he was "last created, as the end of the rest, an Epitome and Mappe of the World, a compendious little other world," he was designed for the highest place, "the last in execution, but first in intention." In him is the whole macrocosm; God said, "FACIAMVS HOMINEM, let vs make Man; that is, a wonderful Creature: and therfore is called in greek MICROCOSMOS, a little world in himself." Actually, "the Philosopher draws man into too narrow a table, when he says he is *Microcosmos*, an Abridgement of the world in little"; he is, instead, *"Mundum Magnum*, a world to which all the rest of the world is but subordinate."

"IT is too little to call Man a *little World;* Except *God*, Man is a *diminutive* to nothing. Man consistes of more pieces, more parts, than the world; than the world doeth, nay than the world is. And if those pieces were extended, and stretched out in Man, as they are in the world, Man would bee the *Gyant*, and the Worlde the *Dwarfe*, the World but the *Map*, and the Man the *World*."[66]*

Man is thus the center and end of all creation. The hope of the world is lodged in his virtue. In the sin of the little world the great world sins, and in his death it, too, must die, for release of the evil forces in man sets free the principles of evil in the world. Man is the *"nexus & naturae vinculum*," binding together all the rest of nature; and when he breaks his own bonds, the whole world as well is unbound. The sins of the microcosm "tainted the whole creation, and brought shame vpon all the frame of heauen, and earth." Man is "this little world, which first set on fire, and inflamed" the great world, which destroys the world's order and deprives it of life.[68]

The signs of old age and death are therefore upon the world as well as upon man, the old age of the world indicating, for the

---

* As microcosm, it may be noted, man must suffer for the evils and corruptions of the whole world; he "could be a *Microcosm*, a world in himself, no other way, except all the misery of the world fell upon him." For our sins, God "brings the heauen, the earth, the ayre, and whatsoeuer was created for mans, vse, to be his enemie"; because man is a very world in himself, his transgressing the law of his nature must draw other evil after it. Having once been the glorious center of all creation, he suffers more poignantly in his present degradation. We know that man has fallen if, designed for the world's ornament, he is now its despoiler, its meanest creature, and its victim.[67]

world as for man, "the decaying parte thereof." Both these worlds "doe now wax ould,"

"That is to say. *Macrocosmus,* and *Microcosmus,* which is to say, the greater world, & the lesser world. And the longer that lyfe doth linger in eyther of them, so much the worse is nature in each of them troubled and vexed."[69]

As it is with the little world, so it must be with the great world; "man changeth and declineth daily, not being now as heretofore he hath been; and so also as a good consequence it must follow, that the greater world doth also suffer change, and, by declining, alteration." If man, *"who is so considerable a* part *of the world, doth decay in his* Species, *'tis a shrewd symptom that the* Whole *is* en decadence, *in a declining state."* If man declines, "then assuredly the whole world cannot be excused from corruption." When we see the decay of the microcosm, we know that the macrocosm, too, can come to no end but corruption and death.[70]

In this concept of the microcosm, which symbolizes an ordered, finite world in which the whole is seen in the part and the end in the beginning, is thus centered the belief in the world's decay. Man is the image of the world, which was created for his use and which is condemned for his sin. The world's corruption depends upon man's corruption, man's corruption upon his Fall, his Fall upon God's original grace. By God's grace the great world was fashioned for the little world, and the whole for God's honor. The process of decay, reflected as it is in the decay of each individual man, is further confirmed by the promise and imminent approach of the end of all.

The problem is urgent because time is running out and the signs of decay and death, once we know that they are the signs of decay and death, may be read in every leaf that falls. Man's corruption has taken root in nature, and the daughter of time is now only death. It is time itself which brings all things to "decay and wither"; it is time itself that "hath wasted and worne out that liuely vertue of Nature," in man and in the whole world. The turning of the hours brings the same decline and end to the world as to man, for the same reasons, and by the same means;

"for this punishment (*morte morieris*) though it principally concernes man, yet the whole world cannot be exempted from it, being directed and ordained onely for mans vse, containing in it selfe the very same seedes, and causes of death and destruction; and as it is most fit and agreeable to our present condition, that being corruptible in our selues, we should likewise dwell in houses of corruption."[71]

It is here in Goodman's fourth and final argument that we may see most clearly the major differences between the two opposing philosophies. Goodman finds decay in a world in which he cannot discover the complete harmony of the presupposed state of perfection. The decay of any part of the world, particularly of its most glorious part, man, is taken as indication of decay in any other part or in the whole; for, once the harmony is destroyed, the state of nature becomes the state of corruption. The appeal to reason and to natural man is justified by the fact that Goodman's world is a world fully understood—in its origins, its way of relating God to man, its complete integration of part and whole.

The decay of the world may be derived from the Fall of man, from any decline in the species or forms of things (such as the decrease in man's size or the declination of the sun), from any anticipation of a natural end of the world, or simply from any disparity between the actual and the exemplary. The irony is greater and the sermon more eloquent when Goodman reminds us that man, who because of his sin is the weakest and most depraved creature in the world, is also the world's image and sum, the microcosm which contains the macrocosm.

This philosophy is replaced by one wherein our knowledge is understood to be fragmentary and the all-inclusive image of microcosm and macrocosm is regarded as a misleading figure of speech. No argument may be so extended from man to nature, it is asserted, for any defection in the part has its compensation in the continuity of the whole. Because the powers of nature are unchanged and unchangeable, any variation in the forms or the state of nature is temporary and local. Hakewill by such reasoning attacks the metaphysical unity of the theory of the world's decay.

Later, even more thoroughly separating the realms of man and nature, reason and faith, natural and supernatural, others deny both the physical basis for the belief in decay and the teleological order which permits the decay to be established by any means other than the physical. The doctrine which had brought despair to Goodman, and to so many others before him, is made untenable when men become unwilling to characterize the whole world either in terms of the mutability of its parts or in terms of the ends for which it was designed or in terms of the ideal which it no longer approximates.

Notes

See the Bibliography for more complete descriptions of works cited in footnotes.

CHAPTER I

1. Godfrey Goodman, *The Fall of Man*, p. 391.
2. John Milton, *Of Education*, in *The Student's Milton*, p. 726.
3. *Pvrchas His Pilgrimage*, p. 42; *Pilgrimes*, I, 25.
4. George Williamson, "Mutability, Decay, and Seventeenth-Century Melancholy."
5. Wilkins, *A Discourse concerning a New World* (1640); Power, *Experimental Philosophy* (1664); Spencer, *A Discourse concerning Prodigies* (1665).

CHAPTER II

1. Now called *The Fall of Adam from Paradice*. It is here that Goodman apologizes for his book as "the worke of a Countrey Parson, not of a Bishop."
2. *Apologie*, Book V, sig. Aaaa2; see also R. F. Jones, *Ancients and Moderns*, p. 292, n. 8. See below, chap. iii, n. 4, for comment on the pagination of the *Apologie*.
3. *Apologie*, sig. [b5], and p. 1.
4. *Fall*, pp. 27–28.
5. *Ibid.*, pp. 27, 64, 108, 128; see also pp. 159–60, 200.
6. *Ibid.*, pp. 214 ff.
7. *Ibid.*, p. 348.
8. *Ibid.*, p. 404.
9. *Ibid.*, sig. A4ᵛ.
10. *Ibid.*, pp. 70–71.
11. *Ibid.*, pp. 6, 11–12.
12. *Ibid.*, pp. 5, 12.
13. *Ibid.*, p. 382.
14. *Ibid.*, p. 11; see also p. 8.
15. *Ibid.*, pp. 400–401, 413; see also pp. 12, 268–69.
16. *Apologie*, V, 93; see also p. 47; V, 80 ff.
17. *Fall*, pp. 387–89.
18. See pp. 29–31.
19. *Fall*, pp. 392–95.
20. *Ibid.*, pp. 401, 444.
21. *Ibid.*, p. 391; see also pp. 262–69.
22. *Ibid.*, pp. 11–13.
23. *Ibid.*, pp. 407–14.
24. *Ibid.*, sig. A4–A4ᵛ and p. 11. This general argument of Goodman's,

that his position more clearly does homage to God, is developed at length by Goodman in the *Apologie* (V, 118 ff., 136), where Hakewill expands on his earlier statement (p. 20) that belief in decay "blunts the edge of vertuous endeavours" and that there can be no credit to God in creating a universe that will run down.

25. *Fall,* pp. 66, 415, 417–18; see also pp. 17, 26–27.

26. *Ibid.,* pp. 418–20; see also pp. 27, 428.

27. *Ibid.,* sig. [a5ᵛ]; see also pp. 13, 17–18, 419.

28. *Ibid.,* p. 182; see also sigs. A3ᵛ–A4ᵛ, [a7]; pp. 85, 109, 158–60, 200, 217–18, 338, 415, 435. Goodman often returns to the figure of the lanced wound (see pp. 160, 274–75, 415).

29. *Ibid.,* sig. [a6] and p. 402. On the text (Mic. 7:8) see F. Y. St. Clair, "The Myth of the Golden Age from Spenser to Milton," p. 146.

30. *Fall,* p. 99; see also sig. [a5]–[a5ᵛ] and pp. 271, 281–82.

31. *Ibid.,* p. 354. Note the debate on this point in *Apologie,* V, 38 ff.

32. *Fall,* p. 441; see also pp. 17–18, 271, 402. This providence of God's is transmitted by means of spirits or angels. We should credit the good angels for our blessings just as we blame, in our corruption, the bad ones for our torments. Not only the actions of men but also those of the physical universe are subject to the control of spirits, those "influences, qualities not materiall," which direct the planets and thereby act upon the earth: "And surely the heauens can bee no otherwise moued then by intelligences, which in effect are Angels: for in nature, no reason can bee assigned why they should moue" by any other means (*ibid.,* p. 30; see also pp. 59, 420, 424).

33. *Ibid.,* p. 229; see also sig. [A5], and pp. 17–18, 65, 415–16, 435–36.

34. *Apologie,* V, 145.

35. *Ibid.,* V, 149.

36. *Fall,* p. 90; see also pp. 33, 160, 432–33.

37. *Ibid.,* p. 91.

38. *Ibid.,* pp. 17–18; for the conflict between man and the creatures see pp. 65–66, 218, 220.

39. *Ibid.,* pp. 68, 107, 423, 427; see also pp. 332, 348.

40. *Ibid.,* pp. 348–49, 107; see also p. 27.

41. *Apologie,* V, 4; VI, 323.

42. *Fall,* pp. 27–28, 33, 337.

43. *Ibid.,* pp. 89, 242–43. Other punishments are discussed later (pp. 36–42) as simple signs of man's corruption, which is the way Goodman presents them. Meanwhile, see *Fall,* pp. 34, 44–45, 107, 231, 331, 393, 437.

44. *Fall,* p. 27.

45. *Ibid.,* pp. 17, 27, 217, 314.

46. *Ibid.,* p. 104; see also pp. 215–20, 226–30.

47. The motion of the heavens "is so strange and so wonderfull, that the minde of man being an intelligent spirit, notwithstanding our studies, our circles, excentric, concentric, epicicle, and the like, yet wee cannot possibly describe the motion, and trace out their paths, but we must be inforced to

vse impossible suppositiõs, that the earth should turne vpon wheeles, and
moue with her owne weight" (*ibid.*, p. 30).

48. *Ibid.*, pp. 16, 432.

49. *Ibid.*, p. 16.

50. *Ibid.*, p. 427.

51. *Ibid.*, pp. 349, 386; *Apologie*, V, 143.

52. *Apologie*, pp. 75-76; V, 101; see also pp. 189-92.

53. *Fall*, pp. 49, 224-27.

54. Anthony à Wood (*Athenae Oxonienses*, Vol. III, col. 256) characterizes
Goodman's treatise as "relating to the eternity of the world, or for the
universal and perpetual decay thereof, whereby Goodman would prove the
fall of man."

55. *Fall*, p. 14.

56. See pp. 29-32.

57. *Fall*, pp. 26-27.

58. *Ibid.*, pp. 14, 15. Hakewill's answer to the whole question of corrupt-
ibility is an unequivocal denial that there is any tendency to decay: "To the
Authour of Nature it is every way as easie to make as unmake" (*Apologie*,
V, 99).

59. *Fall*, p. 350.

60. *Apologie*, V, 134, 172; see also *Fall*, p. 382.

61. *Fall*, pp. 390, 422.

62. *Apologie*, V, 44-45.

63. *Fall*, p. 24.

64. *Ibid.*, pp. 390-91.

65. *Ibid.*, pp. 99, 271, 281-82, 416.

66. *Ibid.*, pp. 14, 26-27, 390, 417, 422, 435. Hakewill denies privation altogether, holds that the generation set in motion by God in the beginning is
stronger than any subsequent corruption, and, finally, argues that privation
cannot be a principle of all nature because no change or corruption is found
in the celestial bodies: "a *generall* decay it cannot imply except you first
prove privation to be in the Heavens" (*Apologie*, V, 3).

67. *Fall*, p. 32; *Apologie*, V, 140.

68. *Fall*, pp. 15, 17-18; see also pp. 19-23, 206-20.

69. "This world you say ... naturally subsisteth of contrary qualities ...
In which position you either include the celestiall bodies, and so make them
to subsist of contrary qualities as well as the elementary, against all experience, reason and authoritie; or you exclude them as being no part of the
world, which are indeed the noblest of all" (*Apologie*, V, 140-41).

70. *Fall*, pp. 15, 22, 24, 416; *Apologie*, V, 40, 143.

71. *Fall*, p. 349. Text reads "iu the vniuersals."

72. *Ibid.*; see also p. 337 and, for debate on this point, *Apologie*, V, 12-14,
18-25, 101-2, 113, 152-54.

73. *Fall*, pp. 343-44; *Apologie*, V, 158.

74. *Fall*, pp. 354, 383-85.

75. *Ibid.*, pp. 383–85; *Apologie*, V, 102–3, 138, 145.

76. *Apologie*, V, sig. Aaaa ff.

77. *Fall*, p. 27.

78. *Ibid.*, p. 310.

79. *Ibid.*, pp. 53, 56–57.

80. *Ibid.*, p. 62.

81. *Ibid.*, pp. 72–75, 85, 311–30, 336, 337, 364, 399.

82. *Ibid.*, pp. 57, 353, 358, 359, 370.

83. *Ibid.*, pp. 47–48; see also pp. 114, 266.

84. *Ibid.*, pp. 44–45; see also pp. 108–15, 134, 389.

85. *Ibid.*, pp. 62, 115–16, 129–49, 153, 183–86, 200, 393.

86. *Ibid.*, pp. 161–75, 187–91, 238–46.

87. *Ibid.*, pp. 54–60, 116–20, 126, 127, 150–51, 211–12, 231–36.

88. "1. That parts of such different condition, the spirit with the flesh, mortall with immortall, should together subsist. 2. That the soule being coupled, should finde such meane and base entertainment. 3. That notwithstanding the contract, there should be a continuall disagreement & opposition between both. 4. That there should be no manner of subordination or subiectiō, such as were requisite in parts, for the vnitie of one person. 5. That being thus parts of one man, yet they should not bee acquainted with each other, but haue actions, priuate and proper to themselues. 6. That the bodie should hinder euery action of the soule, the senses falsely informing and distracting the vnderstanding. 7. The will deluded with showes, vaine hopes, false promises, receiuing no manner of contentment. 8. The body secretly and cunningly conspires with the faculties of the soule, to set a faction and opposition betweene them. 9. That the comelinesse of parts, the gifts of the body, will not together accompanie the gifts of the minde; but are estranged from each other, and that all the actions of the bodie either betoken 10, shame, 11, or punishment, 12, or slauerie" (*ibid.*, pp. 62–63; see also pp. 28, 36).

89. *Ibid.*, pp. 31, 34–37.

90. *Ibid.*, pp. 51–52, 124–25, 206–7.

91. *Ibid.*, p. 212.

92. *Ibid.*, pp. 2–3, 21; see also pp. 5, 250–61, 271-74, 352, 354, 366, 377; *Apologie*, V, 121.

93. *Fall*, p. 248; see also pp. 350–52, 369, 372, 373–76; *Apologie*, V, 177–78. Goodman shares a general complaint against enclosures (see William Stafford, *Compendious or Briefe Examination of Certayne Ordinary Complaints*, pp. 15–16; Phillip Stubbes, *The Anatomie of Abuses*, p. 117, and *The Second Part of the Anatomie of Abuses*, p. 27; William Vaughan, *The Golden-Groue*, sig. C3ᵛ, etc.). But nowhere does Goodman attribute any of the blame for such conditions to the lords of the manors, as does, for example, Richard Brathwaite, who sees the decay of noble houses as God's punishment for the "enclosing of Landes, racking and raysing of rente, with extreme fining of poore Tenants" (*Some Rules and Orders for the Government*

of the House of an Earle, p. 7); see also St. Clair, "Myth of the Golden Age,"
p. 152.

94. *Apologie*, V, 132, 171; see also *Fall*, pp. 376–77.

95. *Fall*, sigs. a^v, a3^v–a4.

96. See p. 75.

97. *Fall*, pp. 16, 19; see also pp. 224–30, 285–86, 366–68.

98. *Ibid.*, pp. 16, 25–26, 379; *Apologie*, V, 61–65.

99. *Fall*, pp. 16–17, 332–33.

100. *Ibid.*, pp. 281, 378.

101. *Apologie*, V, 172–73.

102. *Fall*, pp. 158, 379; see also pp. 269, 332–33, 378–79, 381; *Apologie*, V, 196–97.

CHAPTER III

1. Goodman's *The Fall of Man*, it will be remembered, appeared first in 1616, then in 1618, and again in 1629.

2. Hakewill states and answers minor objections to his thesis (Book IV, chap. xiii, secs. 7, 8), adds further authorities to the long list already invoked in his behalf (IV, i, 2), illustrates his case in somewhat greater detail (IV, x, 4, 5), and, in general, expands the work without affecting the argument. He appends several "Advertisements to the Learned Reader," in which he reprints testimonials, reviews changes made, and anticipates further changes.

3. Book I, chap. iv, sec. 5; II, ix, 3, 7; III, i, 3; III, ii, 4; III, v, 2, 7; IV, iv, 12; IV, vii, 9; IV, x, 6, 7; IV, xi, 10, 11, 12; IV, xii, 6.

4. Manuscripts of Hakewill's arguments against Goodman, differing in many respects from the printed versions (see *DNB*, "Hakewill"), are in Ashmolean MSS 1284 and 1510. The *Apologie* has a continuous pagination for Books I–IV and a separate pagination for Books V–VI. All references to passages from Books I–IV are made without indicating the number of the book. References to Books V and VI are so specified. Unless otherwise designated, all references to the *Apologie* indicate the 1635 edition.

5. *Apologie*, sig. [b5]; see also p. 1, where Hakewill opens his argument by saying that the "opinion of the Worlds Decay is so generally received, not onely among the Vulgar, but of the Learned, both Divines and others, that the very commonnesse of it makes it currant with many, without any further examination."

6. *Ibid.*, VI, 272–73; see also "The Epistle Dedicatory," sig. a2^v.

7. *Ibid.*, sig. [b6^v]. In the second edition this was followed by Hakewill's respectful note (Hakewill was an archdeacon, Goodman a bishop) that Goodman had raised certain objections which would be met as soon as possible (*Apologie* [1630 ed.], sig. [Aaa6^v]); in the third edition the testimonial remains, but the note is deleted, replaced by the debate in Book V.

8. *Apologie*, V, sig. Aaaa.

9. *Ibid.*, V, sigs. Aaaa^v–Aaaa2^v and pp. 49, 78.

10. *Ibid.*, V, 191. Text reads *"agitation of of."*

11. *Ibid.*, sigs. a3^v–[a4], [b5].

12. *Ibid.,* sig. c4.
13. *Ibid.,* pp. 16–17.
14. *Ibid.,* p. 18; see also pp. 45–46.
15. *Ibid.,* VI, [228], 248. The quotations extend through pp. [228]–248 and include, pointedly, several passages from Goodman, passages which ostensibly make Hakewill's point but which, restored to context, show Goodman to be either explaining why the rate of decline, especially in the heavens, is no faster than it is or else contending that God by his special providence sustains the universe which otherwise would return to chaos.
16. *Ibid.,* p. 20; VI, 319–28.
17. *Ibid.,* pp. 20, 22; V, 132.
18. *Ibid.,* p. 23; see also VI, 308–19, 327.
19. *Ibid.,* p. 25.
20. *Ibid.,* p. 26; V, 133.
21. See pp. 80–82. R. F. Jones (*Ancients and Moderns,* p. 33) gives more emphasis to the hopefulness implied in Hakewill's position: "He sounds a rallying call for man to use the powers given him, and he will find that neither time nor necessity has sway over him." But the constant vision of annihilation remains for Hakewill, and not until this also is tempered or destroyed is the mind of man directed more to the present than to the past.
22. Books V and VI of the *Apologie,* appended to the third edition in answer to objections of the unconvinced, are organized independently of the rest of the text.
23. *Apologie,* pp. 44–45.
24. Some estimate of Hakewill's emphasis on the various parts of his demonstration may be seen in the fact that he spends some 41 pages refuting decay of the heavens, 54 pages on the elements, 82 on man's body, 77 on his mind, and 227 on his manners and morals, a subject on which the fullest evidence is, of course, available.
25. *Apologie,* V, 57. Text reads *"your booke hee full."* The arguments themselves in this book and the sixth are discussed in conjunction with the points of the controversy which they illuminate.
26. See pp. 51–53.
27. *Apologie,* V, 84–93.
28. *Ibid.,* p. 47; V, 88, 93–94.
29. *Ibid.,* V, 161–62. Text reads "reasonables."
30. *Ibid.,* V, 111–12; VI, 273–307.
31. *Ibid.,* V, 170; VI, 248.
32. *Ibid.,* V, 38, 119; VI, 265; see also "Argvment," opp. half-title page, and V, 106, 141.
33. *Ibid.,* p. 46; V, 126; see also V, 26.
34. *Ibid.,* p. 114.
35. *Ibid.,* V, 115, 117, 143–44; see also V, 48, 156, 163.
36. *Ibid.,* pp. 87, 150; V, 144, 161.
37. *Ibid.,* pp. 56, 150; V, 48.

38. *Ibid.,* V, 17.

39. *Ibid.,* p. 79; see also p. 48; V, 32.

40. *Ibid.,* pp. 92, 100, 102 ff., 111.

41. *Ibid.,* pp. 86–88, 98, 106.

42. *Ibid.,* pp. 135, 169; V, 173.

43. *Ibid.,* p. 84.

44. *Ibid.,* p. 75; V, 101; see also V, 2, 21, 48, 143–44, 167–68.

45. *Ibid.,* pp. 56, 79; V, 7, 32, 115.

46. *Ibid.,* VI, 323; V, 51, 119, 148–49.

47. *Ibid.,* p. 119. See VI, 325–26, for a statement of the conventional ordering of fire, air, water, and earth in the spheres of the universe.

48. *Ibid.,* p. 36; V, 55, 117.

49. *Ibid.,* pp. 147, 163.

50. *Ibid.,* pp. 151, 153.

51. *Ibid.,* pp. 139–42; V, 62, 65.

52. *Ibid.,* pp. 36, 126–27.

53. *Ibid.,* p. 162; V, 4; VI, 265.

54. *Ibid.,* p. 32; V, 13.

55. *Ibid.,* p. 170.

56. *Ibid.,* pp. 42–43, 186. This last passage follows in detail a statement made by Sir Walter Ralegh (*The History of the World,* p. 77). See p. 134.

57. *Apologie,* pp. 207, 222–24, 229; V, 58.

58. *Ibid.,* pp. 36, 129, 244–48, 251; V, 5, 13.

59. *Ibid.,* pp. 253, 268; V, 130.

60. *Ibid.,* pp. 283–85, 287, 290, 298–305.

61. *Ibid.,* pp. 294, 306–12, 316, 319, 323–30, 530; V, 166–67, 177–78.

62. *Ibid.,* pp. 276, 278, 299–300, 302.

63. *Ibid.,* pp. 268–69, 331–32, 346–47; V, 121–22; see also sig. a3; pp. 1 ff., 262–67, 342, 450, 475–76, 547; V, 127–29.

64. *Ibid.,* pp. 364–99, 502–3, 506–24; V, 166–67, 183–89; see also pp. 270–71, 357–59, 494, 547–48.

65. *Ibid.,* pp. 407, 461–63, 468–69.

66. *Ibid.,* sig. b3ᵛ; V, 134; see also p. 27. This idea, developed by Bacon (see pp. 130–31), was a common one later in the century.

67. R. F. Jones, *The Background of the Battle of the Books,* p. 114: "Hakewill showed how a tangible basis of comparison might be obtained by observing discoveries and inventions." Like Jones, St. Clair ("Myth of the Golden Age," p. 187, n. 24) stresses the "importance of Hakewill's use of this method."

68. *Apologie,* V, 99; see also pp. 22–27.

69. *Apologie,* V, 2, 97.

70. *Ibid.,* p. 33; V, 140–41, 147.

71. *Ibid.,* pp. 57, 59; V, 9, 131.

72. *Ibid.,* p. 33; V, 5, 19, 22–23, 101, 141; VI, 266.

73. *Ibid.,* V, 7, 101–2, 119, 140–41, 148; see also pp. 62, 65–66.

74. *Apologie,* V, 7, 12, 22–23, 101–2, 118, 145, 148.

75. *Ibid.,* p. 153; V, 13, 20, 167.

76. *Ibid.,* V, 2.

77. *Ibid.,* sig. c; see also *Apologie* (1630 ed.), sig. Bbb.

78. *Apologie,* pp. 52, 58, 103–4, 127, 222, 251; V, 4. It does not occur to Hakewill that the cranes and the rats, too, might be reduced in scale.

79. *Ibid.,* pp. 54, 259; see also pp. 40, 50.

80. *Ibid.,* sig. b2; V, 58, 101–2, 119, 125, 192; see also pp. 55–56.

81. *Apologie,* V, 42–43. It is even possible that the creation was instantaneous, only to be "distinguished by *Moses,* into the workes of severall dayes for our better apprehension" (*ibid.,* V, 142).

82. *Ibid.,* pp. 24, 50, 553; V, 144.

83. *Ibid.,* V, 43–44.

84. *Ibid.,* pp. 18, 45, 559; V, 103, 118, 159; see also opp. half-title page.

85. *Ibid.,* sig. e; pp. 589, 597, 602, 604; V, 145–46, 149.

86. *Ibid.,* pp. 565, 568; V, 146–47, 152, 156; VI, 331–60.

87. *Ibid.,* V, 103, 138–39, 145–47, 149, 152–55, 164.

CHAPTER IV

1. *An Abridgemēt of the Notable Worke of Polidore Vergile,* fol. v–vᵛ.

2. Palingenius, *The Zodiake of Life,* pp. 117, 221; see also pp. 115, 161, 211, 216, 217; Pedro Mexia, *The Forest or Collection of Historyes,* fols. 1ᵛ, 2, 23. Mexia's *Silva de varia leccion* (1542) was translated into French in 1552 and thence into English by Thomas Fortescue.

3. *The Whole Workes,* pp. 55, 407. The rubric (p. 55) reads: "The condition of the worlde shall waxe worse and worse." See also *Doctrinal Treatises,* p. 17. For similar statements by another early reformer see *The Decades* of Henry Bullinger: Decade I, Sermon viii, in I, 153; Decade III, Sermon x, in II, 362; and *passim.*

4. *Luther on the Creation,* I, 16.

5. *Ibid.,* pp. 83, 115, 118, 121, 136–37, 153.

6. *Ibid.,* pp. 81, 83, 116, 118, 135–39, 153, 166, 314–17.

7. *Ibid.,* pp. 137, 153, 165, 314. For the destruction of Paradise by the Flood see pp. 150, 164, 352; for various other effects see pp. 81, 315–16, 318.

8. *Ibid.,* pp. 320, 330; see also pp. 150, 316, 317, 319, 331; *Conversations with Luther,* p. 229; see also pp. 147, 245, 250. See also *ibid.,* p. 236, for another statement that "things are constantly getting worse."

9. *Les Devins, ov commentaire des principales sortes de devinations,* pp. 468, 479–80. The work was first published in 1553, the French translation in 1584. The translator may have been Simon Goulart, who in his commentary on Du Bartas refers to the work of Peucer.

10. *The Poetical Works of Sir David Lyndsay,* I, 227, 265–66, 269, 274, 280–82; II, 230, 272; III, 133–40. The first edition of the *Dialog* is dated 1554; for comment see Laing's notes (III, 173–77). This material was called to my attention by Miss Marjorie Nicolson.

Ursinus, *The Summe of Christian Religion,* sig. [A4] and pp. 181, 183–84,

333. The Heidelberg Catechism, from which this was developed, was approved and adopted by the German Calvinists.

11. *A World of Wonders,* trans. R. Carew, pp. 21, 30, 48, 57.

12. Marjorie Nicolson, "The 'New Astronomy' and English Literary Imagination," and "The Microscope and English Imagination."

13. The work, a review of current scientific and philosophical problems, was written in 1575, published a year later, and translated as *The Wonderfull Woorkmanship of the World* in 1578.

14. *Wonderfull Woorkmanship,* fols. 81–83.

15. *The Spanish Mandeuile of Miracles,* fols. 23^v, 52. The rubric on fol. 23^v reads: "The longer the world lasteth the lesser are the people in stature."

16. *The Sermons,* pp. 169, 172. These passages are in the ninth sermon, preached at the death of Charles IX in 1574.

17. *Ibid.,* Sermon 18. Other complaints over the moral failings of the times are found in the sermons of Thomas White, preached in 1576 and 1577, published in 1578 (*A sermō,* sig. Aiii and *passim*). Many popular ballads of the period also urge repentance for the sins which corrupt the earth with monsters and bring miseries to man (see *Ancient Ballads & Broadsides Published in England in the Sixteenth Century*).

18. *Works,* II, 222, 234.

19. *The French Academie,* pp. 82 (including rubric), 170, 331, 334–35, 438, 458. Part I was translated into English in 1586, Part II in 1594, Part III in 1601, and Part IV in 1618. The work was enormously popular both in England and on the Continent.

20. *Ibid.,* pp. 290, 528, 554, 698, 997.

21. *Ibid.,* pp. 403, 697.

22. *Ibid.,* p. 698.

23. *La seconde semaine,* a series of biblical stories beginning with the Fall of man, followed in 1584, after which the two parts regularly appeared together. Urban Holmes lists over forty editions of *Les Semaines,* and the poet was exceedingly popular in England as well. Sylvester's translations were published in part in 1592, 1595, and 1598, and complete in 1605, 1608, 1611, 1613, 1621, 1633, and 1641.

24. *Du Bartas His Divine Weekes and Workes,* in *The Complete Works of Joshuah Sylvester,* Vol. I. See especially *First Week,* I, 374–491; II, 249–54, 1031–62; *Second Week,* I, i, 196–211, 292–99, 726–29; I, iii, 132–83, 208–43, 768 ff.; I, iv, 756–85.

25. See V. K. Whitaker, "Du Bartas' Use of Lucretius."

26. *The Six Bookes of a Commonweale,* pp. 406 ff.

27. *Methodvs historica,* pp. 298–310.

28. *Of the Interchangeable Covrse, or Variety of Things in the Whole World,* trans. Robert Ashley, sig. [A3]. Several French editions were published some twenty years earlier; an Italian translation was issued in 1585; Ashley's is the only English version (1594).

[213]

29. *Ibid.*, fols. 124^v–125.

30. *Ibid.*, sig. B; fols. 3, 30^v, 127^v, 129^v. The notion that the elements, though mutable, are indestructible and that nothing is utterly annihilated appears also in John Rastell's *The Nature of the Four Elements* (1519). The Aristotelian principle that, though *"all other thinges in the worlde by tyme be consumed,"* the heavens are inalterable is accepted by Robert Recorde in *The Castle of Knowledge* (1556), sig. a4^v; p. 7, and *passim.*

31. *Interchangeable Covrse,* sig. B; fols. 1^v–3.

32. *Ibid.,* fols. 3, 30^v, 126^v.

33. *Ibid.,* fols. 32^v, 107–107^v, 111, 112^v, 114–20, 123^v, 125^v–126, 127^v–128^v.

34. Quoted in J. Lewis McIntyre, *Giordano Bruno,* p. 221.

35. Jones, *Ancients and Moderns,* p. 292, n. 4; Montaigne, *Essayes,* Book II, chap. xxxvii; Book III, chap. vii; Banister, *Historie of Man,* sig. Bii.

36. *A Discourse of Constancy,* trans. Nathaniel Wanley (1670), "To the Reader," sig. [*8]; pp. 86, 88–91, 95. Earlier translations appeared in 1595 and 1650.

37. *Ibid.,* pp. 95, 195, [252]–[254], 284.

38. *Ibid.,* pp. 156–65 and *passim.*

39. *A Blazyng Starre,* sig. aii^v.

40. *Ibid.,* sigs. Aiiii^v, Av, Biii, Diii.

41. *Ibid.,* sigs. Aiiii^v–Av.

42. *The Anatomie of Abuses,* pp. 187–88.

43. *Ibid.,* pp. viii, 24, 55; see also *The Second Part of the Anatomie of Abuses,* p. 3.

44. Twyne, *Shorte and Pithie Discourse,* p. 18; Rogers, *General Session,* sig. ¶iiii; pp. 59, 61, 79. Rogers translates and supplements Sheltoo à Geveren's work on the end of the world.

45. *A Worke concerning the Trewnesse of Christian Religion,* trans. Philip Sidney and Arthur Golding, sig. B2; pp. 89, 107, 251, 267.

46. Fols. 46^v, 48, 52–53^v, 56^v, 65, and *passim.*

47. *Batman vppon Bartholome,* fols. 118^v, 120, 121, 135^v, 141^v, 152^v, 165.

48. *A Golden Chaine,* p. 11; *The Foundation of Christian Religion,* p. 1034, and *An Exposition of the Symbole or Creede of the Apostles,* p. 422, both bound with *A Golden Chaine.* See also Thomas Tymme, *A Plaine Discouerie of Ten English Lepers;* Thomas Nash, *Christ's Tears over Jerusalem,* pp. 123 ff.; and Nash's *Pierce Penilesse,* pp. 86–88.

49. *The Complete Poems,* pp. 64, 66–68, and *passim; The Triumphs over Death; Marie Magdalen's Funerall Teares.*

50. *Pavl,* pp. 277, 368; *Genesis,* pp. 13, 63; *Daniel,* pp. 58, 86, 234, 477.

51. *The Workes,* I, 29.

52. *The Theatre of Gods Ivdgements,* sig. [Avi]–[Avi^v], and pp. 1, 3.

53. *A Learned Summary upon the Famous Poeme of William of Saluste Lord of Bartas,* sig. A2^v; Part I, pp. 83, 193; Part II, pp. 67, 83, 145–46. In another sense, as Goulart points out, God's constant care preserves the integrity of the universe, so that the corruption should be regarded as super-

ficial. He makes clear, however, that without this active providence of God the world would have perished many times (Part I, pp. 304–6). Goulart's commentary on *La Semaine* was published in 1583, and the commentary on *La seconde semaine* had appeared by 1589.

54. *Learned Summary,* Part I, pp. 26, 83–84, 97, 138, 156, 176; Part II, pp. 67, 76, 80, 83, 89, 140–41. Both Du Bartas and Goulart oppose, however, the practice of foretelling the future from the disposition of the stars (Part I, pp. 58, 162).

55. *Ibid.,* "To the Reader," sig. [*3ᵛ]; Part II, pp. 119, 131, 138–40, 145–46, [242].

56. Thomas Fuller, *Anglorum speculum, or the Worthies of England,* p. 441.

57. *Satires,* pp. 49, 51; and *A Farewell Sermon* (1624), in *The Works,* pp. 464–65.

58. *Times Lamentation,* pp. 147, [191], 194, 195, 234.

59. *Ibid.,* pp. 3, 10, 22, 133, 135, 138, 447.

60. *A Defence of Ivdiciall Astrologie,* pp. 100–101, 132, 364, etc.; *An Astrological Discourse,* pp. 33–35.

61. *The Felicitie of Man,* pp. 3, 5, 6, 375, 483, 618, 631–32, 645–46, 658, 664, 666.

62. *Ibid.,* pp. 35, 67, 95, 98, 154, 194, 318, 321, 329, 330, 332, 337–39, 350, 353, 355–56, 359, 362, 622, 630, 635, 639, 641, 643, 645, 646, 659.

63. *Ibid.,* sig. [A5].

64. *Right Reckoning of Yeares,* pp. 42, 57, 78–82, 91, 100, 104.

65. *Ibid.,* pp. 35, 42, 82, 83.

66. *Ibid.,* pp. 81, 100, 104.

67. *Lapis philosophicvs,* p. 957. See also Don Cameron Allen, "The Degeneration of Man and Renaissance Pessimism," p. 221.

68. *The Accomplishment of the Prophecies,* p. 251. It is interesting to note that in later French editions Du Moulin does not insist that this sign actually portends the destruction of the world but lets it suggest merely the end of some notable period in its history. For further description of the Fall and of the corruption, death, and misery resulting therefrom see *The Bvckler of the Faith,* pp. 69, 79, 89–90; *The Anatomy of Arminianisme,* pp. 41–42, 46–47, 80–81; *Dv combat chrestien; A Treatise of Peace & Contentment of Mind,* p. 6.

69. *The Practise of Pietie,* sig. A3 and p. 91.

70. Pp. 92–93. Dove is cited by John Swan in proving the physical corruption, particularly the decay of man.

71. *Aristotles Politiqves,* sig. Aiii; Vaughan, *Golden-Groue,* sigs. [D6], G2ᵛ, [N8ᵛ], [X7ᵛ]; Dent, *Plain Man's Pathway to Heaven,* pp. 81, 84; Sutton, *Disce vivere,* pp. vi, 434–35 (and *Disce mori* for more evidence of interest in the effects of sin); Camerarius, *Living Librarie,* pp. 34 ff., 147–49; Hieron, *Sermons,* Part I, pp. [328], 330, 640; Part II, p. 175; Stafford, *Staffords Niobe: Or His Age of Teares,* pp. 5, 8–9, and *Staffords Niobe, Dissolv'd into a Niɨvs,* pp. 82, 84, 101.

72. *The Faerie Queene*, V, Prologue, 1–7; II, vii, 16; IV, viii, 30–31; VII, vi, 6.

73. *Ibid.*, VII, vii, 17–26, 49–59.

74. *A Progress of Piety*, pp. 57, 75, 83–84, 107, 119.

75. *Vicissitudo rerum*, sig. A3; and stanzas 38–40, 47, 52, 107, 108, 156. Miss Kathrine Koller shows that Norden used Ashley's English translation of Leroy, and she makes essentially the same evaluation of Norden that I set forth here. Perhaps Norden's failure to do more with Leroy may be explained by the strong pietistic bias indicated in Norden's *A Pensive Man's Practice, A Progress of Piety*, etc.

76. Davies, *The Works*, I, 142; Daniel, *The Whole Workes*, pp. 329–30; Fletcher, *Poetical Works*, I, 19, 75.

77. Fitzgeffrey, *Poems*, pp. 23, 29; Bastard, *Poems*, pp. 53, 55; Lane, *Tom Tel-Troths Message*, p. [111]; Thynne, *Emblemes and Epigrames*, p. 29; Dekker, *Old Fortunatus*, pp. 290, 314; Tofte, *Honovrs Academie*, Part III, pp. 94–95; also sig. Oo^v; and Part I, pp. 37, 45, 75.

78. *The Muses Sacrifice*, pp. 50–51, in *Works*, Vol. II. Nature is said to be out of frame also in *Wittes Pilgrimage* (1611) in *Works*, Vol. II; and signs of the end are described in "Rights of the Living and the Dead," which appeared as an appendix to *The Muses Sacrifice* (see esp. pp. 78, 87, in *Works*, Vol. II).

79. *Dramatic Works*, III, 171; Γυναικεῖον, pp. 85–86; *Hierarchie*, pp. 113–15, 144–50.

80. *Abuses Stript, and Whipt*, sig. B3; pp. 22–23; *An Improvement of Imprisonment*, pp. 50–51, 112–14; *Britain's Remembrancer*, fols. 8–9, 121^v, 201, and *passim*. It may be pointed out here that Wither translated and published *The Natvre of Man*, by the Greek philosopher Nemesius, a work in which man is shown to have sinned and thereby lost his favored place in a completely teleological world, but in which the process of corruption is shown to be completely balanced by the complementary process of generation (pp. 152, 245, and *passim*).

81. *The Poetical Works*, II, 56–57, 59, 68–71, 109–10.

82. *Ibid.*, I, 27, 36, 37, 80–81, 109, 172, 263, 264, 285; II, 514–15.

83. *Complete Poetry and Selected Prose*, pp. 335, 339. Though there is no decay, nature is shown, however, to be corrupted (see also *ibid., Paradox VIII*, pp. 341–43).

84. *The Poems*, I, 155–56; see also 113–16, 169.

85. *Ibid.*, pp. 295, 302.

86. *Ibid.*, pp. 233, 237, 238, 241.

87. *Ibid.*, p. 237.

88. *Ibid.*, pp. 232, 234–36, 239, 243, 244.

89. *Ibid.*, pp. 201–2, 246–47, 251–53, 262; II, 188.

90. *Complete Poetry and Selected Prose*, pp. 508, 523.

91. *Fifty Sermons*, No. xvii, p. 142; *LXXX Sermons*, No. xxxvi, p. 357; No. xlviii, p. 481; No. lxxx, p. 823.

92. *LXXX Sermons*, No. xiii, p. 129; *XXVI Sermons*, No. xv, p. 207; No. xxvi, p. 402.

93. *Novum organum*, Book I, aphorism lxxxiv, in *The Physical and Metaphysical Works*, pp. 417–18. The idea that "the present time is the real antiquity" appeared earlier in *The Advancement of Learning*, Book I (*Physical and Metaphysical Works*, p. 50).

94. *Novum organum*, Book I, aphorism lxxxix, in *Physical and Metaphysical Works*, p. 423.

95. *Advancement of Learning*, Book I; Book VIII, chap. iii; in *Physical and Metaphysical Works*, pp. 51, 366–67.

96. *Of the Advancement and Proficience of Learning*, sigs. A2, ¶¶2.

97. *Novum organum*, Book I, aphorism xcii; *Advancement*, Book IX; in *Physical and Metaphysical Works*, pp. 375, 425.

98. Purchas' "voyages of discovery" are recounted in *Pvrchas His Pilgrimage* (1613); *Pvrchas His Pilgrim* (1619); and *Hakluytus posthumus, or Purchas His Pilgrimes* (1625).

99. *Pilgrimage*, sig. [¶4]; pp. 22–25, 42; *Pilgrim*, pp. 150–51, 300 ff., 309 ff., 368 ff.; *Pilgrimes*, I, 19, 166; II, 3.

100. *History of the World*, sig. E^v; pp. 76–77, 83.

101. *Ibid.*, p. 77; *Apologie*, p. 186.

102. *History of the World*, pp. 76–77, 81–82, 84–85. Ralegh (p. 78) compares the contemporary practice of physic with the prodigious bloodletting of Galen's day, proving thereby "what reedes we are in respect of those Cedars of the first age."

103. *History of the World*, p. 182; *Apologie*, p. 52.

104. *The Honestie of This Age*, pp. 30–32.

105. Generally attributed to Gervase Markham, but see the *Cambridge Bibliography*.

106. W. Browne, *Britannia's Pastorals*, Book I, Song 4 and Book II, Song 3 in *Works*, Vol. I; Markham, *Conceyted Letters*, sig. B, as cited by St. Clair in "Myth of the Golden Age," pp. 154–55; Brathwaite, *Essays*, p. 67, *Schollers Medley*, pp. 5, 18, 85–86, and *Natures Embassie*, pp. 3, 289; Reynolds, *Triumphs*, sig. A3 and pp. 425, 437.

107. *The Philosophers Banqvet*, pp. 137–39, 289, 310, 315, 331, 340, 353. The 1633 edition, used here, does not seem to represent a further expansion over the 1614 version.

108. *Mystical Bedlam*, pp. 2–3, 81. For more detailed use of the microcosm-macrocosm design see pp. 3, 9.

109. *The Gallants Bvrden*, in *Workes*, p. 19; and *The Sinners Passing-Bell*, in *Workes*, pp. 246–47. The whole of this latter work (pp. 246–70) is devoted to the iniquities of men and the punishment that they 'must suffer. The identification of man and the little world reappears incidentally in a number of places, as in the *Meditations* (*Workes*, p. 1128).

110. *The Spirituall Nauigator*, in *Workes*, pp. 409–10. At one point in *A Divine Herball*, Adams seems to depart from his pattern and to hold that

the world is mutable but not corruptible. The earth "often changeth her burden, without any sensible mutation of her selfe." The parts are altered, but the whole is constant. This apparent inconsistency grows out of Adams' comparison of a faithful heart and the immovable earth, the world thus appearing to be particularly stable by contrast with the corrupt and wandering soul of a man who has not received God (*Workes*, p. 1019).

111. *The Spirituall Nauigator*, in *Workes*, pp. 406, 409; *The Sinners Passing-Bell*, in *Workes*, p. 247.

112. *An Exposition vpon the Epistle to the Colossians*, I, 115; III, 63–64.

113. *The Principles or, the Patterne of Wholesome Words*, pp. 87, 104, 109, 426.

114. *The Philosophers Satyrs*, sigs. A2, [B3^v], [C3^v]–[C4^v]; pp. 11, 14, 52, and *passim*.

115. *A Help to Discourse*, pp. 213–14; see also pp. 5–6, 7, 42, 136–37, 288. Authorship has been attributed to W. Basse, or to W. Baldwyn and E. Philips. The earliest known edition is that of 1619.

116. *The Anatomy of Melancholy*, pp. 1, 584; also "Democritus to the Reader," p. 28.

117. *Ibid.*, pp. 250–52; also "Democritus to the Reader," p. 8.

118. Parrot, *Mastiue*, sigs. H3^v–H4, as cited by St. Clair, in "Myth of the Golden Age," p. 131, n. 88; Hagthorpe, *Visiones rervm*, especially "Principium & mutabilitas rerum," stanzas 17, 23–24, 41; Hannay, *Poetical Works*, p. 203.

119. *Poetical Works*, I, 4, 90, 127.

120. *Ibid.*, II, 5, 20–21, 59.

121. *Ibid.*, II, 73, 78.

122. *Resolves*, pp. 132, 145, 169; Nos. xli, xlvi, liv. Another consideration of the world's mutability is found in James Cole's *Of Death a Trve Description* (1629). The elements are particularly susceptible, though the heavens, too, will be dissolved (pp. 19, 138, and *passim*).

123. *Resolves*, pp. 154–57; No. xlix.

124. *Achitophel*, pp. 10, 49; *Geography*, Book I, pp. 82, 99–100.

125. *Geography*, Book II, pp. 8–9, 174–75, 179–80, 186–87.

126. *Ibid.*, Book I, pp. 76, 97.

127. *Ibid.*, Book I, pp. 12, 15, 82, 116; Book II, pp. 7–10, 74.

128. Jerome, *Moses His Sight of Canaan*, 2d pagination, pp. 163, 250; Peyton, *Glasse of Time*, stanza 161, p. 165; Marandé, *Ivdgment of Humane Actions*, sig. [A6]–[A6^v]; Lake, *Sermons*, p. 533.

129. *Treasvrie*, I, 22, 342, 367 (rubric), 369 ff.; II, 711.

130. *Works*, I, 87, 364, 505, 506; III, 209, 324, 327; IV, sigs. v*–vi*.

131. *Cosmography*, I, 5. This work, which first appeared in 1652, is an expansion of an earlier treatise entitled Μικρόκοσμος: *A Little Description of the Great World*, first published in 1621. At least eight editions of each version are known to have been printed in the seventeenth century.

132. *A Treatise Containing the Originall of Vnbeliefe*, pp. 32–35.

133. *Works*, Vol. I: *The Letting of Hvmovrs Blood*, satyre 7, p. 83; Vol. II: *Melancholie Knight*, pp. 12–18; *A Paire of Spy-Knaves*, p. 1; Vol. III: *Heavens Glory*, pp. 117–18. The *CBEL* suggests that *Heavens Glory* may not be by the same man who wrote the other works in the 1880 edition.

134. *Timber*, in *Works*, p. 874; see also *The Golden Age Restored*, in *Works*, pp. 714–16.

135. *Critical Essays of the Seventeenth Century*, I, 144, 149, 154, and *passim*.

136. *Christ Revealed*, pp. 169–70; *Certain Catechistical Exercises*, in *Works*, pp. 111, 113, 132. Taylor died in 1632; many of his works, previously circulated only in manuscript, were collected and published in 1653.

137. *The Famine of the Word*, in *Works*, p. 293; *Catechistical Exercises*, in *Works*, p. 106; *Christ Revealed*, p. 15.

138. "Decay," in *Works*, p. 99.

139. *The Purple Island*, Canto I, stanzas 1, 17–36, 49.

140. *Varieties*, pp. 6–7, 157; Book V, pp. 85, 87–88. See also pp. 29–30, where again the "sinne in Man" and the "naturall corruption" are coupled in explanation of the world's decline. References to Book V indicate its separate pagination.

141. *Speculum mundi*, pp. 1, 3, 5–12, 15–25, 27, 78–80, 323–24, 337, 344–45, 363, 495, 503–4.

142. *Ibid.*, p. 78. Swan here cites John Dove as one of his authorities. See also p. 3, where Swan argues that "if the parts of the world be subject to corruption, then must likewise the whole world also: but the parts are (as we daily see) and therefore the whole."

143. *Ibid.*, pp. 77–81, 107–17.

144. *Ibid.*, pp. 77–78, 80–81, 315, 319–21, 323–24.

145. *Man Become Guilty*, pp. 11, 330, 332, 334. *L'Homme criminel* was published in 1644, this translation in 1650.

146. *Ibid.*, sig. B2–B2^v; pp. 8, 11, 332, 385. See also p. 337, for Basil's assertion that the sun "doth no longer distribute his heat equally." The whole view of unhappy man living in the world that he pulled down upon his head is given again in Senault's *The Christian Man*. Here the burden of the argument is that perfect felicity cannot be found in this world. Because the earth is cursed, the seasons are irregular, the elements hostile, beasts rebellious, and "man is exceedingly more miserable then happy" (p. 361).

147. *Man Become Guilty*, pp. 319–23, 327–28.

148. Featley, *Clavis mystica*, p. 633; Overton, *Mans Mortallitie;* Amyraut, *Treatise concerning Religions*, pp. 3, 229, 233, 237, and *passim; Lord Mayors' Pageants*, II, 119.

149. *Threnoikos*, pp. 169, 251–52, 452–56, 474, 490.

150. *Pseudodoxia epidemica*, p. 20; *Religio medici*, chap. i, sec. xxxi, pp. 63–64.

151. *Christian Morals*, pp. 41, 129; *Religio*, pp. 34–35, 88; "Letter to a Friend," and *Hydrotaphia*, reprinted with *Religio*, pp. 181, 343.

152. *Christian Morals*, pp. 106, 128; *Hydrotaphia*, p. 343.

153. *Works,* III, 470, 471, 481; IV, 389; IX, 2; and *passim.*

154. Dove, *Almanac for 1653,* sig. [C5].

155. See Lilly, *Almanac for 1671;* and also Lilly's prophecies in *Catastrophe mundi,* apparently based on the *De mundi catastrophe* of Giovanni Francisco Spina, published earlier in the century. The 1683 version, which George Wharton says was *"Genuinely* English'd by the Polite Quill of my Oaken Friend *Elias Ashmole" (Works,* p. 130), reprints a High Dutch prophecy that great tumults, if not the very end of the world, will come in 1588 (pp. 17–18); suggests that the new star of 1572 might have fulfilled the sibylline prophecy and anticipated the end (pp. 89–90); and, in general, testifies to a considerable interest in the date and signs of that final destruction.

156. "Daphnis, an Elegiac Poem," in *Works,* II, 659. The same thought is contained in another poem, in which it is said that man "drew the Curse upon the world, and Crackt The whole frame with his fall" (*Works,* II, 440).

157. *Works,* I, 170–71.

158. *The Parly of Beasts,* sigs. a, b, b2ᵛ; *Familiar Letters,* Part II, Letter lxvi, p. 394.

159. Peacham, *Valley of Varietie,* p. 18; also *Coach and Sedan,* sig. G3ᵛ; *Comedies and Tragedies Written by Francis Beaumont and Iohn Fletcher,* sig. c; L'Estrange, *Poor Robins Visions;* also *Account of the Growth of Knavery;* Cowley, *Poems,* sig. a; also *Four Ages,* p. 3; Winstanley, *Muses Cabinet,* p. 45; Waller, "Of Divine Poesy," *Poems,* II, 133; also "Of Divine Love," *Poems,* II, 126.

160. *Works,* p. 350; see also *Something Touching the Nature of Eclipses* (*ca.* 1655), in *Works,* p. 104.

161. Suckling, *Works,* p. 143; Burgess, *Doctrine of Original Sin;* Camfield, *Theological Discourse,* sig. A3ᵛ; King, *Essay on the Origin of Evil.*

162. *The Harmony of Divine Attributes,* in *Works,* I, 203–9, 475; *Considerations of the Existence of God,* in *Works,* I, 29–30.

163. Ussher, *Works,* I, 109; Richard Parr, *The Life of the Most Reverend Father in God, James Usher,* p. 398.

164. *A Body of Divinity,* pp. 74, 126, 136, 446 ff.

165. *Peripateticall Institutions,* pp. 371–72, 396–97, 422.

166. *Sacred Theory of the Earth,* I, 229, 231, 236, 243, 258.

167. *Ibid.,* I, 237; II, 6, 7, 64, 124, 132.

168. *Ibid.,* II, 17, 18, 33, 45, 47–48, 51, 58.

169. J. B. Mullinger, *The University of Cambridge,* II, 69, 112, 114, 144–45, 190; III, 435.

170. *Considerations Touching the Likeliest Means To Remove Hirelings Out of the Church* (1659), in *The Student's Milton,* p. 897.

171. *Poetical Works,* pp. 151–53, 588–89.

172. *Prose Works,* IV, 180, 253–84, 475–94; *The Student's Milton,* p. 448.

173. *Paradise Lost,* IX, 1000–1004; X, 651–56, 660–61, 668–79, 693–95, 720–21, 728–29; XII, 459. See also the matter of the earth's axis as handled by White and Burnet, pp. 157–58.

174. *Paradise Lost*, III, 353–57; IV, 214 ff.; XII, 469–78, 537–51.

175. *Apologie*, sig. [b6]; *An History of the Constancy of Nature*, pp. 1–6, and *passim*. Unable to obtain either the original Latin or the English version of Johnstone's text, I take this description of the work from Jones, *Ancients and Moderns*, pp. 38–39.

In connection with Hakewill, another minor point may be made here: as part of his proof that the earth has not decayed, Hakewill (*Apologie*, p. [143]) cites Edmund Deane on the present virtues of English medicinal waters (see Deane, *Spadacrene anglica*, p. 92).

176. *A Discourse concerning a New Planet*, pp. 130–31.

177. *The Discovery of a New World* (3d ed. of *The Discovery of a World in the Moone*), pp. 119–21.

178. *Ibid.*, pp. 40–47, 116–17.

179. *Mathematical Magick*, in *The Mathematical and Philosophical Works*.

180. *Naturall Philosophie Reformed by Divine Light*, pp. 28, 31, 70, 74–75, 77, 127, 238.

181. *An Elegant and Learned Discourse of the Light of Nature*, p. 16.

182. *The Darknes of Atheism Dispelled by the Light of Nature*, pp. 289–90; *Physiologia Epicuro-Gassendo-Charltoniana: or a Fabrick of Science Natural*, Book IV, chap. i.

183. *Experimental Philosophy*, p. 188.

184. *Ibid.*, pp. 153–54, 162, 190.

185. *Ibid.*, pp. 164, 184.

186. *Ibid.*, pp. 188–92.

187. *Discourse concerning Vulgar Prophecies*, pp. 5–6, 25, 115, 118, 124.

188. *Discourse concerning Prodigies*, sig. A2–A2^v; pp. 279–80, 295.

189. *Ibid.*, p. 70.

190. *Ibid.*, pp. 279–81.

191. *Leviathan*, Part I, chap. xiii; see also Part I, chaps. xii, xiv, xv; Part II, chaps. xxvii, xxviii, xxxi; Part III, chaps. xxxiii–xxxviii, xliii; Part IV, chaps. xliv–xlvii.

192. Ζῳοτομία, pp. 243–44, 276; see also pp. 208, 210, 211, 218–20.

193. *Two Choice and Vseful Treatises*, p. 146; *The Way of Happiness*, pp. 10–14.

194. *The Vanity of Dogmatizing*, pp. 136, 137, 141, 174, 240; *Scepsis scientifica*, p. 104 and *passim*.

195. *Conversations on the Plurality of Worlds*, pp. 15–16, 64–68, 160, 162, 163, 170, 191.

196. *Poesies pastorales. Avec un traité sur la nature de l'eglogue, & une digression sur les anciens & les modernes*, pp. 108, 123, in *Œuvres diverses*, Vol. II.

197. Osborne, *Miscellany*, pp. 57–58, 75; Hall, *Humble Motion*, p. 6; Dryden, *Discourse concerning the Original and Progress of Satire*, and *Essay of Dramatic Poesy*, in *Essays*, I, 21 ff.; II, 25–26; Farquhar, *Discourse upon*

Comedy, in *Critical Essays of the Eighteenth Century*, pp. 263–64; Young, *Conjectures*, pp. 12, 21, 31–32.

198. Webster, *The Displaying of Supposed Witchcraft*, p. 3; Creech's translation of Lucretius, p. 23.

199. *Miscellaneous Discourses concerning the Dissolution and Changes of the World*, pp. 40–41.

200. *Ibid.*, pp. 21, 23, 41–42, 174–76, 177–79, 181–84, 189.

CHAPTER V

1. Goodman, *Fall*, sig. [a5ᵛ]; pp. 17, 402, 416. See also Barckley, *Felicitie of Man*, pp. 362, 666; Du Moulin, *Bvckler of the Faith*, pp. 72, 77, 90; Donne, *LXXX Sermons*, No. xiii, p. 129; Daneau, *Wonderfvll Woorkmanship*, fol. 86ᵛ; Bury, *Idea of Progress*, pp. 20–23; Burtt, *Types of Religious Philosophy*, pp. 72–73, 81–82.

2. *Apologie*, V, 126.

3. Daneau, *Wonderfvll Woorkmanship*, fol. 64ᵛ; Burtt, *Metaphysical Foundations*, p. 91; Burtt, *Religious Philosophy*, p. 57.

4. Cudworth, *True Intellectual System*, III, 466, n. 10.

5. If any evidence is required to establish the very nearly universal currency of the teleological idea, see Du Bartas, *Little Bartas*, pp. 230–33; La Primaudaye, *French Academie*, pp. 5, 6, 39, 340, 424, 449, 633; Scribonius, *Natvrall Philosophy*, p. 49; Peucer, *Les Devins*, pp. 235, 479; Hooker, *Ecclesiastical Politie*, Book I, pp. 7, 23; Bacon, *De sapientia veterum*, in *Works*, VI, 747; John King, *Sermon*, p. 316; Barckley, *Felicitie of Man*, pp. 658, 667; Davies of Hereford, *Mirum in modum*, p. 12, in *Works*, Vol. I; Davies of Hereford, "Rights of the Living and the Dead," appendix to *Muses Sacrifice*, p. 68, in *Works*, Vol. II; Austin, *Haec homo*, p. 1; Donne, *LXXX Sermons*, Nos. lxv, lxxvi, pp. 655, 770; Purchas, *Pilgrimage*, p. 22; Ralegh, *History of the World*, pp. 22, 27; Scott, *Philosophers Banqvet*, p. 4; Goodman, *Fall*, pp. 11, 17, 68–69; Hakewill, *Apologie*, p. 114; Adams, *Mystical Bedlam*, p. 16; Adams, *Workes*, p. 1124; Thomas Taylor, *Works*, pp. 104, 105, 119; Harris, *Arraignement*, p. 211; Swan, *Speculum mundi*, p. 495; Browne, *Religio*, pp. 70–71; Heylyn, *Cosmography*, Book I, p. 3.

For the belief in the perfect creation see Daneau, *Wonderfvll Woorkmanship*, fol. 80ᵛ; Barckley, *Felicitie of Man*, pp. 656–57; Du Moulin, *Bvckler of the Faith*, pp. 78–79; Donne, *XXVI Sermons*, No. xxiii, p. 314; Purchas, *Pilgrimage*, pp. 23, 25; Goodman, *Fall*, p. 415; Adams, *Workes*, p. 1129; T. Taylor, *Works*, p. 111; Glanvill, *Two Choice and Vsefvl Treatises*, p. 72.

Specific opposition to the accidental creation or the operation of fortune, a principal point for Du Bartas (see the entire argument of the first day), is found also in Goodman, *Fall*, pp. 410–11; Daneau, *Wonderfvll Woorkmanship*, fol. 37ᵛ; Lipsius, *Discourse of Constancy*, p. 74; Person, *Varieties*, Book V, pp. 60 ff. The position of the Cambridge Platonists is examined by C. T. Harrison ("The Ancient Atomists and English Literature of the Seventeenth Century").

6. Gilson, *Spirit of Mediaeval Philosophy*, p. 364; Burtt, *Metaphysical Foundations*, pp. 78–79.

7. Goodman, *Fall*, p. 16; Donne, *LXXX Sermons*, No. v, p. 44; Donne, *Devotions*, No. x, in *Complete Poetry and Selected Prose*, p. 523; see also Purchas, *Pilgrimes*, I, 19; Goulart, *Learned Summary*, Part I, pp. 119, 120.

8. *Experimental Philosophy*, pp. 153–54, 164.

9. Galileo, *Systeme of the World*, Part I, pp. 44–45, 238; Descartes, *Principles of Philosophy*, III, 3, in *Philosophical Works*, Vol. I; see also Lovejoy, *Great Chain of Being*, pp. 186–89; Burtt, *Metaphysical Foundations*, pp. 78–80, 96, 173.

10. Wilkins, *Discovrse concerning a New Planet*, p. 131; Spencer, *Discourse concerning Prodigies*, p. 280; Blount, *Natural History*, sig. A4; Power, *Experimental Philosophy*, p. 162.

11. See pp. 163–68.

12. *Fall*, sig. [a7]; pp. 5, 6, 8, 11–13, 70, 400, 401; Hakewill, *Apôlogie*, V, 136. See pp. 194–97, where the mortality of the world and the urgent need for piety are suggested as further reasons for believing that the decay is incremental.

13. *Fall*, p. 382; *Apologie*, V, 172.

14. See pp. 69–75.

15. *Apologie*, V, 171–72.

16. Hooker, *Ecclesiastical Politie*, pp. 19, 105, 107; see also pp. 8–9, 17–22, 78, 97–107. Hooker's treatment of this matter is found particularly in Book I, chaps. viii–x, and Book III, chaps. viii–ix. Purchas maintains a similar position, specifically showing man's Fall to be discernible by reason (*Pilgrimage*, p. 26). See also Ursinus, *Summe of Christian Religion*, p. 443; and Senault, *Man Become Guilty*, p. 3.

17. *Fall*, p. 389; Heylyn (*Cyprianus anglicus*, Book IV, p. 125) and William Laud (*Works* [see index]) refer to Goodman's Catholic sympathies. For other comment on this point see Bredvold, *Intellectual Milieu of John Dryden*, pp. 16–20; White, *English Devotional Literature, 1600–1640*, pp. 216–17; Bredvold, "Religious Thought of Donne."

18. Bacon, *Advancement of Learning*, Book IX, in *Physical and Metaphysical Works*, p. 369.

19. Browne, *Religio*, p. 21; Wilkins, *Discovery of a New World*, pp. 119–21; Daneau, *Wonderfvll Woorkmanship*, sig. Aii^v, and fols. 6^v–7, 67, 69^v, 72; Daneau, *Frvitfvll Commentarie*, pp. 95, 97, 101–2, 369–70, 502–3; Du Bartas, *Little Bartas*, p. 234; Northampton, *Defensative*, fols. 24^v, 32; Barckley, *Felicitie of Man*, sig. A4^v; Ralegh, *History of the World*, pp. 7, 130, 272–74; Donne, *LXXX Sermons*, pp. 23, 178, 227, 429, 611; Donne, "To the Countesse of Bedford," *Poems*, pp. 189–90; Thomas Taylor, *Christ Revealed*, pp. 323, 325; Person, *Varieties*, p. 191; Senault, *Man Become Guilty*, pp. 74–80; Jeremy Taylor, *Works*, XI, 430–65; Ussher, *Body of Divinity*, p. 76; William King, *Essay on the Origin of Evil*, II, 454; and *Sermon on the Fall of Man*, 2d pagination in same volume, p. 77.

20. On the origin and nature of sin see Goodman, *Fall,* pp. 390, 417–22; La Primaudaye, *French Academie,* p. 575; Lipsius, *Discourse of Constancy,* p. 79; Goulart, *Learned Summary,* Part I, pp. 304–5, Part II, p. 70; Barckley, *Felicitie of Man,* pp. 5, 664–66; Topsell, *Times Lamentation,* pp. 428–29; Perkins, *Golden Chaine,* p. 13, and *Exposition of the Creede,* p. 244; Davies of Hereford, *Mirum in modum,* p. [5], in *Works,* Vol. I; Purchas, *Pilgrimage,* p. 23; Jerome, *Moses His Sight of Canaan,* 2d pagination, p. 250; Willet, *Pavl,* pp. 258, 276; Du Moulin, *Bvckler of the Faith,* p. 69; Du Moulin, *Anatomy of Arminianisme,* pp. 41–42, 51–52; Phineas Fletcher, *Way to Blessednes,* p. 180; Adams, *Workes,* p. 1184; Swan, *Speculum mundi,* p. 344; Bates, *Works,* I, 209, II, 297; Burgess, *Doctrine of Original Sin,* p. 112; Tulloch, *Christian Doctrine of Sin,* pp. 124–25.

21. On the infection of nature see Scott, *Philosophers Banqvet,* p. 289; Purchas, *Pilgrimage,* p. 24; Purchas, *Pilgrim,* p. 151. On the effect of the Flood see Goulart, *Learned Summary,* Part II, pp. 139–40; Goodman, *Fall,* pp. 281–82, 285–86; Carpenter, *Geography,* Book II, pp. 9–10; Burnet, *Sacred Theory of the Earth,* I, 243. We are not here concerned with the "mountain controversy" in which Burnet is so important a figure; but, for a typical statement denying that the Flood caused the formation of mountains, seas, and other variations upon the earth, see Wilkins, *Discovery of a New World,* pp. 116–17.

Among the many works in which a natural corruption is attributed to sin, and particularly to original sin, may be listed Goodman, *Fall,* pp. 17, 27–28, 314, 348–49; La Primaudaye, *French Academie,* p. 528; Du Bartas, *Weekes, Second Week,* I, iii, 1–21; Northampton, *Defensative,* fol. 65; Daneau, *Frvitfvll Commentarie,* pp. 316–17; Daneau, *Wonderfvll Woorkmanship,* fols. 81–84; Bastard, *Chrestoleros,* Book I, Epigram 5, in *Poems,* p. 7; Goulart, *Learned Summary,* Part II, p. 67; Peucer, *Les Devins,* pp. 479–80; Barckley, *Felicitie of Man,* pp. 6, 658; Topsell, *Times Lamentation,* pp. 147, [191], 194–95; Norden, *Progress of Piety,* p. 57; Alexander, *Doomes-Day,* Fourth Hour, stanza 2, in *Poetical Works,* II, 109; Mornay, *Trewnesse of Christian Religion,* "Epistle Dedicatory," sig. B2; Carpenter, *Achitophel,* p. 49; T. Taylor, *Works,* pp. 113, 122; Willet, *Pavl,* p. 277; Swan, *Speculum mundi,* pp. 344–45, 503–4; Person, *Varieties,* Book V, pp. 87–88; Senault, *Man Become Guilty,* sig. B2^v; pp. 3, 328–29, 334, 385; White, *Theological Appendix,* in *Peripateticall Institutions,* pp. 371–72.

For particular statements holding man's sin responsible for corruption of the heavens see, e.g., Goulart, *Learned Summary,* Part I, p. 83, Part II, p. 83; Davies of Hereford, *Muses Sacrifice,* p. 50, in *Works,* Vol. II; Senault, *Man Become Guilty,* pp. 330, 335, 337; *Catastrophe mundi,* sig. A3^v.

For comment on the early history of these ideas see also Tennant, *Sources of the Doctrines of the Fall and Original Sin,* esp. pp. 92, 102, 127, 150–51, 183, 215–16, 271; Williams, *Ideas of the Fall and of Original Sin;* Thorndike, *History of Magic and Experimental Science,* I, 410, II, 201. Gilson (*Spirit of Mediaeval Philosophy,* pp. 420–21) offers the thesis that Church Fathers and medieval doctors make a clear distinction between nature's corruption and nature itself.

22. *Apologie*, V, 44, 113, and *Fall*, p. 24; Daneau, *Wonderfvll Woorkmanship*, fol. 82ᵛ; Lipsius, *Discourse of Constancy*, p. 86; Ralegh, *History of the World*, pp. 76, 83; Person, *Varieties*, pp. 29–30. See also La Primaudaye (*French Academie*, p. 290), Jerome (*Moses His Sight of Canaan*, 2d pagination, 268), and Vergil (*Abridgmēt*, fol. v), where nature's corruptibility is assumed if the world is to be mortal.

23. Senault, *Man Become Guilty*, p. 48 (see also pp. 361–62, where Seneca is given as a source of such heresies); Ursinus, *Summe of Christian Religion*, pp. 183–84; Goodman, *Fall*, p. 14.

24. *Fall*, sig. [a5ᵛ]; pp. 17–18, 441; Hakewill, *Apologie*, V, 26, 36; Goulart, *Learned Summary*, Part I, pp. 26, 97, 306. The notion that God's power subjugates the otherwise dominant evil principle is found also in Plato (see Lovejoy, *Primitivism and Related Ideas in Antiquity*, pp. 157–58).

25. *Apologie*, V, 48; see also pp. 55–57; V, 149; Leroy, *Interchangeable Covrse*, fol. 3; Wilkins, *Discovery of a New World*, pp. 116–17; Spencer, *Discourse concerning Prodigies*, sig. A2ᵛ.

26. Lucretius *De rerum natura* ii. 1150–74, pp. 67 ff.; v. 830–36, p. 165; Hakewill, *Apologie*, pp. 63–65.

27. Seneca *Epist. mor.* xc. 34 ff.; Pliny, *Natvrall Historie*, I, 164–65; Cyprian, *Epistles*, Nos. lviii, pp. 142–43, and lxvii, p. 214; see also Donne, *LXXX Sermons*, No. xxxvi, p. 357; Hakewill, *Apologie*, pp. 70–73; Cudworth, *True Intellectual System of the Universe*, II, 345, n. 1.

28. Daneau, *Wonderfvll Woorkmanship*, fol. 82; Shakelton, *Blazyng Starre*, sig. Av; Alexander, *Doomes-Day*, Second Hour, stanza 97, in *Poetical Works*, II, 69. For Hakewill's views, see pp. 76–79, 84. See also Lipsius, *Discourse of Constancy*, p. 95; Viret, *Worlde Possessed with Deuils*, sig. Aviᵛ, as cited by Allen, "The Degeneration of Man and Renaissance Pessimism," p. 220; Giles Fletcher, "Christs Victorie in Heaven," stanza 7, and "Christs Triumph after Death," stanza 3, *Christs Victorie, & Triumph in Heaven, and Earth*, in *Poetical Works*, I, 19, 75; Goodman, *Fall*, p. 246; Hakewill, *Apologie*, p. 549; V, 101–2; Donne, "To the Countesse of Huntingdon," in *Poems*, I, 202; Carpenter, *Geography*, Book II, pp. 8–9; Sutton, *Disce vivere*, pp. 434–35; Phineas Fletcher, *Purple Island*, Canto I, stanzas 1, 36, pp. 1, 10; Heywood, *Hierarchie*, p. 150; Swan, *Speculum mundi*, pp. 77–78; Comenius, *Naturall Philosophie Reformed by Divine Light*, pp. 80, 127; Bates, *Harmony of Divine Attributes*, in *Works*, I, 475; Wharton, *Works*, p. 350.

29. Purchas, *Pilgrimage*, p. 6; La Primaudaye, *French Academie*, pp. 724–25; Ross, *Philosophicall Touch-Stone*, sig. A2.

30. Aristotle *Metaphysics* iv. 1. 1004ⁿ14–17; see also *Met.* ix. 1. 1046ᵃ29–31.

31. Ross, *Philosophicall Touch-Stone*, p. 79. The italics are mine. See also Goodman, *Fall*, pp. 390–91.

32. Aristotle *Met.* v. 22. 1022ᵇ22–34; ix. 1. 1046ᵃ32–36; Ursinus, *Summe of Christian Religion*, p. 47; Purchas, *Pilgrimage*, p. 6; Fludd, *Mosaicall Philos-*

ophy, p. 77; Hakewill, *Apologie*, V, 97. See also Carpenter, *Geography*, Book I, p. 22; Thomas Taylor, *The Parable of the Sovver and of the Seed*, p. 94; Peucer, *Les Devins*, pp. 474–75; Scott, *Philosophers Banqvet*, p. 342; Goulart, *Learned Summary*, Part II, p. 98; Joseph Hall, *Holy Observations*, in *Works*, p. 147; Jerome, *Moses His Sight of Canaan*, 2d pagination, p. 250; Drummond, *Cypresse Grove*, in *Poetical Works*, II, 70.

33. *Apologie*, V, 1. Hakewill's answer here (p. 2) is that the *"non ens* before the creation included rather a pure negation, then a relative privation; as a stone is said to bee blinde negatively, not privatively, because there is in it no inclination or preparative disposition to sight."

34. Fludd, *Mosaicall Philosophy*, pp. 51, 74; Abernethy, *A Christian and Heavenly Treatise*, p. 20; Drummond, *Cypresse Grove*, in *Poetical Works*, II, 70; King, *Essay*, I, xix. King himself (I, 146) shows natural evils to arise from the origin of things in matter.

Privation as a disruptive influence tending toward decay is indicated also by Batman, *Bartholome*, fol. 152^v; Anton, *Philosophers Satyrs*, sig. [C4]; Adams, *Workes*, p. 76; *Threnoikos*, p. 31. How widely the idea of privation was accepted may be seen from such miscellaneous appearances of the term as those in Leroy, *Interchangeable Covrse*, fol. 6; Du Bartas, *Little Bartas*, p. 242; Goulart, *Learned Summary*, Part I, pp. 48, 81, 196, Part II, p. 91; Lipsius, *Discourse of Constancy*, p. 101; Wright, *Passions of the Minde*, pp. 50–51; Davies of Hereford, *Summa totalis*, p. 18, in *Works*, Vol. I; Du Moulin, *Anatomy of Arminianisme*, pp. 51–52; Person, *Varieties*, p. 7.

35. Goodman, *Fall*, pp. 417, 422; Barckley, *Felicitie of Man*, p. 666; La Primaudaye, *French Academie*, p. 575; Perkins, *Golden Chaine*, pp. 13–14; Davies of Hereford, *Mirum in modum*, p. 23, in *Works*, Vol. I; Phineas Fletcher, *Way to Blessednes*, p. 180; Willet, *Pavl*, p. 276; Du Moulin, *Anatomy of Arminianisme*, pp. 51–52; Bates, *Works*, I, 209, II, 297; Adams, *Workes*, p. 1184; Burgess, *Doctrine of Original Sin*, p. 112.

36. Aristotle *Met.* v. 9. 1018^{a}18–19.

37. Goodman, *Fall*, pp. 15–16, 349–50; Hakewill, *Apologie*, V, 1–7, 167; Goulart, *Learned Summary*, Part I, pp. 164, 197; Pont, *Right Reckoning of Yeares*, p. 65; Crooke, Μικροκοσμογραφία, p, 1; Comenius, *Naturall Philosophie Reformed*, pp. 74–75, 77.

38. Hakewill, *Apologie*, V, 113; Jerome, *Moses His Sight of Canaan*, 2d pagination, p. 347; see also Goodman, *Fall*, pp. 15–18, 32; Batman, *Bartholome*, fol. 165; Recorde, *Castle of Knowledge*, p. 7; La Primaudaye, *French Academie*, p. 696; Goulart, *Learned Summary*, Part 1, pp. 26, 97, Part II, p. [76]; Norden, *Vicissitudo rerum*, stanzas 82, 107, 108; Jerome, *Moses His Sight of Canaan*, 2d pagination, pp. 250, 268; Alexander, *Tragedy of Darius*, in *Poetical Works*, I, 172–73, and *Doomes-Day*, Fourth Hour, stanza 25, in *Poetical Works*, II, 115; Drummond, *Cypresse Grove*, in *Poetical Works*, II, 81; Burnet, *Sacred Theory*, I, 258; Davies of Hereford, *Mirum in modum*, p. 25, in *Works*, Vol. I.

39. See Leroy, *Interchangeable Covrse*, sig. B, and fols. 5^v, 6^v, 7; Daneau,

Wonderfull Woorkmanship, fols. 85–86; Galileo, *Systeme*, pp. 26 ff., esp. p. 27; Hakewill, *Apologie*, pp. 91–92, 95–96; V, 113–14, 147. For various lesser objections to and modifications of Goodman's system, see Palingenius, *Zodiake of Life*, pp. 211–12; Du Bartas, *Weekes, First Week*, II, 249–54; Norden, *Vicissitudo rerum*, stanzas 83–87; Alexander, *Alexandrean Tragedy*, in *Poetical Works*, I, 314, 316; Batman, *Bartholome*, fols. 121, 154; La Primaudaye, *French Academie*, sig. ¶3ᵛ; p. 696.

40. Goulart, *Learned Summary*, Part I, p. 48; also pp. 15, 16, 41–42, 49; and see Purchas, *Pilgrimage*, p. 6; Carpenter, *Geography*, Book I, pp. 7–8; Heylyn, *Cosmography*, Book I, pp. 2–3.

41. Purchas, *Pilgrimage*, p. 6; Goulart, *Learned Summary*, Part I, p. 48.

42. *Apologie*, V, 195–97; Goulart, *Learned Summary*, Part I, pp. 41–42.

43. *Apologie*, pp. 78–79; V, 27, 29–35, 198–99. For other opposition to the idea of a double matter see Willet, *Genesis*, p. 2; Swan, *Speculum mundi*, pp. 315, 365; Carpenter, *Geography*, Book I, p. 7.

44. *Apologie*, p. 78; see also V, 196–97. Among the modern schoolmen see Batman, *Bartholome*, fols. 135ᵛ, 118ᵛ, 120, 168ᵛ; Person, *Varieties*, pp. 6–9; Ross, *Philosophicall Touch-Stone*, p. 82.

45. "I shall not mention their arguments, since 'tis already confest, that they are none of them of any necessary consequence" (*Discovery of a New World*, p. 41). See also Heywood, *Hierarchie*, p. 113; Swan, *Speculum mundi*, pp. 77–78, 319–20; Ray, *Miscellaneous Discourses*, pp. 189–90.

46. Representative descriptions and explanations of the inviolability of the heavens may be found in Hakewill, *Apologie*, pp. 78–79, 91–92; V, 2, 17, 51, 167–68; VI, 264; Cardan, *De subtilitate*, p. 80; Acosta, *Natural & Moral History*, I, 7; Palingenius, *Zodiake of Life*, pp. 117, 161, 211; Recorde, *Castle of Knowledge*, sig. a4ᵛ and p. 7; Batman, *Bartholome*, fols. 120, 121, 141ᵛ; La Primaudaye, *French Academie*, pp. 403, 696 (but see also p. 699); Du Bartas, *Weekes, First Week*, II, 1031, 1040–62; Northampton, *Defensative*, fol. 56ᵛ; Goulart, *Learned Summary*, Part I, pp. 26, 41–42, 70, 156–57; Peucer, *Les Devins*, pp. 468, 480; Norden, *Vicissitudo rerum*, stanza 87; Person, *Varieties*, pp. 6–9; Heywood, *Hierarchie*, pp. 113–14; Basset, *Curiosities*, p. 128; Ross, *Philosophicall Touch-Stone*, p. 82.

47. Following are some of the texts in which mutability of the heavens is indicated, either in support of the doctrine of decay or in opposition to it: Goodman, *Fall*, p. 378, and *Apologie*, V, 195–97; Lucretius *De rerum natura* v. 751–70, p. 163; Ovid *Met.* xv. 453–55; Leroy, *Interchangeable Covrse*, fols. 1ᵛ, 2ᵛ–3 (but see also fol. 129ᵛ); sig. B; Lipsius, *Discourse of Constancy*, pp. 88–90; Galileo, *Systeme*, pp. 26–30, 38; Alexander, *Doomes-Day*, Second Hour, stanzas 95–96, in *Poetical Works*, II, 68–69; Willet, *Pavl*, p. 368; Burton, *Anatomy of Melancholy*, p. 250 (but see also p. 252); Drummond, *Cypresse Grove*, in *Poetical Works*, II, 73, 78; Carpenter, *Geography*, Book I, pp. 81–82, 99–100, Book II, pp. 11, 30; Swan, *Speculum mundi*, pp. 77–80, 319–20, 321, 324; Wilkins, *Discovery of a New World*, pp. 40–47; Comenius, *Naturall Philosophie Reformed*, pp. 80, 127; Glanvill, *Vanity of Dog-*

matizing, p. 174; Lilly, *Almanac for 1671,* sigs. [A8]–B; Lilly, *Englands Propheticall Merline,* sig. F2; Wharton, *Works,* p. 350; Spencer, *Discourse concerning Prodigies,* p. 295; Ray, *Miscellaneous Discourses,* pp. 189–90.

48. Lucretius' antiteleological position is indicated in *De rerum natura* ii. 167–83, p. 40, and 1090–1104, p. 66.

Among those who, holding for the decay of the world, reject the Epicurean-Lucretian philosophy as atheistic, are Vergil, *Abridgemēt,* fol. iv–iv^v; La Primaudaye, *French Academie,* p. 629; Carpenter, *Achitophel,* p. 28; Adams, *Workes,* p. 1114; and Person, *Varieties,* Book V, pp. 60 ff.

Du Bartas, greatly indebted to Lucretius in other ways, is particularly severe (esp. *Weekes, First Week,* I and VII) in his attack upon a chance, nonprovidential creation. Hakewill makes the most of this weakness in his opponents' position by arguing that the Lucretian advocacy of decay rests upon this denial of God's providence; "your lordship," he says to Goodman (*Apologie,* V, 87), "togeather with these *Epicureans* defend the worlds decay." For the church's fight against the atomistic philosophy, particularly in the second half of the seventeenth century, see C. T. Harrison, "The Ancient Atomists and English Literature of the Seventeenth Century."

Ross (*Philosophicall Touch-Stone,* pp. 16, 57, 60) and Glanvill (*Vanity of Dogmatizing,* p. 146) illustrate the very common opposition between Aristotelians and atomists. See also G. B. Stones, "The Atomic View of Matter in the XVth, XVIth, and XVIIth Centuries," in this connection.

On plurality of worlds see Lucretius *De rerum natura* ii. 1048–76, pp. 64–65; and in denial, Du Bartas, *Weekes, First Week,* I; Daneau, *Wonderfvll Woorkmanship,* fol. 25; Batman, *Bartholome,* fol. 119; Perkins, *Exposition of the Creede,* p. 223; T. Taylor, *Works,* p. 91; Adams, *Workes,* p. 1123; Swan, *Speculum mundi,* p. 120; Person, *Varieties,* Book V, pp. 58–59. Burton (*Anatomy of Melancholy,* pp. 252–55) discusses the plurality of worlds in relation to the whole controversy in modern astronomy. Wilkins (*Discovrse concerning a New Planet,* pp. 130–31) indicates the opposition between teleology and the plurality of worlds. See also Grant McColley, "The Seventeenth-Century Doctrine of a Plurality of Worlds."

For man's advance from primitive savagery see Lucretius *De rerum natura* v. 324–37, p. 150; 1448–57, pp. 184–85. The compensating operation of cycles is described by Leroy, *Interchangeable Covrse,* fols. 32^v, 112^v, 126; by Barclay, *Icon animorum,* pp. 43, 45, 54; and by Hakewill, *Apologie,* V, 144–45, 192; and is opposed by Bates, *Works,* I, 29–30.

49. *Apologie,* p. 54.

50. *De rerum natura* i. 214–18, p. 9.

51. *Ibid.* v. 64–109, pp. 141–42; see also v. 821–36, p. 165; Donne, *Anatomie of the World,* in *Poems,* I, 229 ff.; Mornay, *Trewnesse of Christian Religion,* p. 89; Lipsius, *Discourse of Constancy,* p. 95; T. Taylor, *Works,* p. 293.

52. *Fall,* p. 383; *Apologie,* pp. 43–45, 57; V, sig. Aaaa-Aaaa^v; V, 24, 43, 80–81, 84–85, 90–93, 98, 113, 118, 136–37, 145–59; see also above, pp. 56–58, 80–82.

53. *Apologie*, V, 81-82, 164; see also p. 559; V, 84-85, 98, 175; Carpenter, *Geography*, Book II, pp. 177-78.

Among the many other refutations of the Aristotelian idea of eternity see Vergil, *Abridgemēt*, fol. v; Du Bartas, *Weekes, First Week*, I; Shakelton, *Blazyng Starre*, sigs. aii[v], Aii; Willet, *Genesis*, p. 16; Anton, *Philosophers Satyrs*, sig. [C3[v]]; p. [74]; Adams, *Workes*, p. 1114; Swan, *Speculum mundi*, pp. 1, 79-80; Heywood, *Hierarchie*, pp. [145], [151]; Ussher, *A Body of Divinity*, p. 95; Daneau, *Wonderfvll Woorkmanship*, fols. 31-37, 64; Cuff, *Differences of the Ages of Mans Life;* Ralegh, *History of the World*, sigs. E[v]-E2.

It is easy to see how this opposition to the world's eternity is argued as a vindication of God's honor; for the discussions of Goodman and Hakewill on this point see *Fall*, p. 271; *Apologie*, pp. 18, 567; V, 136, 152, 157-63; see also Person, *Varieties*, Book V, pp. 60 ff.

54. *Speculum mundi*, p. 5. Hakewill's more elaborate distinctions are found in *Apologie*, p. 565.

55. Burnet, *Sacred Theory*, II, sig. [A5].

The quarrel between Goodman and Hakewill in this respect is developed in *Apologie*, V, 136-39, 145-47, 149, 152-54, 156-57, 162-64, 192; see also pp. 565-71 and the whole of Book VI, chap. vi. The purification or renovation of the world is held also by Ursinus, *Summe of Christian Religion*, p. 332; La Primaudaye, *French Academie*, p. 647; Shakelton, *Blazyng Starre*, sig. [Avi]; Goulart, *Learned Summary*, Part I, pp. 83-84; Perkins, *Exposition of the Creede*, p. 424; Joseph Hall, *Farewell Sermon*, in *Works*, pp. 464-65; Boehme, *Works*, II, 34; Davies of Hereford, *Muses Sacrifice*, p. 50, in *Works*, Vol. II; Drummond, *Flowers of Zion*, in *Poetical Works*, II, 20-21; Alexander, *Doomes-Day*, Fourth Hour, stanzas 25-33, in *Poetical Works*, II, 115-17; Adams, *Workes*, p. 254; Swan, *Speculum mundi*, pp. 5-9; Browne, *Religio*, pp. 98-99; Senault, *Man Become Guilty*, p. 387; Jeremy Taylor, *Works*, III, 481; Glanvill, *Two Choice and Vsefvl Treatises*, p. 146; Burnet, *Sacred Theory*, II, 7; Ray, *Miscellaneous Discourses*, pp. 23, 189 ff.; Ralegh, *History of the World*, sig. E.

56. *Fall*, p. 385.

57. For general statements showing the end to be near see Goodman, *Fall*, pp. 354, 383, 384; *Apologie*, V, 101, 171; Cyprian, *De unitate ecclesiae*, p. 57; Cyprian, *Epistles*, No. lviii, pp. 142-43, No. lxvii, p. 214; Edwin Sandys, *Sermons*, No. ix, p. 169, No. xx; Leroy, *Interchangeable Covrse*, fols. 2[v]-3, 126[v]; Shakelton, *Blazyng Starre*, sigs. Av, Biiii; Stubbes, *Anatomie of Abuses*, pp. 24, 187-88; Pont, *Right Reckoning of Yeares*, pp. 57, 91, 104; Boehme, *Mercurius Teutonicus*, pp. 3, 7-8, 10, 12; Stafford, *Staffords Niobe, Dissolv'd into a Nilvs*, p. 84; Davies of Hereford, *Muses Sacrifice*, pp. 51, 78, in *Works*, Vol. II; Davies of Hereford, *Wittes Pilgrimage*, p. 40, in *Works*, Vol. II; Drummond, *Poetical Works*, I, 90; Rainolds, *Prophecies of Obadiah*, p. 110; Scott, *Philosophers Banqvet*, pp. 352-53; T. I., "Preface," *The Miracle of Miracles*, as cited by Wright, *Middle-Class Culture in Elizabethan England*,

p. 460, n. 101; *Threnoikos*, p. 474; Feltham, *Resolves*, pp. 156–57; Swan, *Speculum mundi*, p. 9; Henry Burton, *Sovnding of the Two Last Trvmpets;* Browne, *Christian Morals*, pp. 106–7, 128–29; Browne, *Letter to a Friend*, printed with *Religio*, p. 181.

Signs of the end are seen in the decline of faith, in the heresies and false prophecies, and in the general moral decline of present times. For representative descriptions of these portents as foreshadowing the world's destruction see Goodman, *Fall*, pp. 354, 385–86; Sandys, *Sermons*, No. ix, p. 170, and the whole of No. xviii; La Primaudaye, *French Academie*, p. 334; Shakelton, *Blazyng Starre*, sig. Cv; Rogers, *General Session*, p. 59; Stubbes, *Anatomie of Abuses*, pp. 24, 187–88; Barckley, *Felicitie of Man*, p. 645; Pont, *Right Reckoning of Yeares*, pp. 78–81, 99; Norden, *Progress of Piety*, pp. 107, 119; Perkins, *Exposition of the Creede*, pp. 420–23; Bayly, *Practise of Pietie*, sig. A3ᵛ; Sutton, *Disce vivere*, pp. 434–35; T. Taylor, *Christ Revealed*, p. 15; *Threnoikos*, pp. 251–52, 454, 456; Browne, *Christian Morals*, p. 128; Dove, *Almanac for 1653*, sig. [C5]; Howell, *Parly of Beasts*, sig. b2ᵛ. See also *Apologie*, pp. 60 ff., for early Christian expressions of the same idea and for Hakewill's refutation.

Another common sign of the approaching end—the revelation of the Antichrist—is discussed in Cyprian, *Epistles*, No. lviii, p. 142, No. lxvii, p. 214; Perkins, *Exposition of the Creede*, pp. 421–23; Willet, *Daniel*, pp. 442–43; Boehme, *Mercurius Teutonicus*, p. 5; and Hakewill, *Apologie*, pp. 553–56.

Physical signs of the end, emphasizing particularly the decay in the heavens, are recounted at length in many works, among them Shakelton, *Blazyng Starre*, sigs. Biiᵛ–Biii; Stubbes, *Anatomie of Abuses*, pp. 187–88; Pont, *Right Reckoning of Yeares*, pp. 82–83, 90–91; Case, *Lapis philosophicvs*, p. 957; Du Moulin, *Accomplishment of the Prophecies*, p. 251; Dove, *Confvtation of Atheisme*, p. 93; Drummond, *Flowers of Zion*, in *Poetical Works*, II, 59, 61; Alexander, *Doomes-Day*, Second Hour, stanzas 62–63, in *Poetical Works*, II, 59; Sutton, *Disce vivere*, pp. 434–35; Adams, *Workes*, pp. 19, 409; *Catastrophe mundi*, pp. 87–89; and Anton, *Philosophers Satyrs*, sigs. [C3ᵛ]–[C4].

Particular dates of the end are suggested in Goodman, *Fall*, p. 385; Napier, *Plaine Discouery*, pp. 16–22 (but see Hakewill, *Apologie*, p. 25); Pont, *Right Reckoning of Yeares*, pp. 78, 101; Du Moulin, *Accomplishment of the Prophecies*, pp. 250–51 (but see Hakewill, *Apologie*, pp. 97–98); Swan, *Speculum mundi*, p. 24; Dove, *Almanac for 1653*, sig. [C5]; *Pepysian Garland*, p. 112; *Catastrophe mundi*, pp. 17, 18, 71, 75, 76, 81; *Whole Prophecies*, pp. 41, 44, 47.

More regularly, however, the date, though we may know it to be near, is understood to be beyond our powers of discovery. For such protestations see Goodman, *Fall*, p. 383; Goulart, *Learned Summary*, Part I, p. 193, Part II, p. 145; Shakelton, *Blazyng Starre*, sig. [Avii]; Ursinus, *Summe of Christian Religion*, p. 333; Rainolds, *Prophecies of Obadiah*, p. 110; Swan, *Speculum mundi,* pp. 9–12, 15–25, 27; *Threnoikos,* p. 453; *Catastrophe mundi,* p. 76; Ray, *Miscellaneous Discourses,* pp. 23, 182–84.

Prophesying the date of the end is characterized by Burton (*Anatomy of Melancholy,* p. 635) as a manifestation of melancholy. Willet (*Daniel,* pp. 58, 220–21), Senault (*Man Become Guilty,* pp. 327–28), Burnet (*Sacred Theory,* II, 45–48, 51), and Ray (*Miscellaneous Discourses,* pp. 174–79) deny that the date of the end may be predicted from the signs of the end. Hakewill (*Apologie,* p. 51) argues that, if the world were decaying, we would thereby be warned of the time of the end; since the end will come without warning, there can be no decay. Ray (*Miscellaneous Discourses,* pp. 181–82) makes a parallel point when he says that we cannot know the date of the end because there is no decay by which to measure it.

Nevertheless, even Hakewill accepts the fact that this is the last age of the world, and the general opinion seems to be that, however long the world still endures, the remaining period is the afternoon of time, the echo of the last trumpet. For illustrations of this belief see Goodman, *Fall,* pp. 246, 384; Cyprian, *Epistles,* No. lxvii, p. 214; Sandys, *Sermons,* p. 170; Boehme, *Mercurius Teutonicus,* p. 12; Shakelton, *Blazyng Starre,* sig. [Avii]; I. D., in *Aristotles Politiqves,* sig. Aiii; Ursinus, *Summe of Christian Religion,* p. 333; Goulart, *Learned Summary,* Part I, sig. A2ᵛ, Part II, pp. 145–46; Pont, *Right Reckoning of Yeares,* pp. 22–23, 35, 42, 90; Perkins, *Exposition of the Creede,* p. 420; Vaughan, *Golden-Groue,* sigs. [D6], G2ᵛ, [N8ᵛ], [X7ᵛ]; Donne, *Fifty Sermons,* No. xvii, p. 142; Anton, *Philosophers Satyrs,* sig. [C4]; Alexander, *Recreations with Muses,* in *Poetical Works,* I, 3; Alexander, *Doomes-Day,* Second Hour, stanzas 30, 84, in *Poetical Works,* II, 51, 65; *Help to Discourse,* p. 6; Bayly, *Practise of Pietie,* sig. A3–A3ᵛ; Purchas, *Pilgrimes,* I, 166, II, 3; Reynolds, *Triumphs of Gods Revenge,* sig. A3; p. 425; *Treasvrie of Avncient and Moderne Times,* I, 342; Downe, *Certaine Treatises,* p. 111; Person, *Varieties,* Book V, p. 10; Heywood, *Hierarchie,* p. 144; *Threnoikos,* p. 474; Howell, *Parly of Beasts,* sig. a–aᵛ; Lilly, in *Catastrophe mundi,* p. 86.

See also Hakewill (*Apologie,* pp. 549–50) and Ray (*Miscellaneous Discourses,* p. 21) for the suggestion that the last times need not indicate an early end, and Gouge (*Progresse of Divine Providence,* pp. 15–19, 40) for the similar suggestion that the last times are not necessarily the worst. The usual implication, of course, is that this final period of the world's duration represents the dregs of time, with the end oppressively near.

58. Shakelton, *Blazyng Starre,* sigs. Aiiii–Av; Feltham, *Resolves,* No. xlix, pp. 156–57. See also Lucretius *De rerum natura* ii. 1150 ff., p. 67; Cyprian, *Epistles,* No. lxvii, p. 214; Sandys, *Sermons,* p. 169; Adams, *Workes,* p. 19.

59. Pont, *Right Reckoning of Yeares,* p. 35; Donne, *LXXX Sermons,* No. xxxvi, p. 357; La Primaudaye, *French Academie,* p. 554. The comparison of man's death and the world's end is found also in Bayly, *Practise of Pietie,* pp. 91–92; Joseph Hall, *Works,* p. 465; Adams, *Mystical Bedlam,* p. 81; Sutton, *Disce vivere,* pp. 434–35; Swan, *Speculum mundi,* pp. 5–6. The part-to-whole

argument, current in many variant forms, may be found in Goodman, *Fall,* pp. 22–23, 349–50; Hakewill, *Apologie,* V, 11, 15, 22; Shakelton, *Blazyng Starre,* sig. Aiiii; Feltham, *Resolves,* pp. 154, 156; T. Taylor, *Works,* p. 106; Swan, *Speculum mundi,* p. 3; Vaughan, *Mount of Olives,* in *Works,* I, 170–71; Dove, *Confvtation of Atheisme,* p. 92; Adams, *Workes,* p. 409. The refutation propounded by Hakewill is that the world's old age, even if granted, need not and will not bring on its death, and, more generally, that the world as a whole is exempt from the mutability and mortality of its parts (see *Apologie,* sig. C2; p. 60; V, 7, 12–13, 19).

60. See Browne, *Religio,* pp. 68–69; Lovejoy, *Primitivism and Related Ideas,* pp. 99–100; Burtt, *Metaphysical Foundations,* pp. 78–79.

61. Purchas, *Pilgrim,* p. 26; Weigel, *Astrology Theologized,* p. 99; Boehme, *Works,* II, 63; G. Fletcher, "Christs Victorie in Heaven," stanza 8, in *Poetical Works,* I, 20; Du Bartas, *Little Bartas,* p. 212; Donne, *LXXX Sermons,* No. lxxx, pp. 823–24.

For further characterizations of man and world in these terms see Batman, *Bartholome,* fol. 118ᵛ; Du Bartas, *Weekes, First Week,* I, 305; *First Week,* II, 1197, 1203; *Little Bartas,* p. 233; La Primaudaye, *French Academie,* pp. 9, 372, 523, 543, 631, 670–72; sig. Iiiᵛ; Goulart, *Learned Summary,* Part I, pp. 123, 201, Part II, p. 237; Perkins, *Exposition of the Creede,* p. 221; Stafford, *Staffords Niobe, Dissolv'd into a Nilvs,* p. 178; Donne, *LXXX Sermons,* No. xxxix, p. 388; Donne, *XXVI Sermons,* No. xiv, p. 196, No. xv, pp. 207–8; Purchas, *Pilgrim,* pp. 25–26, 30 ff.; Ralegh, *History of the World,* pp. 30–32; Zouche, *Dove,* p. 10; Joseph Hall, *Contemplations,* in *Works,* p. 813; Bayly, *Practise of Pietie,* pp. 91–92; Jackson, *Raging Tempest Stilled,* p. 36; Sutton, *Disce vivere,* p. 434; Adams, *Workes,* p. 1128; Adams, *Mystical Bedlam,* pp. 3, 9, 81; Harris, *Arraignement,* p. 83; Carpenter, *Chorazin and Bethsaida's Woe,* sig. A2ᵛ; P. Fletcher, *Purple Island,* Canto I, stanza 43, p. 12; P. Fletcher, "An Hymen at the Marriage of My Most Deare Cousins Mr. W. and M. R.," and "Upon the Contemplations of the B. of Excester [*sic*]," in *Purple Island,* 2d pagination, pp. 57, 84; Swan, *Speculum mundi,* pp. 5–6, 153–54, 496; Heywood, *Hierarchie,* p. 338; Person, *Varieties,* p. 27; Book V, pp. 88–89; Austin, *Haec homo,* p. 32; Heylyn, Μικρόκοσμος, p. 18, and *Cosmography,* p. 4; Ross, Πανσέβεια, sig. A3; Comenius, *Naturall Philosophie Reformed,* pp. 16, 46–47, 226–27; Bates, *Works,* I, 182; Weigel, *Astrology Theologized,* pp. 55, 81, 98; Whitlock, Ζωοτομία, pp. 321, 395; Walkington, *Optick Glasse of Humors,* p. 163.

62. *Apologie,* V, 119; see also V, 7.

63. *Essays on Ancient & Modern Learning and on Poetry,* p. 30.

64. See Hakewill, *Apologie,* V, 4, 7, 51, 101–2, 118–19, 141, 143–44, 148, 156–57; Bacon, *Advancement of Learning,* Book I, in *Physical and Metaphysical Works,* p. 51; Wotton, *Reliquiae Wottonianae,* p. 529; Osborne, *Miscellany,* p. 106; Spencer, *Discourse concerning Prodigies,* pp. 70–71, 280–81.

65. Purchas, *Pilgrimes,* I, 25; Davies of Hereford, "Rights of the Living

and the Dead," appendix to *Muses Sacrifice*, p. 68, in *Works*, Vol. II; Browne, *Religio*, p. 99.

66. Purchas, *Pilgrimage*, pp. 10–11; Stubbes, *Anatomie of Abuses*, p. iii; Donne, *XXVI Sermons*, No. xxv, p. 370; Donne, *Devotions*, No. iv, in *Complete Poetry and Selected Prose*, p. 511.

For other examples of the very common connection between teleological doctrines and the analogy of microcosm and macrocosm see also Goodman, *Fall*, pp. 107, 423; J. King, *Funeral Sermon*, p. 316; Bastard, *Chrestoleros*, Book I, Epigram 4, in *Poems*, p. 6; Allott, *Wits Theater of the Little World*, sig. A3; Davies of Hereford, *Microcosmos*, pp. [6], 85, in *Works*, Vol. I; Purchas, *Pilgrimes*, I, 15, 25, 29, 135, 136–37, and *Pilgrimage*, p. 26; Scott, *Philosophers Banqvet*, p. 4; Anton, *Philosophers Satyrs*, sig. B3ᵛ; Fludd, *Mosaicall Philosophy*, pp. 160, 163–64, 215; Crooke, Μικροκοσμογραφία, pp. 2–3, 6; Person, *Varieties*, p. 93; Weigel, *Astrology Theologized*, pp. 76–77.

67. Donne, *Fifty Sermons*, No. xx, p. 166; Adams, *Workes*, p. 246. See also Hooker, *Ecclesiastical Politie*, Book I, p. 23; Donne, *Devotions*, No. i, in *Complete Poetry and Selected Prose*, p. 508; Goodman, *Fall*, p. 107; Comenius, *Janua linguarum reserata*, chap. xx, sentence 227, sig. [H5]; Burton, *Anatomy of Melancholy*, p. 1.

68. Goodman, *Fall*, pp. 17, 27; Hall, *Farewell Sermon*, in *Works*, p. 464.

69. Pont, *Right Reckoning of Yeares*, p. 35; Gascoigne, *Drum of Doomsday*, in *Works*, II, 234. For other examples of the world's decline described in the same terms see Estienne, *World of Wonders*, p. 21; Torquemada, *Spanish Mandeuile of Miracles*, fols. 23ᵛ, 52; Goodman, *Fall*, pp. 348, 386; *Apologie*, V, 101; Viret, *Worlde Possessed with Deuils*, sig. Aviᵛ, as cited by Allen "The Degeneration of Man and Renaissance Pessimism," p. 210; Adams, *Workes*, p. 246.

70. Howell, *Parly of Beasts*, sig. b; Swan, *Speculum mundi*, p. 78; Goodman, *Fall*, pp. 348–49; see also *Help to Discourse*, p. 288; Person, *Varieties*, p. 232.

71. Goodman, *Fall*, pp. 348–49; Ralegh, *History of the World*, pp. 76–77; see also Bacon, *Novum organum*, Book I, aphorism lxxxiv, in *Physical and Metaphysical Works*, p. 418.

Bibliography

REFERENCE AND CRITICISM

ALLEN, DON CAMERON. "The Degeneration of Man and Renaissance Pessimism," *Studies in Philology*, XXXV (1938), 202–27.

BREDVOLD, LOUIS I. *The Intellectual Milieu of John Dryden: Studies in Some Aspects of Seventeenth-Century Thought*. Ann Arbor: University of Michigan Press, 1934.

———. "The Religious Thought of Donne in Relation to Medieval and Later Traditions," *Studies in Shakespeare, Milton and Donne*. ("University of Michigan Publications. Language and Literature," Vol. I.) New York: Macmillan Co., 1925.

BURTT, E. A. *The Metaphysical Foundations of Modern Physical Science*. London: Kegan Paul, Trench, Trübner & Co., Ltd., 1925.

———. *Types of Religious Philosophy*. New York: Harper & Bros., [1939].

BURY, J. B. *The Idea of Progress*. London: Macmillan & Co., Ltd., 1924.

Cambridge Bibliography of English Literature. Edited by F. W. BATESON. 4 vols. Cambridge: At the University Press, 1941.

COFFIN, CHARLES M. *John Donne and the New Philosophy*. New York: Columbia University Press, 1937.

COLLIER, K. B. *Cosmogonies of Our Fathers: Some Theories of the Seventeenth and the Eighteenth Centuries*. New York: Columbia University Press, 1934.

Dictionary of National Biography. Various articles.

GILSON, ÉTIENNE. *The Spirit of Mediaeval Philosophy*. Translated by A. H. C. DOWNES. ("Gifford Lectures, 1931–1932.") New York: Charles Scribner's Sons, 1936.

HARRISON, C. T. "The Ancient Atomists and English Literature of the Seventeenth Century," *Harvard Studies in Classical Philology*, XLV (1934), 1–79.

HOLMES, ELIZABETH. *Henry Vaughan and the Hermetic Philosophy*. Oxford: Basil Blackwell, [1932].

HUIZINGA, JOHAN. *The Waning of the Middle Ages*. London: E. Arnold & Co., 1924.

JOHNSON, FRANCIS R. *Astronomical Thought in Renaissance England: A Study of the English Scientific Writings from 1500 to 1645*. Baltimore: Johns Hopkins Press, 1937.

JONES, RICHARD FOSTER. *Ancients and Moderns: A Study of the Background of the Battle of the Books*. ("Washington University Studies. New Series. Language and Literature," No. VI.) St. Louis, 1936.

————. *The Background of the Battle of the Books.* ("Washington University Studies. Humanistic Series," No. VII.) [St. Louis, 1920.]

KOLLER, KATHRINE. "Two Elizabethan Expressions of the Idea of Mutability," *Studies in Philology,* XXXV (1938), 228–37.

LOVEJOY, ARTHUR O. *The Great Chain of Being.* Cambridge, Mass.: Harvard University Press, 1936.

LOVEJOY, ARTHUR O., and BOAS, GEORGE. *Primitivism and Related Ideas in Antiquity.* Baltimore: Johns Hopkins Press, 1935.

McCOLLEY, GRANT. "The Seventeenth-Century Doctrine of a Plurality of Worlds," *Annals of Science,* I (1936), 385–430.

McINTYRE, J. LEWIS. *Giordano Bruno.* London: Macmillan & Co., Ltd., 1903.

MOLONEY, MICHAEL F. *John Donne: His Flight from Mediaevalism.* Urbana: University of Illinois Press, 1944.

MULLINGER, J. B. *The University of Cambridge.* 3 vols. Cambridge: At the University Press, 1873–1911.

NICOLSON, MARJORIE. "The Microscope and English Imagination," *Smith College Studies in Modern Languages,* XVI, No. 4 (July, 1935), 1–92.

————. "The 'New Astronomy' and English Literary Imagination," *Studies in Philology,* XXXII (1935), 428–62.

————. "The Telescope and Imagination," *Modern Philology,* XXXII (1935), 233–60.

OSENBURG, FREDERIC CHARLES. "The Ideas of the Golden Age and the Decay of the World in the English Renaissance." Unpublished Ph.D. dissertation, department of English, University of Illinois, 1939.

ST. CLAIR, FOSTER YORK. "The Myth of the Golden Age from Spenser to Milton." Unpublished Ph.D. dissertation, department of English, Harvard University, 1931.

SMITH, PRESERVED. *A History of Modern Culture,* Vol. I: *The Great Renewal, 1543–1687.* New York: Henry Holt & Co., [1930].

STONES, G. B. "The Atomic View of Matter in the XVth, XVIth, and XVIIth Centuries," *Isis,* X (1928), 445–65.

STRONG, EDWARD W. *Procedures and Metaphysics: A Study in the Philosophy of Mathematical-Physical Science in the Sixteenth and Seventeenth Centuries.* Berkeley: University of California Press, 1936.

TENNANT, F. R. *The Sources of the Doctrines of the Fall and Original Sin.* Cambridge: At the University Press, 1903.

THORNDIKE, LYNN. *A History of Magic and Experimental Science.* 6 vols. New York: Macmillan Co., 1923–41.

TILLYARD, E. M. W. *The Elizabethan World Picture.* London: Chatto & Windus, 1943.

TULLOCH, JOHN. *The Christian Doctrine of Sin.* New York: Scribner, Armstrong & Co., [1876?].

WHITAKER, V. K. "Du Bartas' Use of Lucretius," *Studies in Philology,* XXXIII (1936), 134–46.

WHITE, HELEN C. *English Devotional Literature, 1600–1640.* ("University of Wisconsin Studies in Language and Literature," No. XXIX.) Madison, Wisconsin, 1931.

WILLEY, BASIL. *The Seventeenth Century Background*. London: Chatto & Windus, 1934.

WILLIAMS, ARNOLD. "A Note on Pessimism in the Renaissance," *Studies in Philology*, XXXVI (1939), 243–46.

WILLIAMS, N. P. *The Ideas of the Fall and of Original Sin*. London: Longmans, Green & Co., Ltd., 1927.

WILLIAMSON, GEORGE. "Mutability, Decay, and Seventeenth-Century Melancholy," *ELH: A Journal of English Literary History*, II (1935), 121–50.

WRIGHT, LOUIS B. *Middle-Class Culture in Elizabethan England*. Chapel Hill: University of North Carolina Press, 1935.

TEXTS

ABERNETHY, JOHN. *A Christian and Heavenly Treatise. Containing Physicke for the Sovle*. London: Felix Kyngston for Iohn Budge, 1622.

ACOSTA, JOSEPH DE. *The Natural & Moral History of the Indies*. Translated by EDWARD GRIMSTON. Edited by CLEMENTS MARKHAM. 2 vols. London: Hakluyt Society, 1880.

ADAMS, THOMAS. *Mystical Bedlam, or the VVorld of Mad-Men*. London: George Purslowe for Clement Knight, 1615.

———. *The Workes of Tho: Adams*. London: Tho: Harper for Iohn Grismand, 1630.

ALEXANDER, WILLIAM. *The Poetical Works of Sir William Alexander, Earl of Stirling*. Edited by L. E. KASTNER and H. B. CHARLTON. 2 vols. Manchester: Manchester University Press, 1921, 1929.

ALLOTT, ROBERT. *Wits Theater of the Little World*. [London]: I. R. for N. L., 1599.

AMYRAUT, MOÏSE. *A Treatise concerning Religions*. London: M.*Simons, for Will. Nealand, 1660.

Ancient Ballads & Broadsides Published in England in the Sixteenth Century, Chiefly in the Earlier Years of the Reign of Queen Elizabeth. London: Whittingham & Wilkins, 1867.

ANTON, ROBERT. *The Philosophers Satyrs*. London: T. C. and B. A. for Roger Iackson, 1616.

ARISTOTLE. *Aristotles Politiqves*. Translated by I. D. London: Adam Islip, 1598.

———. *The Basic Works of Aristotle*. Edited by RICHARD MCKEON. New York: Random House, 1941.

ASHMOLE, ELIAS. *Theatrum chemicum Britannicum*. London: J. Grismond for Nath: Brooke, 1652.

AUSTIN, WILLIAM. *Haec homo*. London: Richard Olton for Ralph Mabb, 1637.

BABINGTON, GERVASE. *The Workes of the Right Reverend Father in God, Gervase Babington*. 5 vols. in 1. London: George Eld, 1615.

BACON, FRANCIS. *Of the Advancement and Proficience of Learning.* Translated by GILBERT WATS. Oxford: Leon. Lichfield, 1640.

———. *The Physical and Metaphysical Works of Lord Bacon.* Edited by JOSEPH DEVEY. London: George Bell & Sons, 1894.

———. *The Works of Francis Bacon.* Edited by JAMES SPEDDING, R. L. ELLIS, and D. D. HEATH. 14 vols. London: Longman & Co., 1857–90.

BANISTER, JOHN. *The Historie of Man.* London: John Daye, 1578.

BARCKLEY, RICHARD. *The Felicitie of Man, or, His summum bonum.* 3d ed. London: R. Y., 1631.

BARCLAY, JOHN. *The Mirrovr of Mindes, or Barclays Icon animorum.* Translated by T[HOMAS] M[AY]. London: I. Norton for T. Walkley, 1631.

BARTHOLOMAEUS ANGLICUS. See BATMAN, STEPHEN.

B[ASSET], R[OBERT]. *Curiosities, or the Cabinet of Nature.* London: N. and I. OKES, 1637.

BASTARD, THOMAS. *The Poems English and Latin of the Rev. Thomas Bastard, M.A.* Edited by A. B. GROSART. [Manchester: Charles E. Simms], 1880.

BATES, WILLIAM. *The Whole Works of the Rev. W. Bates, D.D.* 4 vols. London: James Black, etc., 1815.

BATMAN, STEPHEN. *Batman vppon Bartholome, His Booke De proprietatibus rerum, Newly Corrected, Enlarged and Amended: With Such Additions as Are Requisite, vnto Euery Seuerall Booke: Taken Foorth of the Most Approued Authors, the Like Heretofore Not Translated in English.* London: Thomas East, 1582.

BAYLY, LEWIS. *The Practise of Pietie.* 5th ed. London: Iohn Hodgets, 1615.

BEARD, THOMAS. *The Theatre of Gods Ivdgements.* London: Adam Islip for Michael Sparke, 1631.

BEAUMONT, FRANCIS, and FLETCHER, JOHN. *Comedies and Tragedies Written by Francis Beavmont and Iohn Fletcher Gentlemen.* London: Humphrey Robinson & Humphrey Moseley, 1647.

BEST, GEORGE. See *The Three Voyages of Martin Frobisher.*

BLOUNT, THOMAS POPE. *A Natural History: Containing Many Not Common Observations: Extracted Out of the Best Modern Writers.* London: R. Bentley, 1693.

BOAISTUAU, PIERRE. *Theatrum mundi.* London: Thomas East for John VVyght, 1581.

BODIN, JEAN. *Methodvs historica.* Basileae: Petri Pernae, 1576.

———. *The Six Bookes of a Commonweale.* Translated by RICHARD KNOLLES. London: G. Bishop, 1606.

BOEHME, JACOB. *Mercurius Teutonicus; or a Christian Information concerning the Last Times.* London: M. Simmons for H. Blunden, 1649.

———. *The Works of Jacob Behmen, the Teutonic Theosopher.* 4 vols. London: M. Richardson, 1764–81.

BRATHWAITE, RICHARD. *Essays upon the Five Senses.* In *Archaica,* Vol. II. London: T. Davison, 1815.

BRATHWAITE, RICHARD. *Natures Embassie.* Boston, Lincolnshire: Robert Roberts, 1877.

———. *The Schollers Medley.* London: N. O. for George Norton, 1614.

———. *Some Rules and Orders for the Government of the House of an Earle.* London: R. Triphook, 1821.

BROWNE, THOMAS. *Christian Morals.* 2d ed. London: Richard Hett for J. Payne, 1756.

———. *Pseudodoxia epidemica.* London: T. H. for Edward Dod, 1646.

———. *Religio medici, A Letter to a Friend, Christian Morals, Urn Burial, and Other Papers.* Boston: Ticknor & Fields, 1862.

BROWNE, WILLIAM. *The Whole Works of William Browne.* Edited by W. C. HAZLITT. 2 vols. [London]: Roxburghe Library, 1868–69.

BULLINGER, HENRY. *The Decades.* Translated by H. I. Edited by THOMAS HARDING. ("Parker Society Publications," Nos. VII–X.) 4 vols. Cambridge: At the University Press, 1849–52.

BURGESS, ANTHONY. *The Doctrine of Original Sin.* London: Abraham Miller for Thomas Underhill, 1659.

BURNET, THOMAS. *The Sacred Theory of the Earth: Containing an Account of Its Original Creation, and of All the General Changes Which It Hath Undergone, or Is To Undergo, until the Consummation of All Things.* 7th ed. 2 vols. London: T. Osborn, etc., 1759.

BURTON, HENRY. *The Sovnding of the Two Last Trvmpets, the Sixt and Seventh.* London: S. Gellibrand, 1641.

BURTON, ROBERT. *The Anatomy of Melancholy.* 4th ed. Oxford: Henry Cripps, 1632.

BYFIELD, NICHOLAS. *An Exposition vpon the Epistle to the Colossians.* London: E. G. for Nathaniel Bvtter, 1617.

———. *The Principles or, the Patterne of Wholesome Words. Containing a Collection of Such Truths as Are of Necessitie To Be Belieued vnto Saluation, Seperated Out of the Bodie of All Theologie.* 3d ed. London: W. Sansby for Phile. Steuens & Christ. Meredith, 1627.

CAMERARIUS, PHILIP. *The Living Librarie.* Translated by IOHN MOLLE. London: Adam Islip, 1621.

CAMFIELD, BENJAMIN. *A Theological Discourse of Angels, and Their Ministries.* London: R. E. for Hen. Brome, 1678.

CARDAN, JEROME. *The First Book of Jerome Cardan's De subtilitate.* Translated by M. M. CASS. Williamsport, Pa.: Bayard Press, [1934].

CARPENTER, NATHANAEL. *Achitophel, or, the Pictvre of a Wicked Politician.* London: M. S., 1629.

———. *Chorazin and Bethsaida's Woe.* London: T. Cotes for Michael Sparke, 1633.

———. *Geography Delineated Forth in Two Bookes.* Oxford: Iohn Lichfield & William Tvrner, 1625.

CARTARI, VINCENT. *The Fovntaine of Ancient Fiction.* Translated by RICHARD LINCHE. London: Adam Islip, 1599.

CASE, JOHN. *Lapis philosophicvs.* Frankfurt: A. Wecheli & A. Hierat, 1600.

Catastrophe mundi: Or, Merlin Reviv'd. London: John How & Thomas Malthus, 1683.

CHARLETON, WALTER. *The Darknes of Atheism Dispelled by the Light of Nature*. London: J. F. for William Lee, 1652.

———. *Physiologia Epicuro-Gassendo-Charltoniana: Or a Fabrick of Science Natural*. London: Tho: Newcomb for Thomas Heath, 1654.

COLE, JAMES. *Of Death a Trve Description*. London: A. M., 1629.

COMENIUS, JOHANN AMOS. *Janua linguarum reserata*. Translated by THO. HORN. Corrected and amended by JOH. ROBOTHAM. Edited by W. D. London: T. R. and N. T. for the Co. of Stationers, 1673.

———. *Naturall Philosophie Reformed by Divine Light: Or, a Synopsis of Physicks*. London: Robert and William Leybourn for Thomas Pierrepont, 1651.

COOPER, THOMAS. *See* [LANQUET, THOMAS].

COWLEY, ABRAHAM. *Poems*. London: H. Moseley, 1656.

———. *See The Four Ages of England*.

CREECH, THOMAS. *See* LUCRETIUS.

Critical Essays of the Eighteenth Century. Edited by WILLARD H. DURHAM. New Haven: Yale University Press, 1915.

Critical Essays of the Seventeenth Century. Edited by J. E. SPINGARN. 3 vols. Oxford: Clarendon Press, 1908–9.

CROOKE, HELKIAH. Μικροκοσμογραφία: *A Description of the Body of Man*. [London]: W. Iaggard, 1616.

CUDWORTH, RALPH. *The True Intellectual System of the Universe*. With notes by J. L. MOSHEIM. 3 vols. London: T. Tegg, 1845.

CUFF, HENRY. *The Differences of the Ages of Mans Life*. London: A. Hatfield, 1607.

CULVERWEL, NATHANIEL. *An Elegant and Learned Discourse of the Light of Nature*. London: T. R. and E. M. for John Rothwel, 1654.

CYPRIAN. *The Epistles of S. Cyprian*. Translated by H. CAREY. Oxford: John Henry Parker, 1844.

———. *De unitate ecclesiae*. Translated by E. H. BLAKENEY. London: Society for Promoting Christian Knowledge, 1928.

DANEAU, LAMBERT. *A Frvitfvll Commentarie vpon the Twelue Small Prophets*. Translated by JOHN STOCKWOOD. Cambridge: Iohn Legate, 1594.

———. *The Wonderfvll Woorkmanship of the World*. Translated by T[HOMAS] T[WYNE]. London: Andrew Maunsell, 1578.

DANIEL, SAMUEL. *The Whole Workes of Samvel Daniel Esquire in Poetrie*. London: Nicholas Okes for Simon Waterson, 1623.

DAVIES, JOHN. *The Works in Verse and Prose of Sir John Davies*. Edited by A. B. GROSART. 3 vols. [Blackburn: C. Tiplady], 1869–76.

DAVIES, JOHN (of Hereford). *The Complete Works of John Davies of Hereford*. Edited by A. B. GROSART. 2 vols. [Edinburgh: Edinburgh University Press], 1878.

DEANE, EDMUND. *Spadacrene anglica*. Bristol: John Wright, 1922.

DEKKER, THOMAS. *Old Fortunatus*. In *Thomas Dekker*. Edited by ERNEST RHYS. ("The Mermaid Series.") London: Ernest Benn, etc., [n.d.].

[DENT, ARTHUR. *The Plain Man's Pathway to Heaven*. 40th ed. Title-page missing.]

DESCARTES, RENÉ. *The Philosophical Works of Descartes*. Translated by E. S. HALDANE and G. R. T. Ross. 2 vols. Cambridge: At the University Press, 1911.

DONNE, JOHN. *Complete Poetry and Selected Prose*. Edited by JOHN HAYWARD. New York: Random House, 1936.

——. *LXXX Sermons Preached by That Learned and Reverend Divine John Donne*. London: Richard Royston, 1640.

——. *Fifty Sermons, Preached by That Learned and Reverend Divine, John Donne*. London: Ja. Flesher for M. F., J. Marriot, & R. Royston, 1649.

——. *The Poems of John Donne*. Edited by H. J. C. GRIERSON. 2 vols. Oxford: Clarendon Press, 1912.

——. *XXVI Sermons (Never Before Publish'd) Preached by That Learned and Reverend. Divine John Donne*. London: Thomas Newcomb, 1661.

[DOVE. *Almanac for 1653*. Title-page missing.]

DOVE, JOHN. *A Confvtation of Atheisme*. London: Edward Allde for Henry Rockett, 1605.

DOWNE, JOHN. *Certaine Treatises of the Late Reverend and Learned Divine, Mr. John Downe*. Oxford: Iohn Lichfield for Edward Forrest, 1633.

DRAYTON, MICHAEL. *The Complete Works of Michael Drayton*. Edited by J. W. HEBEL. 5 vols. Oxford: Shakespeare Head Press, 1931–41.

DRUMMOND, WILLIAM. *The Poetical Works of William Drummond of Hawthornden*. Edited by L. E. KASTNER. 2 vols. Edinburgh: William Blackwood & Sons, 1913.

DRYDEN, JOHN. *Essays of John Dryden*. Edited by W. P. KER. 2 vols. Oxford: Clarendon Press, 1900.

DU BARTAS, GUILLAUME. *Du Bartas His Divine Weekes and Workes*. See SYLVESTER, JOSHUAH, *The Complete Works of Joshuah Sylvester*, Vol. I.

——. *Little Bartas: Or Brief Meditations, on the Power, Providence, Greatnes, & Goodnes of God*. See SYLVESTER, JOSHUAH, *The Parliament of Vertues Royal*, Vol. I.

——. *The Works of Guillaume de Salluste, Sieur du Bartas: A Critical Edition*. Edited by URBAN T. HOLMES, etc. 3 vols. Chapel Hill: University of North Carolina Press, 1935–40.

DU MOULIN, PIERRE. *The Accomplishment of the Prophecies*. Oxford: Ioseph Barnes, 1613.

——. *The Anatomy of Arminianisme*. London: Nathanael Newbery, 1626.

——. *The Bvckler of the Faith*. London: R[ichard] F[ield] for Nathanael Newbery, 1620.

——. *Dv combat chrestien*. 4th ed. Genève: Pierre Avbert, 1632.

——. *A Treatise of Peace & Contentment of Mind*. 3d ed. London: R. White for John Sims, 1678.

EDEN, RICHARD. See *The First Three English Books on America.*

ESTIENNE, HENRI. *A World of Wonders: Or an Introdvction to a Treatise Touching the Conformitie of Ancient and Moderne Wonders: Or a Preparatiue Treatise to the Apologie for Herodotvs.* [Translated by R. CAREW.] London: Iohn Norton, 1607.

FEATLEY, DANIEL. *Clavis mystica.* London: R. Y. for N. Bourne, 1636.

FELTHAM, OWEN. *Resolves. A Duple Century.* 3d ed. London: Henry Seile, 1628–29.

The First Three English Books on America. Compiled and translated by RICHARD EDEN. Edited by EDWARD ARBER. Birmingham [Edinburgh: Turnbull & Spears], 1885.

FITZGEFFREY, CHARLES. *The Poems of the Rev. Charles Fitzgeoffrey.* Edited by A. B. GROSART. [Manchester: Charles E. Simms], 1881.

FLETCHER, GILES and PHINEAS. *Poetical Works.* Edited by F. S. BOAS. 2 vols. Cambridge: At the University Press, 1908–9.

FLETCHER, PHINEAS. *The Purple Island, or the Isle of Man: Together with Piscatorie Eclogs and Other Poeticall Miscellanies.* Cambridge: Printers to the Universitie, 1633.

———. *The Way to Blessednes, a Treatise or Commentary, on the First Psalme.* London: I. D. for Iames Boler, 1632.

FLUDD, ROBERT. *Mosaicall Philosophy: Grounded upon the Essentiall Truth or Eternal Sapience.* London: Humphrey Moseley, 1659.

FONTENELLE, BERNARD LE BOVIER DE. *Conversations on the Plurality of Worlds.* Translated by WILLIAM GARDINER. London: A. Bettesworth & E. Curll, 1715.

———. *Œuvres diverses,* Vol. II: *Poesies pastorales. Avec un traité sur la nature de l'eglogue, & une digression sur les anciens & les modernes.* Londres: Paul & Isaak Vaillant, 1707.

The Four Ages of England. London: J. C. for Tho: Dring & Joh. Leigh, 1675.

[FULLER, THOMAS.] *Anglorum speculum, or the Worthies of England.* London: John Wright, etc., 1684.

GALILEI, GALILEO. *The Systeme of the World: In Four Dialogues. See* SALUSBURY, THOMAS.

GASCOIGNE, GEORGE. *The Complete Works of George Gascoigne.* Edited by J. W. CUNLIFFE. 2 vols. Cambridge: At the University Press, 1907–10.

GLANVILL, JOSEPH. *Plus ultra: Or, the Progress and Advancement of Knowledge since the Days of Aristotle.* London: James Collins, 1668.

———. *Scepsis scientifica.* London: E. Cotes for Henry Eversden, 1665.

———. *Two Choice and Vsefvl Treatises: The One Lux orientalis; or an Enquiry into the Opinion of the Eastern Sages concerning the Præexistence of Sovls. . . .* London: James Collins & Sam Lowndes, 1682.

———. *The Vanity of Dogmatizing.* New York: Columbia University Press for Facsimile Text Society, 1931.

———. *The Way of Happiness.* London: E. C. & A. C. for James Collins, 1670.

GOODMAN, GODFREY. *The Fall of Man, or the Corrvption of Natvre, Proved by the Light of Our Naturall Reason.* London: Felix Kyngston, 1616.

———. See HAKEWILL, GEORGE. *An Apologie or Declaration of the Power and Providence of God . . .* (1635 ed.), Book V.

GOUGE, WILLIAM. *The Progresse of Divine Providence.* London: G. M. for Ioshua Kirton, 1645.

GOULART, SIMON. *A Learned Summary upon the Famous Poeme of William of Saluste Lord of Bartas.* London: Iohn Grismand, 1621.

HAGTHORPE, JOHN. *Visiones rervm.* London: Bernard Alsop, 1623.

HAKEWILL, GEORGE. *An Apologie or Declaration of the Power and Providence of God in the Government of the World. Consisting in an Examination and Censvre of the Common Errovr Tovching Natvres Perpetuall and Vniversall Decay, Divided into Fovre Bookes.* Oxford: William Turner, 1630.

———. *An Apologie or Declaration of the Power and Providence of God in the Government of the World. Consisting in an Examination and Censvre of the Common Errovr Tovching Natvres Perpetuall and Universall Decay, Divided into Six Bookes.* Oxford: William Turner, 1635.

———. *An Apologie of the Power and Providence of God in the Government of the World.* Oxford: Iohn Lichfield & William Tvrner, 1627.

HALL, JOHN. *An Humble Motion to the Parliament of England.* London: John Walker, 1649.

HALL, JOSEPH. *Satires.* Chiswick: C. Whittingham for R. Triphook, 1824.

———. *The Works of Joseph Hall.* London: Nath. Butter, 1625.

HANNAY, PATRICK. *The Poetical Works of Patrick Hannay, A.M.* [Glasgow: R. Anderson], 1875.

HARRIS, ROBERT. *The Arraignement of the Whole Creatvre, at the Barre of Religion, Reason, and Experience.* London: B. Alsop & Tho: Favvcet, 1631.

A Help to Discourse: Or, More Merriment Mixt with Serious Matters. 16th ed. London: S. G. for Andrew Crook, 1667.

HERBERT, GEORGE. *The Works of George Herbert.* Edited by F. E. HUTCHINSON. Oxford: Clarendon Press, 1941.

HEYDON, CHRISTOPHER. *An Astrological Discourse.* London: J. Macock for Nathaniel Brooks, 1650.

———. *A Defence of Ivdiciall Astrologie.* Cambridge: Iohn Legat, 1603.

HEYLYN, PETER. *Cosmography in Four Books.* London: A. C. for P. Chetwind & Anne Seile, 1677.

———. *Cyprianus anglicus.* Dublin: James Carson for John Hyde, etc., 1719.

———. Μικρόκοσμος: *A Little Description of the Great World.* 8th ed. Oxford: William Turner, 1639.

HEYWOOD, THOMAS. *Dramatic Works.* 6 vols. London: John Pearson, 1874.

———. Γυναικεῖον: *Or, Nine Bookes of Various History concerninge Women.* London: Adam Islip, 1624.

———. *The Hierarchie of the Blessed Angells.* London: Adam Islip, 1635.

Hieron, Samuel. *The Sermons of Master Samuell Hieron.* 2 vols. in 1. London: John Beale, 1635.

Hobbes, Thomas. *Leviathan.* ("Everyman's Library.") London: J. M. Dent & Sons, Ltd., 1937.

Hooker, Richard. *Of the Lawes of Ecclesiastical Politie.* London: Will. Stansby, 1617.

Howell, James. *Familiar Letters on Important Subjects, Wrote from the Year 1618 to 1650.* 10th ed. Aberdeen: F. Douglass & W. Murray, 1853.

——. Θηρολογία. *The Parly of Beasts.* London: W. Wilson for William Palmer, 1660.

Innocent III. *The Mirror of Mans Lyfe.* Translated by Humphrey Kirton. London: H. Bynneman, 1576.

Jackson, Thomas. *The Raging Tempest Stilled.* London: Iohn Haviland for Godfrey Emondson, etc., 1623.

——. *A Treatise Containing the Originall of Vnbeliefe, Misbeliefe, or Misperswasions concerning the Veritie, Vnitie, and Attributes of the Deitie.* London: I. D. for Iohn Clarke, 1625.

Jerome, Stephen. *Moses His Sight of Canaan. With Simeon His Dying-Song.* London: Roger Iackson, 1619.

Jonson, Ben. *The Works of Ben Jonson.* Edited by William Gifford. Boston: Phillips, Sampson, & Co., 1854.

King, John. *A Sermon Preached at the Funeral of the Most Reverend Father, John, Late Archbishop of York . . . 1594.* In *Lectures vpon Jonah.* Edinburgh: James Nichol, 1864.

King, William. *An Essay on the Origin of Evil . . . and a Dissertation concerning the Principle and Criterion of Virtue. . . . To Which Are Added Two Sermons by the Same Author . . . the Latter on the Fall of Man.* Translated by Edmund Law. 2d ed. 2 vols. London: J. Stephens for W. Thurlbourn, 1732.

Lake, Arthur. *Sermons with Some Religious and Diuine Meditations.* London: W. Stansby for Nathaniel Butter, 1629.

Lane, John. *Tom Tel-Troths Message.* Edited by F. J. Furnivall. ("New Shakspere Society Publications," Ser. VI, No. 2.) London: N. Trübner & Co., 1876.

[Lanquet, Thomas.] *Coopers Chronicle.* [London], 1565.

La Primaudaye, Pierre de. *The French Academie.* London: Thomas Adams, 1618.

Laud, William. *The Works of the Most Reverend Father in God, William Laud.* 7 vols. in 9. Oxford: J. H. Parker, 1847–60.

Leroy, Louis. *Of the Interchangeable Covrse, or Variety of Things in the Whole World.* Translated by R[obert] A[shley]. London: Charles Yetsweirt, 1594.

L'Estrange, Roger. *An Account of the Growth of Knavery.* London: H. H. for Henry Brome, 1678.

——. *Poor Robins Visions.* London: A. Boldero, 1677.

[LILLY, WILLIAM. *Almanac for 1671*. Title-page missing.]

LILLY, WILLIAM. *Englands Propheticall Merline*. London: John Raworth for John Partridge, 1644.

LIPSIUS, JUSTUS. *A Discourse of Constancy*. Translated by NATHANIEL WANLEY. London: J. Redmayne for James Allestry, 1670.

Lord Mayors' Pageants. Edited by F. W. FAIRHOLT. ("Percy Society Publications," No. X.) London: T. Richards, 1843–44.

LUCRETIUS. *T. Lucretius Carus. The Epicurean Philosopher, His Six Books De natura rerum Done into English Verse*, [by Thomas Creech] *with Notes*. 2d ed. Oxford: L. Lichfield for Anthony Stephens, 1683.

LUTHER, MARTIN. *Conversations with Luther*. Translated and edited by PRESERVED SMITH and H. P. GALLINGER. Boston: Pilgrim Press, [1915].

———. *Luther on the Creation: A Critical and Devotional Commentary on Genesis*, Vol. I. In *The Precious and Sacred Writings of Martin Luther*. Edited by J. N. LENKER. Minneapolis: Lutherans in All Lands Company, 1903–10.

LYNDSAY, DAVID. *The Poetical Works of Sir David Lyndsay*. Edited by DAVID LAING. 3 vols. Edinburgh: William Paterson, 1879.

MARANDÉ, LÉONARD. *The Ivdgment of Humane Actions*. Translated by JOHN REYNOLDS. London: A. Mathewes for Nicholas Bourne, 1629.

[MARKHAM, GERVASE.] *Conceyted Letters Newly Layde Open*. London: B. Alsop, 1618.

MEXIA, PEDRO. *The Forest or Collection of Historyes*. Translated by THOMAS FORTESCUE. London: John Day, 1576.

MILLES, THOMAS. See *The Treasvrie of Avncient and Moderne Times*.

MILTON, JOHN. *The Poetical Works of John Milton*. New York: Oxford University Press, 1938.

———. *The Prose Works of John Milton*. 5 vols. London: Henry G. Bohn, 1861–68.

———. *The Student's Milton*. Edited by F. A. PATTERSON. New York: F. S. Crofts & Co., 1931.

MONTAIGNE, MICHEL DE. *The Essayes of Michael, Lord of Montaigne*. Translated by JOHN FLORIO. London: George Routledge & Sons, [1885].

MORNAY, PHILIPPE DE. *A Worke concerning the Trewnesse of Christian Religion*. Translated by PHILIP SIDNEY and ARTHUR GOLDING. London: Robert Robinson for I. B., 1592.

NAPIER, JOHN. *A Plaine Discouery of the Whole Reuelation of Saint Iohn*. Edinbvrgh: Robert Walde-Graue, 1593.

NASH, THOMAS. *Christ's Tears over Jerusalem*. London: Longman, Hurst, Rees, etc., 1815.

———. *Pierce Penilesse*. Edited by G. B. HARRISON. ("Bodley Head Quartos," No. XI.) London: John Lane, [1924].

NEMESIUS. *The Natvre of Man*. Translated by GEORGE WITHER. London: M. F. for Henry Taunton, 1636.

NORDEN, JOHN. *A Progress of Piety*. ("Parker Society Publications," No.

XXXI.) Cambridge: At the University Press, 1847.

———. *Vicissitudo rerum, an Elegiacall Poeme, of the Interchangeable Courses and Varietie of Things in This World.* ("Shakespeare Association Facsimilies," No. 4.) London: Oxford University Press, 1931.

NORTHAMPTON, HENRY HOWARD, EARL OF. *A Defensative against the Poyson of Supposed Prophecies.* London: W. Iaggard, 1620.

OSBORNE, FRANCIS. *A Miscellany of Sundry Essayes, Paradoxes, and Problematicall Discourses.* London: J. Grismond for R. Royston, 1659.

O[VERTON], R[ICHARD]. *Mans Mortallitie.* Amsterdam: John Canne, 1643.

OVID. *Ovid's Metamorphosis.* Translated by GEORGE SANDYS. 6th ed. London: J. F. for A. Roper, 1669.

PALINGENIUS, MARCELLUS. *The Zodiake of Life.* Translated by BARNABIE GOOGE. London: Raufe Newberie, 1576.

PARR, RICHARD. *The Life of the Most Reverend Father in God, James Usher.* London: Nathanael Ranew, 1686.

[PARROT, HENRY.] *The Mastiue, or Young-Whelpe of the Old-Dogge.* London: Thomas Creede for Richard Meighen & Thomas Jones, 1615.

PEACHAM, HENRY. *Coach and Sedan.* London: Frederick Etchells & Hugh Macdonald, 1925.

———. *The Valley of Varietie.* London: M. P. for Iames Becket, 1638.

A Pepysian Garland. Edited by H. E. ROLLINS. Cambridge: At the University Press, 1922.

[PERKINS, WILLIAM. *Works.*] *A Golden Chaine: Or, the Description of Theologie.* [Bound in continuous pagination with *An Exposition of the Symbole or Creede of the Apostles; An Exposition of the Lords Prayer;* etc.] Cambridge: Iohn Legat, 1600.

PERSON, DAVID. *Varieties.* London: Richard Badger for Thomas Alchorn, 1635.

PETER MARTYR. See *The First Three English Books on America.*

PEUCER, KASPAR. *Les Devins, ov commentaire des principales sortes de devinations.* Translated by S. G. S. Anvers: Hevdrik Connix, 1584.

PEYTON, THOMAS. *The Glasse of Time.* New York: John B. Alden, 1886.

PLINY. *The Historie of the World. Commonly Called the Natvrall Historie of C. Plinivs Secvndvs.* Translated by PHILEMON HOLLAND. 2 vols. in 1. London: Adam Islip, 1601.

PONT, ROBERT. *A Newe Treatise of the Right Reckoning of Yeares, and Ages of the World, and Mens Liues, and of the Estate of the Last Decaying Age Thereof, This 1600. Yeare of Christ, (Erroniouslie Called a Yeare of Jubilee) Which Is from the Creation, the 5548. Yeare.* Edinburgh: Robert Waldegrave, 1599.

POWER, HENRY. *Experimental Philosophy, in Three Books: Containing New Experiments Microscopical, Mercurial, Magnetical.* London: T. Roycroft for John Martin & James Allestry, 1664.

PURCHAS, SAMUEL. *Hakluytus posthumus, or Purchas His Pilgrimes.* 20 vols. Glasgow: James MacLehose & Sons, 1905 ff.

PURCHAS, SAMUEL. *Pvrchas His Pilgrim. Microcosmvs, or the Historie of Man.* London: W. S. for Henry Fetherstone, 1619.

———. *Pvrchas His Pilgrimage.* London: William Stansby for Henrie Fetherstone, 1613.

RAINOLDS, JOHN. *The Prophecies of Obadiah.* Oxford: Joseph Barnes, 1613.

RALEGH, SIR WALTER. *The History of the World.* London: Walter Bvrre, 1614.

RASTELL, JOHN. *The Nature of the Four Elements.* ("Tudor Facsimile Texts.") London: T. C. and E. C. Jack, 1908.

RAY, JOHN. *Miscellaneous Discourses concerning the Dissolution and Changes of the World.* London: Samuel Smith, 1692.

[RECORDE, ROBERT.] *The Castle of Knowledge.* [London: R. Wolfe, 1556.]

REYNOLDS, HENRY. *Mythomystes.* See *Critical Essays of the Seventeenth Century,* Vol. I.

REYNOLDS, JOHN. *The Triumphs of Gods Revenge.* London: William Lee, 1635.

RICH, BARNABE. *The Honestie of This Age.* ("Percy Society Publications," No. XI.) London: T. Richards, 1844.

ROGERS, THOMAS. *The General Session, Conteining an Apologie of the Most Comfortable Doctrine concerning the Ende of this World, and Seconde Comming of Christ.* London: Henrie Middleton for Andrew Maunsell, 1581.

ROSS, ALEXANDER. Πανσέβεια: *Or, a View of All Religions in the World.* London: James Young for John Saywell, 1653.

———. *The Philosophicall Touch-Stone: Or Observations upon Sir Kenelm Digbie's Discourses of the Nature of Bodies, and of the Reasonable Soule.* London: James Young, 1645.

ROWLANDS, SAMUEL. *The Complete Works of Samuel Rowlands.* 3 vols. [Glasgow]: The Hunterian Club, 1880.

SALUSBURY, THOMAS. *Mathematical Collections and Translations: The First Tome. In Two Parts.* London: William Leybourne, 1661.

SANDYS, EDWIN. *The Sermons of Edwin Sandys.* ("Parker Society Publications.") Cambridge: At the University Press, 1842.

SCOTT, MICHAEL. *The Philosophers Banqvet.* London: Nicholas Vavasour, 1633.

SCRIBONIUS, W. A. *Natvrall Philosophy: Or a Description of the World, and of the Severall Creatures Therein Contained.* Corrected and enlarged by DANIEL WIDDOVVES. 2d ed. London: Thos. Cotes for John Bellamie, 1631.

SENAULT, JEAN FRANCIS. *The Christian Man: Or, the Reparation of Nature by Grace.* London: M. M., etc., 1650.

———. *Man Become Guilty, or the Corruption of Natvre by Sinne.* Translated by HENRY, EARL OF MONMOUTH. London: William Leake, 1650.

SENECA. *Ad Lucilium epistulae morales.* Translated by R. M. GUMMERE. ("Loeb Classical Library.") 3 vols. New York: G. P. Putnam's Sons, 1917–25.

SHAKELTON, FRANCIS. *A Blazyng Starre or Burnyng Beacon, Seene the 10. of October Laste (and Yet Continewyng) Set on Fire by Gods Prouidence, To Call All Sinners to Earnest & Speedie Repentance.* London: Ihon Kyngston for Henry Kirkham, 1580.

SOUTHWELL, ROBERT. *The Complete Poems of Robert Southwell.* Edited by A. B. GROSART. [London: Robson & Sons], 1872.

——. *Marie Magdalen's Funerall Teares.* London: Charles Baldwyn, 1823.

S[OUTHWELL], R[OBERT]. *The Triumphs over Death.* In *Archaica,* Vol. I. London: T. Davison, 1815.

SPENCER, JOHN. *A Discourse concerning Prodigies.* 2d ed. London: J. Field for Will Graves, 1665.

——. *A Discourse concerning Vulgar Prophecies.* [Bound with *A Discourse concerning Prodigies.* Separate pagination.]

SPENSER, EDMUND. *The Complete Poetical Works of Edmund Spenser.* [Edited by R. E. N. DODGE.] ("Student's Cambridge" ed.) Boston: Houghton Mifflin Co., [1908].

STAFFORD, ANTHONY. *The Gvide of Honovr.* London: T. C. for T. Slater, 1634.

——. *Staffords Niobe: Or His Age of Teares. The First Part.* 2d ed. London: Humfrey Lownes, 1611 [Bound with *Staffords Niobe, Dissolv'd into a Nilvs: Or, His Age Drown'd in Her Owne Teares: Serving as a Second Part to the Former Treatise.* London: H. L. for Mathew Lownes, 1611.]

S[TAFFORD], W[ILLIAM]. *Compendious or Briefe Examination of Certayne Ordinary Complaints.* ("New Shakspere Society Publications," Ser. VI, No. 3.) London: N. Trübner & Co., 1876.

STRODE, GEORGE. *The Anatomie of Mortalitie.* 2d ed. London: William Iones for Thomas Weaver, 1632.

STUBBES, PHILLIP. *The Anatomie of Abuses.* Edited by F. J. FURNIVALL. ("New Shakspere Society Publications," Ser. VI, Nos. 4 and 6.) London: N. Trübner & Co., 1877–79.

——. *The Second Part of the Anatomie of Abuses.* Edited by F. J. FURNIVALL. ("New Shakspere Society Publications," Ser. VI, No. 12.) London: N. Trübner & Co., 1882.

SUCKLING, JOHN. *The Works of Sir John Suckling.* London: H. H., 1696.

SUTTON, CHRISTOPHER. *Disce mori.* London: I. Windet for Cuthbert Burby, 1602.

——. *Disce vivere.* Oxford: John Henry Parker, 1841.

SWAN, JOHN. *Speculum mundi or a Glasse Representing the Face of the World.* Cambridge: T. Buck & R. Daniel, 1635.

SYLVESTER, JOSHUAH. *The Complete Works of Joshuah Sylvester.* Edited by A. B. GROSART. 2 vols. [Edinburgh: Edinburgh University Press], 1880.

——. *The Parliament of Vertues Royal.* 2 vols. [London: H. Lownes, 1614.]

TAYLOR, JEREMY. *The Whole Works of the Right Rev. Jeremy Taylor.* 15 vols. London: C. Rivington, etc., 1828.

[247]

TAYLOR, THOMAS. *Christ Revealed.* London: M. F. and R. Dawlman & L. Fawne, 1635.

———. *The Parable of the Sovver and of the Seed.* London: Iohn Dawson for Iohn Bartlet, 1623.

———. *The Works of That Faithful Servant of Jesus Christ, Dr. Thom. Taylor.* London: T. R. and E. M. for John Bartlet the elder & John Bartlet the younger, 1653.

TEMPLE, WILLIAM. *Sir William Temple's Essays on Ancient & Modern Learning and on Poetry.* Edited by J. E. SPINGARN. Oxford: Clarendon Press, 1909.

The Three Voyages of Martin Frobisher. Edited by VILHJALMUR STEFANSSON. 2 vols. London: Argonaut Press, 1938.

Threnoikos. The House of Movrning. London: John Dawson for R[alph] M[abb], 1640.

THYNNE, FRANCIS. *Emblemes and Epigrames.* Edited by F. J. FURNIVALL. ("Early English Text Society.") London: N. Trübner & Co., 1876.

T[OFTE], R[OBERT]. *Honovrs Academie.* London: Thomas Creede, 1610.

TOPSELL, EDWARD. *Times Lamentation: Or an Exposition on the Prophet Ioel, in Sundry Sermons or Meditations.* London: Edm. Bollifant for George Potter, 1599.

TORQUEMADA, ANTONIO DE. *The Spanish Mandeuile of Miracles. Or the Garden of Curious Flowers.* Translated by FERDINANDO WALKER. London: I. R. for Edmund Matts, 1600.

The Treasvrie of Avncient and Moderne Times. Translated and edited by THOMAS MILLES. 2 vols. London: W. Iaggard, 1613–19.

TWYNE, THOMAS. *A Shorte and Pithie Discourse, concerning the Engendring, Tokens, and Effects of All Earthquakes in Generall.* London: Richarde Iohnes, 1580.

TYMME, THOMAS. *A Plaine Discouerie of Ten English Lepers.* London: Peter Short, 1592.

TYNDALE, WILLIAM. *Doctrinal Treatises and Introductions to Different Portions of the Holy Scriptures.* ("Parker Society Publications," No. XLIII.) Cambridge: At the University Press, 1848.

[———. *The Whole Workes of W. Tyndall, John Frith and Doct. Barnes, Three Worthy Martyrs, and Principall Teachers of This Churche of England.* London: John Daye, 1573. Title-page supplied.]

URSINUS, ZACHARIAS. *The Summe of Christian Religion, Delivered by Zacharias Ursinus, First by Way of Catechisme, and then Afterwards More Inlarged by a Sound and Judicious Exposition.* London: Robert Young, 1633.

USSHER, JAMES. *A Body of Divinity, or the Svmme and Svbstance of Christian Religion.* 3d ed. London: M. F. for Tho. Dovvnes and Geo. Badger, 1648.

———. *The Whole Works of the Most Rev. James Ussher.* Edited by C. R. ELRINGTON. 17 vols. Dublin: Hodges, Smith & Co., 1864.

VAUGHAN, HENRY. *The Works of Henry Vaughan*. Edited by L. C. MARTIN. 2 vols. Oxford: Clarendon Press, 1914.

VAUGHAN, WILLIAM. *The Golden-Groue*. 2d ed. London: Simon Stafford, 1608.

[VERGIL, POLYDORE. *An Abridgemēt of the Notable Worke of Polidore Vergile*. London: R. Grafton, 1546. Title-page supplied.]

VIRET, PIERRE. *The Worlde Possessed with Deuils*. London: I. Perin, 1583.

W[ALKINGTON], T[HOMAS]. *The Optick Glasse of Humors*. London: G. Dawson, 1664.

WALLER, EDMUND. *The Poems of Edmund Waller*. Edited by G. THORN DRURY. 2 vols. London: A. H. Bullen, 1901.

WEBSTER, JOHN. *The Displaying of Supposed Witchcraft*. London: J. M., 1677.

WEIGEL, VALENTIN. *Astrology Theologized*. London: George Redway, 1886.

WHARTON, GEORGE. *The Works of That Late Most Excellent Philosopher and Astronomer, Sir George Wharton*. London: H. H. for John Leigh, 1683.

WHATELY, WILLIAM. *Prototypes*. London: G. M. for George Edwards, 1640.

WHITE, THOMAS. *Peripateticall Institutions. In the Way of That Eminent Person and Excellent Philosopher Sr. Kenelm Digby*. London: R. D., 1656.

———. *A Sermō Preached at Pawles Crosse on Sunday the Thirde of Nouember 1577 in the Time of the Plague*. London: Francis Coldock, 1578.

WHITLOCK, RICHARD. Ζωοτομία, *or Observations on the Present Manners of the English*. London: Tho. Roycroft, 1654.

The Whole Prophecies of Scotland, England, Ireland, France & Denmark. Glasgow: J. and M. Robertson, 1806.

[WILKINS, JOHN.] *A Discourse concerning a New World & Another Planet* [containing *The Discovery of a New World* and *A Discovrse concerning a New Planet*]. [London]: Iohn Maynard, 1640.

WILKINS, JOHN. *The Mathematical and Philosophical Works*. London: J. Nicholson, etc., 1708.

WILLET, ANDREW. *Hexapla in Danielem*. [Cambridge]: Leonard Greene, 1610.

———. *Hexapla in Genesin*. 3d ed. London: Assignes of Thomas Man, Pavl Man, and Ionah Man, 1632.

[———.] *Hexapla . . . Pavl* [Cambridge]: Cantrall Legge, 1620

WINSTANLEY, WILLIAM. *The Muses Cabinet*. London: F. Coles, 1655.

WITHER, GEORGE. *Abuses Stript, and Whipt*. London: Humfrey Lownes for Francis Burton, 1617.

———. *Britain's Remembrancer Containing a Narration of the Plagve Lately Past*. London: J. Grismond, 1628.

———. *An Improvement of Imprisonment, Disgrace, Poverty, into Real Freedom*. London, 1661.

WOOD, ANTHONY à. *Athenae Oxonienses: An Exact History of All the*

Writers and Bishops...of Oxford. 4 vols. London: F. C. & J. Rivington, 1813–20.

WOTTON, HENRY. *Reliquiae Wottònianae.* London: Thomas Maxey for R. Marriot, etc., 1651.

WRIGHT, THOMAS. *The Passions of the Minde.* London: Miles Flesher, 1630.

YOUNG, EDWARD. *Conjectures on Original Composition.* Edited by E. J. MORLEY. Manchester: Manchester University Press, 1918.

ZOUCHE, RICHARD. *The Dove; or, Passages of Cosmography.* Oxford: H. Slatter, 1839.

Index

INDEX